His Only Son

His Only Son

Leopoldo Alas

Translated from the Spanish, with an Introduction,
by Julie Jones

Louisiana State University Press
Baton Rouge and London

Designer: Patricia Douglas Crowder
Typeface: Linotype Garamond
Typesetter: Service Typesetters
Printer: Thomson-Shore, Inc.
Binder: John Dekker & Sons, Inc.

LIBRARY OF CONGRESS CATALOGING IN PUBLICATION DATA
Alas, Leopoldo, 1852–1901.
  His only son.
  I. Title.
PQ6503.A4S813   863'.5   80–20837
ISBN 0-8071-0759-X

This translation is dedicated to my parents in grateful recognition of their help over the years.

Introduction

Born in 1852, Leopoldo Alas lived most of his life in Oviedo, capital of the northern Spanish province of Asturias and a city of some twenty thousand inhabitants at the time. There he attended the local school and later the university, from which he received a degree in law in 1871. Alas' family was moderately well-to-do; his father, a small landowner, occupied himself with politics, serving at different times as civil governor of Zámora (Alas' birthplace) and León. In addition to his house in Oviedo, he owned property in Carreño, a small country town set in a green valley near the sea. Carreño served as a model for the description of Bonifacio Reyes' ancestral home in *His Only Son*, just as Oviedo provided the model for the provincial capital where the action of the novel is centered.

With graduation, Alas became restless and made the decision to continue his studies at the University of Madrid. He lived in Madrid for seven years, taking his doctorate in civil and canon law in 1878. There he was exposed to Krausismo, a movement founded on the tenets of the German philosopher Karl C. F. Krause, which in Spain took a form more cultural than philosophic. It became a liberalizing force, directed toward reforming the schools, the church, the government. At first, Alas was one of the more eager disciples. Although he never sacrificed art to utility, he did see in literature, especially the novel, a medium for reform. Later he became increasingly skeptical of the value of principles devoid of religious meaning in the rather traditional sense in which he understood religion; yet, despite his disaffection with Krausismo, all his life Alas continued to use fiction as a weapon for combating moral and cultural evils. Through satire, he attempted to warn his fellowmen of their intellectual and spiritual poverty. He lamented the dominion of "the crystallized formula over the spiritual juice of things," a malaise he saw as peculiarly Spanish.*

During his residence in Madrid, he began to publish articles, for the most part literary. In 1875, he first signed his pen name, Clarín (the Trumpet), to an article in *El Solfeo*, a review dedicated to the arts. The name stuck, and the articles continued to appear.

Returning to Oviedo, Alas married Onofre García, a rather serious, intelligent young woman, though unfortunately crippled. Perhaps Leopoldo, very short, very near sighted, very timid in respect to the ladies, found her less intimidating than others of her sex. Their marriage, which resulted in three children, seems to have been ideal; at least, Juan Antonio Cabezas, Alas' sentimental biographer, comments, "It would be hard to find a pair with less flesh and more spirit between them than these two dreamers."† But in view of the strong undercurrent of sensuality in the novels and short stories, and the obessively repeated theme of frustrated love, one may perhaps be inclined to question Cabezas' assessment.

In 1883, Alas accepted a position as professor of Roman law at the University of Oviedo. There he remained until his death in 1901. During this eighteen-year period, he taught and contributed literary articles to a vast number of periodicals, which commandeered most of his time. He also published short stories, novellas, and two major novels, *La Regenta* (*The Judge's Wife*), in 1884–1885, and *Su único hijo* (*His Only Son*), in 1890. He was esteemed by his contemporaries as a literary critic rather than as a fiction writer; but more recent readers have reversed this judgment, finding the criticism (if they read it at all) dated and often wrongheaded, and the novels and many of the short stories of enduring value.

---

* Leopoldo Alas, *Doctor Sutilis (Cuentos)* (Madrid: Renacimiento, 1916), 273 (my translation).

† Juan Antonio Cabezas, *"Clarín," el provinciano universal* (Madrid: Espasa-Calpe, 1936), 126 (my translation).

To a great degree, Alas' mature fiction is concerned with the problem of finding and maintaining some sort of ideal, no matter how humble, in the face of an existence both hostile and unimaginative. In *His Only Son*, we find an acquisitive, meanspirited society on one hand and on the other a hero—a buffoon and a weakling, perhaps, but a hero nonetheless—who is trying to extract some personal meaning from, and impose a sort of order, even though it be imaginary, on, the chaos that confronts him. Bonifacio Reyes, the protagonist, erects one ideal after another: art, love, fatherhood. The first two fail him; if the third succeeds, it is only through his strength of will and blind determination.

Although, as the title indicates, the ideal of fatherhood culminates Bonifacio's spiritual progression, the real interest of the novel centers on art and love, ideals that tend to become confused in the hero's mind. Bonifacio suffers from bovarism (Flaubert greatly influenced Alas' writing). Like Emma, a great reader of romantic novels, Bonifacio judges life by the standards of literature and finds it sadly wanting. Only with the advent of Serafina Gorgheggi, the star of a run-down Italian opera company reduced to playing the provinces, does he find that for once life measures up to art: "He compared himself to the heroes of those novels he read before going to sleep. . . . He was a hero. All of his acts and adventures became the embodiment of that which other imaginations could only scribble about." Bonifacio's tendency to launch himself into verbal transports, wilder than any imaginable liaison, provides Alas with the opportunity to satirize both the language and the thought of the Romantic movement, which reached Spain fairly late and which hung on in a decadent form in the provinces long after it had disappeared from the capital. To be more precise, Alas' target is what he felt was a legacy of that movement: a cultivated sentimentalism that had become a stock posture, another "crystallized formula," denying true emotion.

Although Bonifacio's shortcomings are readily apparent, Alas treats him gently. He is, after all, well intentioned albeit confused. The satirist reserves his real indignation for the society of unscrupulous miscreants and pickthanks who surround him—characters who are out solely for their own gratification and whose moral and intellectual vacuity is evidenced by their glib use of clichés and received ideas. Here, too, language is an index of inner value, but whereas Bonifacio bumbles into his linguistic excesses in an effort to maintain *some* sort of ideal, no matter how thin, these creatures use it to deceive or to hurt—each other or, more frequently, the hapless hero.

In emphasizing Alas' satire of the language, I am discussing only one facet of a rich and complex novel: the aspect most interesting to a translator. The passages in which Alas parodies the language of romantic novels provide special difficulties in translation. Rendered literally, they can be terribly stilted or simply unintelligible. I have, therefore, been sometimes fairly free with literal meanings, adding words, clarifying or rephrasing when I thought it necessary to make the intention clear or the passage smooth. I have done this with some of the "straightforward" passages as well, Alas' style being, at all times, baroque. I have tried, when I had to alter the literal sense, to pay very close attention to tone and imagery; and I hope that I have not softened, but only diverted, the energy of the original.

Alas' writing is liberally laced with colloquialisms. Whenever possible, I have retained them in the original form; however, when this has not been possible, I have tried to find a near equivalent that would not disrupt the feeling of the line. I have avoided using peculiarly American or English expressions for fear that they would strike a false note in this context.

I have standardized the punctuation and dropped the italics with which Alas underscored the clichés and trite remarks that he ordered so carefully. The italics I found somewhat heavy for contemporary usage and altogether unnecessary, since the reader will surely have no trouble in detecting the platitudes.

His Only Son

Chapter One

Emma Valcárcel was an only child, and spoiled. When she was fifteen, she fell in love with her father's clerk. The clerk, Bonifacio Reyes, came from an honorable family which had been eminent a century ago, but which in the last two or three generations had fallen on bad times. Bonifacio was a peaceable man, mild, languid, very sentimental, extremely tenderhearted, addicted to music and fanciful stories, a faithful patron of the local lending library. He was handsome in the romantic fashion, of average height, slender, with a pale oval face, wavy chestnut-colored hair, a small foot and a good leg. He was hopeless at any kind of serious or regular work. His handwriting was pretty and delicately traced, but he took a long time to fill a page, and his spelling was very strange and fanciful; it could hardly be considered spelling at all. Words to which he gave great importance were written in capital letters, for example: Love, Charity, Sweetness, Pardon, Epoch, Autumn, Erudite, Soft, Music, Sweetheart, Appetite and a number of others. On the same day that Emma's father (a man of noble lineage and a famous lawyer) decided to dismiss poor Reyes because his writing made the lawyer look like a fool in front of judges and juries, Emma decided to elope with her sweetheart. Bonifacio had allowed himself to be loved. He tried in vain to avoid being spirited away, but Emma carried him off by force, the force of love, and the Civil Guard, justifying its good name, surprised the fugitives on the first stage of their flight. Emma was shipped off to a convent; the clerk disappeared from the town (a third-rate capital, dull and melancholy) and was not heard of for a long time. Emma remained in her religious prison for several years. With her father's death, she returned as though nothing had happened. Rich and arrogant, she treated her only guardian, an uncle, as if he were her butler. Certain though she was of her physical purity, her pride demanded that the townspeople acknowledge that fact as well. She determined either to marry or to die—to marry in order to prove the purity of her honor. Acceptable suitors, however, did not appear. Valcárcel's daughter still imagined that she was in love with the clerk whom she had loved at the age of fifteen; yet she did not know what had become of him, and even if he had appeared she would not have given him her hand simply because that would have been tantamount to an admission of guilt. She wanted another husband first. Yes, almost without realizing it, Emma thought to herself, "another husband *first*." The *afterwards* which she hoped for and vaguely speculated upon, almost took for granted, was not adultery but rather the death of the first husband, followed, of course, by the second wedding—a wedding she firmly believed was her due. Two years after her release, the first husband appeared. A coarse, sickly, taciturn and pious man, he had returned to Spain after making his fortune in Latin America. He married Emma for a selfish reason; he wanted a pair of soft hands to take care of him when he was indisposed. The husband lasted a year. A year later, Emma ceased mourning, and thanks to this small tyrant's ukase, the guardian-butler, along with a host of cousins (all Valcárcels, most of them secretly in love with Emma), embarked on an extensive search for the fugitive, poor Bonifacio Reyes. Reyes turned up in Puebla, Mexico, where he had gone to seek his fortune. He had not found it, becoming instead the inept editor of a libelous review that referred to everyone as either a bungler or a simpleton. Although his life was sad and needy, he was quiet, tranquil and resigned to his fate; in fact, he was hardly aware of it. A merchant's agent put the Valcárcels in touch with Bonifacio. How could they bring him back to Spain? How could they broach the proposal respectably? They offered him a position in a small village three leagues distant from the capital. It was a humble position but certainly better than the one with the Mexican review. Bonifacio accepted and returned to his own country. When he asked whom he should thank for the favor, he was conducted into the presence of one of Emma's cousins, Sebastian, who had been in love with her since he was twenty. The following week, Emma and Bonifacio saw each other. Three weeks later, they were married. Eight days after that, Emma realized that this was not the Bonifacio of her dreams. Although mild, he was far more annoying than the guardian and less poetic than the cousin.

After two months of marriage, Emma began to experience an intense and overwhelming affection for every member of her family, living and dead. She surrounded herself with relatives. She spent a small fortune having ancestral portraits restored; then, finally, without telling a soul, she fell hopelessly in love—with the remarkable Don Diego Antonio Valcárcel y Meras, founder of the Valcárcel line, a famous warrior who had both made and lost his name and fortune in the Alpujarras War. Armed in full regalia, tanned and frowning, his gaze as penetrating and shining as the sun, owing to a new coat of varnish, this mysterious person on the canvas appeared to Emma's dreamy eyes as the paradigm of all dead, irretrievable grandeur. To fall in love with her grandfather, a symbol of the chivalric life, was a passion worthy of a woman who made every effort to distinguish herself from those around her. The impulse to draw away from the ordinary, to break every rule, to defy rumors, overcome impossibilities and provoke scandals, was not in Emma a hollow show or the pedantic vanity of a woman misled by foolish books; it sprang, rather, from the spontaneous perversion of her spirit, a sick prurience. With the restoration of that family icon, Cousin Sebastian lost ground. If Emma, perhaps, had been three fingers from the abyss of marital infidelity—a hypothesis never to be proved—her secret and purely ideal infatuation saved her from any positive danger. A piece of old canvas had fallen between Sebastian and his cousin. One evening they were strolling through the portrait gallery together. It was almost dark. Sebastian was preparing a sentence that in a few words would explain the consideration he had earned through loving so many years without trying to take advantage of his passion or even so much as voicing it. Suddenly, Emma stood in front of him. In a peremptory tone, she ordered her cousin to light a lamp and hold it up to the portrait of that illustrious grandfather.

"You do resemble each other somewhat," she said, "but it's quite clear that our line has degenerated. He was much better looking and stronger than you. Nowadays, you Valcárcels are made of sugar paste. In that armour, you'd look ridiculous."

Thus, by necessity, Sebastian's love for Emma continued to be secret and hopeless. The warrior of Alpujarras kept close watch on his family's honor.

Bonifacio suspected neither the cousin nor the grandfather. After his wife had put a stop to the honeymoon—and that did not take long—he found time heavy on his hands (at Emma's express command, the uncle continued to look after the estate), so Bonifacio began to look for someone to love, something that would fill his life. In spite of his good looks, Bonifacio's speech and manners were artless, his appearance unexciting, his gestures, actions, words, all prosaic and unmemorable. Nonetheless, it is worth noting that "inside," as he used to say, he was a dreamer, a dreamy dreamer, and when he spoke to himself, he used an elevated, romantic style without even realizing it. Casting about, then, for something to fill his life, he found a flute. It was an ebony flute with silver keys, which turned up among some of his father-in-law's papers. Even though he had been a bit old for such things, that Fellow of the illustrious Law Society had indulged in romantic tendencies when he was alone. He had played the flute with a great deal of feeling, but never in public. After some consideration, Emma agreed to let her father's flute pass on into her husband's hands. The husband rubbed it with oil and repaired it so that the instrument was as good as new, and then dedicated himself, body and soul, to music, his favorite pastime. He was somewhat more talented than average, had a good embouchure and played with great feeling. The sweet, peaceful, monotonous, almost nasal tone of the instrument (which, like his hair, smelled of almond extract) harmonized with the character of the player. The position in which Reyes held his head to play, a position he exaggerated, contributed to the total effect by giving him the appearance of a blessed soul. Playing the flute, Reyes resembled the saintly musicians of Pre-Raphaelite painting. Above the black mouthpiece, between the silky, chestnut-colored moustaches, the tip of his clean, healthy tongue occasionally flashed. His limpid blue eyes, which were large and tender, reached like a mystic's toward the highest point of their orbit; but in spite of this fact, they focused not on heaven, but, instead, on the wall in front, for Reyes had his head lowered as though he were about to charge. He marked time by beating on the floor with the tip of his foot, and during particularly moving passages his entire body swayed as though his waist were a hinge. In the *allegros*, he rocked with a force and animation peculiar in a man who often appeared to be so apathetic; his eyes, lifeless before and intent on nothing except the music as if they were an integral part of the flute or at least dependent on it for some hidden resource, became lively, warm and shining, and they revealed inexpressible afflictions, as do the eyes of an intelligent animal begging for help. At these critical moments, Bonifacio looked more than anything like a drowning castaway who searches about in vain for his life raft. Reyes believed that his strained face, his feverish cheeks and the intensity of his gaze must express the profundity of his emotions, his great passion for melody; but they resembled more closely the symptoms of an irremediable asphyxia, an attack of apoplexy or some other horrible physical crisis, anything, in short, but this music lover's beautiful heart, which was simple as a dove's.

To avoid bothering anyone or spending his wife's money—he himself had none—by purchasing sheets of music, Bonifacio borrowed the polkas and the scores for Italian operas, which were his chief delight, and he copied by hand those torrents of harmony and melody represented in each of the beloved notes of the musical staff. Emma did not ask any questions about his avocation or about the better part of each day, which he devoted to it. She only demanded that he be dressed, and well dressed, when they went out for walks or on visits. *Her* Bonifacio was no more than a clotheshorse who had no common sense or even feelings but who cut a good figure and was useful as an escort to make the local ladies envious. She showed off her husband. She bought him fine clothes which he wore with distinction, and she reserved for herself the right to call him a simpleton. At first he appeared to be content with his lot. He had no say in the management of the house. He spent no more on his personal needs than would a poor student, since the expensive and luxurious clothes were not bought on his account but to satisfy his wife's vanity. He enjoyed being well dressed, but he could have foregone that sartorial extravagance without so much as a sigh; furthermore, he was scandalized by his wife's insistence that his trousers and frock coats be cut in Madrid. Such excessive dandyism was unheard of in the town. He was acquainted with a humble tailor, a flutist as well, who for a modest sum could make a suit as handsome as any designed by the corrupt *artistes* of the court. Bonifacio thought this, but he dared not mention it. He allowed himself to be outfitted. His sole resolution was to inconvenience the Valcárcels as little as possible and, on every account, to maintain silence.

Chapter Two

Emma was the head of the family and was even, as we have seen, its tyrant. Uncles, cousins and nephews obeyed her orders and respected her caprices. Although this domination of soul is not explained entirely by economic motives, doubtless they formed an important part of it. All of the Valcárcels were now poor. They were, too, famous throughout the province for their fertility. The Valcárcel females were pregnant more often than not, and their sisters-in-law did not lag far behind them. Wholesale procreation and laziness seemed to be the insignia of that family line. During the entire century, the only worker had been Emma's father, the lawyer, who had also been less prolific than his relations—within the confines of his family. Since Emma was an only child, she was sole heir to the romantic lawyer, sometime flutist; however, the diligent solicitor's savings reached her in somewhat diminished quantities. It seems that Don Diego Valcárcel's vaunted continence had been rather overrated; his real virtues had been prudence and secrecy, for he fully realized that bad example and scandal are the most formidable enemies of any well-organized society. Since it was impossible for him to remain a chaste widower, between seducing the house maids, his daughter's governesses and, prompted by temptation, even respectable clients, bereaved ladies who rushed to his office in search of judicial-moral illumination, and regimenting his vice—the inevitable expansions of weak flesh—he opted for the latter course, organizing the service of Aphrodite, as he called it, with consummate skill. In the nearby hamlets to which he was often taken by his own business as well as his clients', he became, if truth be told, the irresponsible Abraham—Pater Orchamus—of a large population of natural children, many the fruit of adultery. When the time came to draw up his will, neither his own conscience nor his confessor's (a priest who had helped him avoid scandal a number of times) nor the threat of embarrassing confessions on the part of a handful of lady sinners would let him forget certain obligations of blood. Thus, always observing the proper formalities, he dropped portions of his fortune here and there, diminishing Emma's rightful inheritance as far as the law allowed. Worse than this, during previous consultation with that same spiritual director, Don Diego had made certain surreptitious promises *inter vivos* regarding the transferral of property, which discretion obliged him to keep, albeit very unwillingly. In short, Emma's fortune was far smaller than her father's. She, however, hardly noticed her loss, since legal papers gave her migraines, arithmetic brought on fainting fits and legal writing revolted her. "Take it to my uncle," she would say of every financial concern. The only thing she really understood was spending. Don Juan Nepomuceno, Emma's one-time guardian and her present steward, would have liked to send packing the relatives who buzzed like flies around that shrunken honeycomb, the inheritance; but this was not feasible, and the profound affection his niece felt toward all Valcárcels, past, present and future, ordained that they be shown the greatest hospitality. Don Juan was forced to content himself with being the sole administrator of this ostentatious prodigality; his influence had no effect whatsoever in reducing the wastage or even in persuading his old ward to restrict her excessive generosity to herself.

During the early part of her marriage, Emma had a miscarriage and very nearly lost her life. She emerged from the crisis with her insides torn and her stomach weak. She lost weight and endeavored to cover up premature wrinkles, but she could not hide the cold, malicious sharpness of her gaze. The mysterious resplendence of her eyes, in times past the subject of serenades, became a hard glitter, the expression of an irascible hypochondriac. Now Emma flirted openly with those cousins who had once been secretly enamored of her, and she came to esteem her husband for nothing except his appearance, despising him more each day.

Reyes understood clearly that through no fault of his own he had become the enemy of his in-laws, a beaten, humiliated enemy, thanks to a wife who handed him over defenseless, tied hand and foot, as it were, to any relative who wanted to make a fool of him.

The Valcárcels, who were originally mountain dwellers, had come to the villages on the plains to find an easier, more comfortable life for themselves. Their only thought was to make advantageous matches; so they seduced the rich old men of the villages with their noble lineage and the family crest, emblazoned in stone on their big, old houses that were tucked away back in the mountains. The tender young ladies they seduced with their fine figures, which revealed an arrogant vigor and a lordly grace inherent in that line. Although heavier set, perhaps, than their heroic grandfather Don Antonio, almost all the Valcárcels were handsome, well-built boys; but without exception, they were also tight lipped, sullen, harsh voiced, secretive and unashamedly proud. They distinguished themselves, too, by an exaggerated attachment to long, wide capes which they wore all the year round in the humid, temperate, lowland hamlets where they canvassed for brides. Audacious beings, some of them—without ever leaving the capes behind—even ventured to the very gates of the provincial capital. Finally, Don Diego, Emma's father, who was without a doubt the family genius, actually entered the city. He was both an enterprising student and a playboy. As soon as he reached maturity and took his degree, his character underwent a sudden change. He became as dedicated as a saint. He opened an office, monopolized the mountain clientele and fawned upon those gentlemen on the fringes of good society, serious magistrates like himself who were very formal and correct in their behavior. He made a good marriage, rose above his poverty and shone in court with the brilliance of a good lighthouse. In spite of the fact that in his own right he was so romantic that he wrote octaves at home and was forced to find safety valves for his sentimentalism in the keys of his flute, he adhered to the letter of the law with singular rigidity; he deplored those irresponsible interpretations which base their appeal on the *spirit* of that sacrosanct law. There is no record of the court's *ever* having the slightest cause to reprimand him. On the contrary, the magistrature did nothing but praise the propriety of his language, which, to tell the truth, Don Diego carried so far that his speech became almost totally euphemistic. His little affectation, however, was forgivable because it was in this way that he emerged as pure as an ermine from the muddy waters of private corruption into which his duties at the bar so frequently dragged him.

In spite of himself, on one occasion he was forced to accuse an unworthy priest of indecency. Although he tried to appear firm, terrible and implacable, he absolutely refused to employ harsh, vivid or even picturesque epithets. At the very climax of the indictment, the strongest language he could bring himself to use was "this misguided priest, if I may be allowed to describe him in these terms." "Misguided," Don Diego remarked afterwards, explaining the adjective. "That is, I suppose the priest would never have been guilty of such immodesty had he not been prompted by someone—probably the Devil."

In his forensic discourses, lawyer Valcárcel had to guard himself against using the coarse and overfamiliar language of his region, a dialect which sometimes threatened to emerge even while he was in court; however, he triumphed over his native tongue, contriving to discover refined equivalents for even the coarsest terms. Once, for example, when he had occasion to refer to the foundations of a granary, known in his area as "legs," he preferred to say "the sustentation of the artifact, dear sir," rather than sully his lips with a word of that sort.

To these qualities, which went a long way toward winning him the respect and sympathy of all the magistrates, he added the by no means insignificant gift of remembering dates with an infallible exactitude; there were more numbers recorded in his brain than in a table of logarithms. Thanks to Don Diego, the name of Valcárcel regained a reputation it had not enjoyed since the days it had been famous for military prowess. The illustrious attorney had earned an honorable name and made a good profit. His relations, so impoverished by their wives' fertility that they had become an unhappy proletariat that threatened to fill the world with Valcárcels, were anxious to make use of these advantages. Due to their disproportionate gift for procreation, "good" marriages alone were not enough to tow them out of penury. Their emigration in search of prosperity, which had first taken them from the mountains to the valley, now reversed its course, sending them once again to the mountains, back to the big, out-of-the-way houses, back to the Valcárcel progeny, which had multiplied without rhyme or reason and was incapable of working, since you cannot really call work, at least in any economic sense, the agonies endured by Emma's relatives around the card table.

When Don Diego died, the Valcárcels lost their sole support, and the retrograde movement toward the mountain accelerated. Now, when they did come down to the valley, they seemed to be wilder and more arrogant with each visit; their dislike of courtesy, of the complicated formulas demanded by the good society of the province, became more pronounced. The poorer they were, the more vain they became and the more they criticized life in the villages and on the plains. The Valcárcels recognized only one institution worthy of respect in "the flats," as they called the lowlands, and that was the card game. They traveled down to the fairs to play, to lose, to pawn, and then returned home.

As they wandered back toward their origin, their race once more became a horde; the whole line regressed to an almost primitive standard of living. For a little while, Emma restrained this alarming tendency. The tribal affection which was so strongly developed in her helped to reconcile many of her relations to civilization and the lowlands. Their trips to the capital became more frequent again. Thanks to Emma's hospitality such visits were cheap and comfortable. They knew that the famous lawyer's house was what he would have called, had he been alive, *jenodokia jenones*, which is to say in Christian, an inn for mountaineers. In times past Emma had disdained, not without a measure of coquetry, the adoration of her cousins and uncles (for she had passionate uncles as well). After the miscarriage had cut short the flower of her beauty and her vivacity, she passed the hours recalling those old, then despised, amatory triumphs, musing endlessly over the sweet impressions of that bygone devotion. She took a voluptuous delight in surrounding herself, as though in a heady and perfumed atmosphere, with those Valcárcels who would once have hurled themselves headfirst into the river for a smile from her.

In at least some of them that love must have faded. Years and fat and the terrible banality of scratching out a poor existence in the mountains would have made any effort at chivalrous constancy appear ridiculous, but that hardly mattered. Emma was satisfied at seeing herself surrounded by men who remembered their now dead love with respect and affection, men who dedicated every attention compatible with their brusque, diffident nature to La Varcárcel, the self-ordained priestess of her own cult. It is possible, of course, that in rendering their homages to the past those courtiers thought more of the present munificence of Don Diego's heir, the only person in the whole family who had more than four *cuartos*. However, as long as her dominion over them was fully recognized, poor Bonifacio's capricious wife did not bother to scrutinize her cousins' recondite motives. It is doubtful that any of these relations saw in Emma the beauty that had, in fact, flown, but a number of them pretended, dissembling with great delicacy, to nourish in secret the embers of an ardent affection which duty and good manners alone forced them to hide. Emma enjoyed their dissimulation, imparting to it a sort of vague, almost unconscious acknowledgment. She delighted in that farrago of undefined love which shared the incertitude of distant music, heard perhaps by the mind, perhaps by the ear. The family followed a rigid dogma: Emma did not age; the trouble with her stomach was nothing; after a miscarriage she had emerged fresher and more exuberant than ever. No one believed this formula because it was so patently untrue, but everyone mouthed it.

The courtiers of that violent and temperamental princess made up for their inevitable humiliation by openly mocking Reyes. Emma came to experience a fondness for her husband analogous in certain respects to the affection felt by the Roman emperor for the horse he made a senator. Another family dogma, a tacit one, was this: the dear child had wrought her own unhappiness by attaching herself to that man. Cousin Sebastian confessed between sighs that the only act in his life of which he repented (and, after all, he was a man who had lost his mother's entire estate on the turn of a single card) sprang from the time when his mad passion for Emma had driven him to agree to undertake all the necessary steps for hunting, finding, employing and marrying off Don Diego's stupid clerk. He could never forgive his weakness, his passionate blindness. And Sebastian would sigh, and the other relatives would sigh, and Emma, too, would sigh occasionally, taking a melancholy pleasure in playing the role of a resigned victim who must suffer the disastrous consequences of a childhood folly for the rest of her life.

Chapter Three

For quite a long time the good-natured husband had not given thought to these insults. In his heart of hearts, in spite of his elegant suits made of English wool, he continued to see himself as the one-time clerk of Don Diego, an employer whose kindness he had repaid with the blackest ingratitude.

All the Valcárcels were young gentlemen in his eyes. During the brief and now remote days of their honeymoon, his enamored wife had exhorted him to maintain an attitude of dignity and firmness in relation to his cousins and uncles, but Bonifacio could not help but look upon them as socially his superiors because of their blood, because of certain class privileges he confusedly valued. Don Juan Nepomuceno terrified him with his ash-gray pair of side whiskers; his cold, chocolate-colored eyes and his double chin, shaved with chancellorlike care. More than anything, the complicated accounts, which Reyes regarded as the very essence of wisdom, frightened him. When Don Juan gave a summary account of the estate's losses to his confused niece, he always insisted that her husband attend as well. Emma and Bonifacio tried ineffectually to do away with the ceremony. "By no means," shouted the uncle. "I want both of you to see everything so that one fine day this one (Bonifacio) won't say I've ruined you by being inept, or worse." The "everything" which "this one" had to see was nothing. The accounts were far from clear, and even if Reyes could have seen something, he would not have looked. For Emma, it was a source of intense irritation to be forced to attend her uncle's ceremonial reckoning, from which she gathered only that things were going very badly. For her husband, it was an insupportable torment. Instead of concentrating on the numbers, he wondered what the expression in his relative's eyes signified. In his own opinion, it meant: who are you to make me give accounts? who are you to check up on my administration? what do you have to do with this family, you worthless plebeian? Yes, plebeian, thought the unhappy man. Although vaguely aware that his ancestors had been well bred, he had almost forgotten that fact, and he realized that no one else, especially not the Valcárcels, wanted to remember anything of the sort.

Finally, he became so sick of those pointless interviews that, for the first time in his life, he exerted his own willpower. He squared his shoulders, as he was to remark later, and refused to attend the unbearable display. Somewhat surprised and more than pleased with himself, he won an easy victory over the uncle, who gave in with no great show of resistance. Emma did not remonstrate with her husband because she knew that her own emancipation would soon follow his. In point of fact, after three months of doing without Bonifacio at these meetings, Emma managed to effect her own absence as well, and the uncle, without the knowledge of anyone but himself and his niece, no longer rendered accounts of income and expenses to any living soul. Each one signed what needed to be signed without reading so much as a line or a number, and no one mentioned the matter.

After this incident, Bonifacio began to brood. His anxiety sprang from two sources: one was a great sorrow, the other a constant nuisance. Both were due to his wife's miscarriage. His grief was the result of knowing that he would never have a son. The perpetual nuisance, encroaching upon and dominating him, was brought about by his wife's little ailments. Emma lost her stomach, and Bonifacio his tranquility, his muse. The changeable temperament of Don Diego's daughter hardened into a set pattern, a solidity of elements which it had heretofore been vain to seek in her. Her attitude became fixed. Her overbearing, if mercurial, whims now no longer changed with every gust of wind. With a sobriety rare in her, Emma resolved to become an unbearable woman for the rest of her life, the torment of her husband. From then on, her manner was dry and harsh with everyone near her, but she reserved the flower of her wrath for the intimacy of the bedroom. There was an element of almost religious zeal in that incessant persecution. She scourged Reyes as though she were given that mission from On High. All of her misfortunes—the recent loss of her figure, her wrinkles, the exaggerated prominence of her cheekbones, which served as a reminder of the skull underneath that pale, faded hide, her consistent lack of appetite, her insomnia, her nausea, the frightening irregularities of the periodical phenomena of her sex—all these were crimes for which Bonifacio's conscience deserved to be racked by ferocious pangs of remorse.

Did Reyes see things in that light? No. His imagination did not carry him so far as his wife wished. He went no further than admitting his ingratitude to Don Diego in permitting himself to be stolen by that man's daughter. As to the rest, it was not he who was to blame, but Emma, or rather the devil, who took pleasure in the fact that he was childless and his wife was physically unfit to play the woman's accustomed role. As soon as they found themselves alone in the sick woman's room, she would slam the door, and from then on nothing was heard but the loud, strident voice of the anemic, who spent her diminished forces on a diatribe of undeniable eloquence and fecundity. The dispute, if these squabbles deserve such a name, generally commenced with a medical consultation.

"Something is the matter with me," she would say, and then she would talk about her personal irregularities. "What do you think could be wrong? What should I do? Should I go on with this medication or should I give it up?" Bonifacio grew pale; his saliva turned to glue. What did he know? He sympathized with his wife— much less, of course, than with himself—but he had no idea what was best for her. He felt reasonably assured that her disorders were fairly serious and that they were the origin of his own desperation because they put an end to his hopes of becoming a father, but what could he say about medicine and diagnosis? Nothing. He would

16

begin to tremble, thinking of those obscure, pathological phenomena she described and foreseeing the storm that his ignorance would give rise to.

"Woman, I can't tell you. I don't understand. We should call the doctor."

"That's it! Call the doctor. Call the doctor for things of this nature. Even though you have no modesty, let me keep mine," Emma screeched. "These things should be kept between husband and wife. The doctor should never be called until it is absolutely necessary. You should know. You should make an effort to find out what I need, if not out of affection, at least for the sake of modesty, of decency, and if you're not even ashamed, then out of contrition, out of . . ." She was only beginning. It has already been pointed out that, at moments such as this, Emma's effusions knew no bounds.

One day, when she imagined that she had an inflammation of the liver, on her left side, she began looking for her husband. She found him in his bedroom, playing the flute. Her indignation found no words. In a situation of that sort, rhetoric was impossible; only silence could speak, or action. She was dying of an attack of the liver, and he was—playing the flute. That was a scene worthy of witnesses, and it had them. Don Juan Nepomuceno, Sebastian and two other cousins came rushing at her summons. Everyone was exasperated. Bonifacio had been caught in *flagrante delicto*. The flute was there, on the table, and Emma's liver was in its place, but utterly wrecked. Bonifacio, who in spite of everything loved his wife more than all the cousins and uncles put together, forgot his own crime and tried to find out what affected her. Stretched out on a sofa, choking her sobs, Emma would do no more than point to her left side.

"But, sweet," he said, not without some daring, "but that's not your liver. The liver is on the other side."

"Brute!" shouted his wife. "You have a nerve to speak. Haven't you always said that you're not a doctor? That you understand nothing about this type of thing? And now, on top of everything you have the cheek to contradict me."

17

Don Juan Nepomuceno, a lover of truth so long as it was not of the mathematical variety, in which he preferred more fanciful lucubrations, declared conscientiously that upon that occasion Bonifacio was not "O rara avis!" altogether wrong, that in fact the liver was on the other side.

"That doesn't matter," returned Sebastian. "It could be a reflex pain."

"What's that?"

"I don't know, but I seem to have heard of it before."

It was no such thing. It was shifting rheumatic twitch. A few minutes later, Emma felt it in her back. But, although her affliction turned out to be nothing of any consequence, *one* thing was certain: Bonifacio had been playing the flute at the very moment when his wife believed herself to be at the sepulcher.

Husband and wife did not sleep together. On the contrary, their rooms were quite far apart, but when Bonifacio awakened in the morning he was obliged to hurry to his wife's room to take care of her. Since the maid was hopelessly clumsy, he prepared everything. In this respect, Emma did Bonifacio the justice of recognizing his capabilities, his soft hands. He broke a great deal of china and crystal, and for this he was severely reprimanded, but he had definite talent as a nurse and chambermaid. In addition to that, Emma, reflecting sometimes on her dead illusions, realized that in spite of his capacity for tasks of that order, her husband was not in the least effeminate in his looks or gestures. He was gentle, somewhat feline, almost unctuous, but, nonetheless, in every way masculine. Reyes' talent for the intimate offices of the bedroom, with the complications brought on by the sick woman's fancies and the wistful languor of convalescence, seemed, moreover, to reveal less the natural aptitude of a devout eunuch or a meticulous old maid than the romantic exaggeration of a quixotic love applied to the trivia of conjugal intimacy.

Emma continued to be proud of the physique of her Bonis, as she called Reyes. Seeing him move through the bedroom, his countenance noble and kind despite the humble tasks with which he busied himself, she experienced the secret contentment of a vanity satisfied. But she would have let herself be torn to pieces before admitting those feelings, and whenever Don Diego's miserable clerk was at his most handsome, that is precisely when she wanted to enslave him most; when he seemed to accept his humiliation with a kind of grace, then she wanted to humiliate him even more. Reproaching Bonis was her single consolation. She could neither do without his attentions nor do without repaying him with shouts and churlish behavior. Who could doubt that her Bonis had been born to tolerate her and to take care of her?

Emma would spend her few moments of relatively good temper in encouraging former suitors. A trace of sentimentality—purely fanciful, reduced, sickly—was the only indication that, in the presence of the Valcárcels and at no other time, revealed any flow of soul within that thin, pale, wrinkled creature. The rest of the time, almost all day long, she appeared to be a rabid animal, driven by instinct to bite, again and again, the same spot: the submissive heart of her gentle spouse.

Bonifacio was no coward, but perhaps more than anything, he loved peace. Regarding his wife's unjust and nervous inventions, what pained him most was the noise. If she would only put all this in writing like Don Diego, who insulted his opponents and inferiors on stamped paper, I myself would endorse it gladly, he thought. It was her loud voice and her harangues, rather than her opinions, as he said, which overwhelmed his spirit.

There were periods of time when, once the daily tasks of the bedroom for which he was indispensable were concluded, Emma would announce that she would not bear to see Bonifacio, that the greatest favor he could do was to disappear until it was time for him to perform another of those services related to his exclusive incumbency. Then, as he opened the door and stepped out into the street, he saw the heavens open up before him.

Chapter Four

On such occasions, Bonifacio would go to a store. He had
three or four favorite groups of acquaintances who gathered around
the different counters. He divided his free time between the apothecary's shop in the plaza, the New Book Store, which rented books,
and the draper's shop in Los Porches, which belonged to Cascos'
widow. In this last establishment, his spirit found the most effective
remedy, a soothing balm which took the form of lazy silences and
tender memories. All the provincial romanticism of the decade of
the forties was to be found in Cascos' shop. It is a point worth
noting that in Bonifacio's small town, as in many others of its type,
the popular notion of romanticism consisted of reading many novels,
no matter who the authors might be, of reciting verses by Zorrilla
and the Duke of Rivas, Larrañaga and Don Heriberto García de
Quevedo (not the other Quevedo) and finally of presenting *The
Troubadour and the Page, Zoraida* and all those other plays characterized by the appearance of a Moor who abandons himself to
sentimental lyricism while luxuriating in tear-jerking hendecasyl-
lables:

> Is it true, Almazor, that my tender arms
> Embrace thee once again?
> May Heaven grant us this.

Along with his contemporaries, Bonifacio would repeat these lines
in a soft and honeyed chant, not unlike the crooning of a nurse.
And they would recite other lines as well, in more forceful tones:
"Boabdil, Boabdil, awaken and arise."

This was the healthiest and best side of their special type of romanticism. Its corollary involved applying reading to behavior and, above all, fabricating great passions, strong enough to carry out the most extravagant projects. All these passions finally coalesced into a single one—love—because the others, such as boundless ambition, aspiration toward the unknown, or profound misanthropy, either were sooner or later vague and boring or were afforded too little opportunity for their application in that village. As a result, romantic energy found its outlet in love, a love accompanied by guitar music and handwritten reviews filled with sentimental verses, which were passed on from person to person. It was a great pity that more often than not this sincere lyricism was coupled with malicious satires in which the poets corrected each other's diction, revealing that envy is compatible with the most exaggerated idealism. As to romantic love, if indeed it had its beginnings in a pure and intellectual form, it soon degenerated into the traditional tendency, for, sad to say, the imagination of these dreamers was much weaker and less constant than the more natural strength of their temperaments. Blind lust, which is never romantic, played havoc with their loftier conceptions just as it did during the Renaissance, during classical times and during every other period in history. In short, all the habitués of Cascos' shop confessed reluctantly that public morality had never left so much to be desired as it did during those blessed years of romanticism. Adulteries abounded then. The somewhat jaded Tenorios who lived in the city during that period used their time to good advantage, and it was common knowledge that many young, single girls of good families had eloped with their lovers, jumping over balconies and skipping out of doors, or, remaining home, had found themselves pregnant without the mediation of any sacrament whatsoever.

The gathering at Cascos' and the shop at Los Porches itself had been, respectively, the occasion of and the place for many of those adventures which unfolded in a spicy air of mystery and, afterwards, became fodder for strange rumors that were no less piquant. Although such extremes were condemned in the name of religion and morality, it cannot be denied that in the same people who gossiped and passed censure one could detect (perhaps for love of art) a hidden admiration for those very deeds they condemned, something like that inspired by fashionable poets, good comedians, Italian opera singers (good or bad) or the best guitarists. As it was represented in society, the romantic mode (in those days the modern preoccupation with reality had not yet been invented) was a more or less superior variety of common aesthetic belief. If the old devotees of *Clair de Lune* who gathered in the draper's shop were forced to admit to the moral laxity of those times (only, that is, in relation to the Sixth Commandment), they could also cite in favor of the period the widespread use of good manners and euphemistic language. Everything was referred to with circumlocution, with opaque phrases; in speaking of illicit love, they would say, for example, "So-and-so is courting So-and-so." In any event, life was much more amusing then, youth more spirited and women more sensitive.

As they reminisced, everyone in Cascos' shop would sigh. Cascos himself had died, leaving his wife an inheritance of fabrics, clientele and old romantics, all of them now too old and preoccupied, and many of them too fat even to consider such acts of transcendental sensibility. That made no difference, however; they kept on sighing, and many of the prolonged silences which made solemn the now imposing obscurity of the shop that was as dark as a cave—silence which gratified Bonifacio so much—were consecrated to invoking memories from the forties. Cascos' widow, a respectable lady of fifty Novembers, was said to have loved and been loved by one of those assiduous habitués, a certain Don Críspulo Crespo, an honest, energetic and intelligent prosecutor with a very bad temper. Yes, they had been in love with each other although without actually committing the "worst wrong." In their friends' opinion, they continued to love each other, and everyone respected their private but constant passion. It was seldom alluded to, but it was regarded as the sole living reminder of better times. The old friends' consideration for that posthumous symbol of the romantic life was revealed only by the fact that a privileged place was always kept behind the counter for Don Críspulo.

Bonifacio, who had been one of the worthiest disciples of that popularized and now moribund romanticism, was at home with the group, and he stayed close to its breast, which was warm as a mother's. One afternoon when Emma had thrown him out of her bedroom for having used the wrong ingredients (uncommon for him) in a cataplasm, Bonifacio left for the draper's shop, more disposed than usual toward their congenial nostalgia. Don Críspulo was in his privileged place. Cascos' widow, who was knitting, sat facing him. Between coughs and long intervals of silence, which seemed to be part of some drowsy and mysterious ritual, the other ex-romantics murmured as they sat in front of the counter in semi-obscurity, reviewing their common memories. Who lived in the plaza across the way in the forties? The paymaster for the clergy, a man with a prodigious memory, recalled one by one each of those who had lived in the sad, dirty edifices, big, old houses, two stories tall. The Gumía sisters had died in forty-six in Havana, where the older one's husband was a magistrate. On the second floor of the Gumía's house the secretary of the civil government, a man named Escandón, had lived. He was a Galician and a very good poet. Years later he had committed suicide in Zamora because, as the treasurer, he had been held responsible for an embezzlement actually committed by the bookkeeper. In number five, the Castrillos had lived: five brothers and five sisters who had had reunions and given theatricals at home. The Castrillos' house had been one of the centers of romantic feeling in the town; it was there, in fact, that the numbers of an anonymous review, later slipped under certain doorways, were surreptitiously written. Perico Castrillo had been a talented youth, but between women and liquor, he was lost; he went mad, then died in a hospital in Valladolid. Antonio Castrillo had been the best ombre player in the province. Afterwards he had gone to play in Madrid and there managed so well that, without giving up ombre, he made a name in politics and served as subsecretary under Istúriz; but Antonio and then the rest of the Castrillo men died of tuberculosis. As for the girls, they had scattered. Three made bad marriages, one became a nun, and the other was seduced and ruined by a man who held a position in the provincial government of Logroño, a Captain Suerro.

When he came to house number nine, the paymaster sighed ostentatiously, "There . . . all of you remember who lived there in the forties."

"The Great Soprano," said a few.

"Yes, La Merlatti," exclaimed others.

The Great Soprano, La Merlatti, had embodied all that was musically romantic in the town. She was an Italian soprano whom these provincials set up against La Grisi and La Malibran without even feeling the necessity of hearing these last two. The gentlemen of the town would in no way concede that any voice in the world could surpass La Merlatti's—and what a figure! And she was so charming! More stately than anyone present, as white as a swan and as soft, she was as graceful as she was well contoured. She rode sidesaddle, knew how to use a pistol, and once, in the middle of the street, she had boxed the ears of her rival, La Volpucci, who was widely known as the Little Contralto and had her own fans as well. The Little Contralto was also graceful and slender as a reed. She outshone the soprano in the *fioriture*, but as to voice, figure and actual presence, there was really no comparison. The Great Soprano was superior. She had gone back to the city from time to time, and finally she married a retired soldier, Colonel Cerecedo, the owner of that very house in the plaza by the theater. There she had lived, year after year, giving concerts at home, sought out and admired by the local music lovers, who were delighted with, even enamored of the ex-soprano's increasingly obvious charms. But who would have guessed it? After a miscarriage, she too had died of consumption.. The Great Soprano! All of those gentlemen, every one of whom had loved her, some secretly, some in public (including Bonifacio himself, who had been very young then) had to confess that their taste for serious opera had developed as a result of listening to the voice of that beautiful girl, with her snow-white breast, tiny, well-shod foot, and pearl-like teeth.

The paymaster continued his review of these inhabitants from the period of the forties. His melancholy account of the dead and the absent seemed to evoke the musk of ruin, of cemeteries. Listening to him, one would think that he was chewing the dust of a demolition and that the bones of a common grave were turning over all at the same time. Suicide, consumption, bankruptcy, elopement, living deaths—all were ground out as though on a torture wheel through those rotten, gap teeth, which touched upon death with a sexton-like indifference. The old man finished his detailed history, his eyes lighted with pride. What a memory I have! he thought. What a world this is! thought everyone else.

That narration reminded Bonis of the sad spectacle represented by the ruins of the house where he was born. Yes, he had seen the yellow painted walls and the walls covered with green-sprigged paper give way. He had seen, upstairs on what had been the third floor of the now floorless building, the crumbling fireplace by the light of which his mother had put him to sleep with wonderful stories. Now, nothing remained of the warmth of that hearth except the hollow for a charcoal grate in a cracked, dust-covered partition. Out in the open air, exposed continually to the indifferent gaze of the public, stood the bedroom in which his father had died. Yes, he had seen the miserable remains up high, the wall stained with the sick man's spittle, the marks of the simple iron bed on the greasy paper. What was left of all that house, of that family which, although poor, had been content in its mutual love? He alone remained, a mere flutist in the clutches of his Emma, a harpy—there was no reason to deny it to himself—an actual harpy. The home had disappeared. The ruins of his house had become a source of scandal for the townfolk. "But when will that filthy façade on the dirty corner of Calle Mercado be torn down?" the local press had demanded month after month, and finally the city government had applied the City Mother's pickax, as the newspaper called it, to the last vestiges of so many sacred memories. And he himself, thought Reyes, what was he but only an old corner, a worthless heap of debris, who was disturbing an entire worthy family with his insistence on living and, because of a lamentable error, being married to his wife? With his reminiscences of the year 1840, that devilish paymaster had awakened all of these melancholy and humiliating ideas which lay dormant in Reyes' unconscious. History! Oh, history in the operas was very entertaining, magnificent: Semiramis, Nebuchadnezzar, the Crusades, Attila. . . . But the Gumía girls, the Castrillos, so many deaths, so many misfortunes, so much dispersion, so much grief—*their* histories weighed down the spirit.

Fortunately, the conversation turned again to the Great Soprano, and they began to think of the operas sung in those days and compare them with the operas sung now. The truth was that, nowadays, operas were no longer performed in their town. For eight years not so much as a second-rate quartet had appeared. The paymaster, who had saddened the whole group with his discussion, only then decided to notify them of an item of news. This decision was contrary to habit, for his custom was usually to deprecate in forceful terms every event, past, present and future, which did not demand great "faculty for retention," as he described memory, in order to be either referred to or instigated. The good man announced peevishly:

"Well, you're going to have opera now, and good opera, because the mayor told me that they have invited the famous Mochi and La Gorgheggi to come from the theater in León."

"La Gorgheggi!" everyone present exclaimed in one voice.

Even the prosecutor made a movement of surprise from where he sat in his chair, half-hidden in the shadow, and Cascos' widow looked at him and sighed discreetly.

A week later, the tenor Mochi, famous in provincial theaters throughout the kingdom, and his protégé, La Gorgheggi, were in town. On opening night, they sang *La Straniera* and, although the most music-conscious newspaper in the capital did not "dare to pass judgment after hearing only one presentation," the less-circumspect public (but also less responsible, it is true, to the history of art) was, of course, enraptured, and it swore en masse that "since the Great Soprano, nothing so wondrous has been heard in town. La Gorgheggi was a nightingale, and beautiful, sweet tempered, attentive to the public and so appreciative of applause!" Truly, she was beautiful. She was an English girl who had been translated by her friend, Mochi, into Italian. She was gentle and graceful in her movements; her skin was translucent, her body strong, her eyes clear and serene. She had a smooth forehead, which shone modestly; and her bright, wavy, chestnut hair was combed in an unusual fashion so that it served as a simple frame for her pale face which even in the daytime, thought Bonis, seemed to reflect moonlight. Bonifacio watched two acts of *La Straniera* on the opening night. With a supreme effort of willpower, he managed to tear himself away from temptation in order to return to his wife. Emma, yellow and sickly, her features distorted and her hair matted, sat in the middle of her bed screaming because her husband had abandoned her, failing to present himself until late, very late—one half-hour after the appointed time, to be precise—to give her the rubdown without which she thought she would die within a few minutes. Reyes arrived. He gave her a rubdown with great energy, but in silence, listening with resignation to his wife's wild reproaches, thinking of the forehead and the voice of La Gorgheggi and of the finale of *La Straniera* being sung at that very moment.

Bonifacio went to bed reflecting: she is very lovely, but her finest feature is her forehead. I still don't know what that soft curve and that gentle wave of hair have to say to my heart. And her voice . . . her voice has an almost maternal quality. She sings with the coquetry a mother might use to make her son fall asleep in her arms; it seems as though she lulls us all, that she rocks us all to sleep; absurd though it seems, hers is an *honest* voice, the voice of a housewife who sings very well. That thick quality, as the prosecutor calls it, must be what sounds to me like a tone of kindliness. Hard-working women must sing like that when they mend clothes or take care of a convalescent. I don't know! That voice somehow reminds me of my mother, although my mother never sang. What nonsense! Ah yes, silly to say, but not to think. But, finally, what have I to do with her? Nothing. Emma probably won't let me go again to the theater. And he fell asleep, thinking of La Gorgheggi's voice, La Gorgheggi's forehead.

The next day at noon there was a rehearsal. Reyes was present, more dead than alive, imagining the scene that his wife was sure to be planning for him upon his return. He had escaped from the house, and he had to confess that the pleasure of being there was all the greater since it represented an act of revolt.

Bonifacio had always been especially fond of rehearsals. He himself did not perfectly understand why he preferred them to the most solemn and magnificent performances, but he had worked it out, in his own way. True theater, theater viewed internally, is a theater of rehearsal. Reyes disliked pretense, even in art. He felt that the tenors and sopranos should never sing behind footlights, between canvas trees, dressed in percale, in front of distracted audiences in narrow, stuffy rooms; rather, they should freely pass like nightingales through secluded forests, or live like sirens on mysterious islands in the clear light of the moon and in the open air, trilling to the rhythms of the branches rocked by the breeze or the melancholy waves striking the beach. All very well, but since this was impossible, Bonifacio preferred to hear the singers at rehearsal. There one saw the artist as he was, not as he pretended to be.

Thanks to an instinct for good taste, of which he was himself unaware, Bonis detested the inartistic school of mere declamation, the blatantly false postures, costumes and gestures of the actors who played in that poor provincial theater. Such deficiencies were particularly evident in the public presentations. In the rehearsals, one did not see a Nebuchadnezzar who looked like the king of clubs or an Attila who resembled a goatherd, but rather an individual gentleman who sang well, a man preoccupied with real problems— for example, low pay, difficulties with his voice or, say, mail which brought bad news. Reyes loved art for the sake of the artist; he greatly admired those people who travel around the whole world, never certain of tomorrow's bread, whose chief concern remains their song. How brave is the man, he mused, who is determined to trust his existence to a bassoon, a cornet, a violoncello or a bass voice as low as his salary. I, for example, would make a passable flutist, he thought further, but for the life of me, I would never have the courage to run away from home and to travel the world over, as far, say, as Russia, stopping up holes in an orchestra. Perhaps, for the sake of my dignity and personal independence, it would be better for me to take up that career, but I would throw myself into the river first. Chance, unforeseen disasters, unpredictable fare—how terrifying! And consequently, because he believed himself incapable of being the kind of artist who would roam through the world with nothing but his flute, his admiration grew for those men who he felt were cut from another cloth.

Now, Bonifacio was fascinated by foreigners and even attracted by that somewhat more common breed, strangers. To come from any place other than that insignificant town where he and his wife were born constituted a distinct advantage; to come from very far away was a marvel. The world, the rest of the world, must be so beautiful! All that he knew was so ugly, so worthless that he felt sure that the beauties of which he dreamed and which the books of poetry and adventure described must certainly be found in unknown places. He had seen little to recommend in Mexico, but then Mexico had been a Spanish colony, and a certain amount of pettiness must have rubbed off. A true foreign country was something else, and it was from such places that the artists and singers came. To be an Italian, to be an artist, to be a musician: honey on top of pancakes and nectar on top of honey! If the foreigner, the artist, the musician was a woman, then Bonifacio's respect and admiration reached the level of religion, of idolatry. For all of these reasons and for the reasons noted before, he preferred to see the players as they naturally were, rather than look upon them as painted priests or stage kings. The rehearsal, that was where one met the artist.

He entered the proscenium box for which, from time immemorial, his friends at Cascos' shop had held season tickets. It was the closest of the "clear" seats, as they used to call the parquet boxes, and because it was near the proscenium and half-hidden by the main wall, it was nicknamed then "the pocket" and years later "the purse." The box was empty. Reyes opened the door, trying to be as quiet as possible. For him, the theater was the temple of art, and music was a species of religion. He sat down, moving like a slow and silent cat. He rested his elbows on the rail and tried to make out the figures which crossed the dark scene like shadows in the half-light. In those days, there were no gas footlights such as were to be found afterwards which could raise the light to a reasonable height. Instead, the plain oil lamps furnished scant light from the stage floor, where they were arrayed like fallen stars made of oil. On the actor's right (Reyes considered such things), around a table poorly lighted by a weak paraffin lamp, there was a cluster of shadows, which eventually became distinguishable: the director, the main prompter, another prompter and a small, fat man with an enormous belly, who was impeccably dressed, quite pale and very fashionable all in all. It was Mochi, the impresario, first and last tenor in the company. Silent groups wandered around backstage; they were part of the chorus. The ladies' section was seated in a circle to the left. Wherever these pallid, poorly dressed women drew together, they fell, by force of habit, into semicircles or circles, depending upon the space.

Reyes had read the *Odyssey* in Castilian, and he remembered Ulysses' compelling visit to the underworld, that gloomy subterranean life of Erebus, where he believed the souls of the dead must endure horrible boredom, and that was now evoked by the drifting players, silent and morose, who crossed the dark scene like specters. There were always gloomy moments during rehearsal, although there were also times of gaiety when everyone came alive. Bonifacio knew that when an artist is not moved by aesthetic enthusiasm, which is for him a kind of spiritual alcohol, he can easily fall into a state of dullness or apathy like a slave of hashish or opium. In his own fashion, Reyes had made a reasonably acute psychological study of the once renowned tenors who used to come to his town, weathered like old boats that drift toward a shore where they can moulder on the sand in peace. He also learned a great deal about shabby sopranos who attempt to pass for stars. Although very young when he had had the opportunity to make these observations, he found that a certain amount of reflection had been a great help to him. He observed with sympathy and admiration, so much so that his analysis cut truly to the heart of the matter. What he did not see was the less attractive side of artists. Everything about them he romanticized. The powerful contrast between their elevated dreams and their backstage life, with its misfortunes and difficulties, a life defined by necessity and poverty, offered Reyes only further reasons for sentimental worship and gave to his idols the aura of martyrdom.

That day he tried, as usual, to attract the attention of the singers— the tenor, soprano, bass and contralto. He managed to do this with a discreet smile when by chance any one of them glanced in his direction, perhaps after "attacking" a note with special élan, after particularly elegant phrasing or even after telling a joke.

Mochi, the short, fat tenor, scampered about like a squirrel and chattered like a dentist, but in incomprehensible Italian. His manners were very elegant. He was talking with the director, who laughed constantly; and Bonifacio, who did not understand a word Mochi said but believed he could divine it, smiled too. Since he was the only spectator in the theater, it did not take the tenor long to notice Bonifacio's presence and his smiles; after a short while, he directed all his *concetti* to Reyes. Bonifacio was so pleased that, when the time came to leave the box, he wondered if he should not acknowledge the tenor with a slight nod of his head. Then, Mochi looked up at Bonis, and Bonis, blushing with embarrassment, jerked his lovely head of hair in a puppetlike bow and went home saturated with the Ideal.

Chapter Five

That night Emma threw Bonifacio out of his home and
hearth for a few hours, and he returned to the rehearsal. Now he
was no longer the only person to be found in the audience. There
were patrons in all the boxes, and in the one frequented by the
habitués of Cascos' shop, the respectable figure of the military
governor of the province stood out clearly. He had honored those
gentlemen by accepting one of their seats in the dark box. Reyes
sat down in the front, and as soon as Mochi glanced in his direction,
he raised his hat. The tenor did not respond immediately, which
disconcerted his good fan principally for fear of what his friends
would think; but, oh, immortal glory, oh, unforgettable moment!
At Mochi's side, in front of the prompter's box, stood a woman
wearing a velvet hood from under which waves of bright, fine,
chestnut hair peeped, and that woman, that lady, had noticed Reyes'
greeting. She touched the tenor familiarly on the shoulder with her
gloved hand, and she must have said to him, "Someone in that box
has greeted you."

Mochi turned around quickly, saw Bonis and made a low bow. In
the box, everyone, including the military governor, was envious;
they were even more envious of the smile with which the lady, who
seemed pleased to have reminded Mochi of his absentmindedness,
accompanied his gesture of courtesy.

Reyes found La Gorgheggi, for she was the lady, gazing up into
his eyes. Often, thinking afterwards of that critical instant in his
life, he had to confess that he had never received a sweeter or

stronger impression in the whole of his fanciful youth. Only a foreigner and an artist, he said to himself at that moment, could look at one like that: modest but daring, chaste but bold. What honest impudence! What innocent coquettishness!

From smiles and gestures, they quickly passed to conversation. Bonifacio and the other gentlemen in the box laughed discreetly at the jokes that Mochi secretly made at the expense of the local orchestra, as out of tune as it could possibly be. One particular dandy, famous for his amorous conquests behind the scenes, tried to act as interpreter between Mochi and a French-horn player whom the tenor had politely reprimanded in Italian. The dandy did not, in fact, know the language of Dante very well, but he did know enough to realize that in speaking of *missure* Mochi was referring to measure; however, the horn player's linguistic ability fell short of that, and Bonis himself, blushing deeply, risked translating another polite admonition—this one on behalf of La Gorgheggi—to the obstinate musician, whose nature was as bad as his ear. The soprano, speaking Spanish as sweetly as a nightingale, had said "measure," but the brass player refused to understand her as well. Bonifacio's translation, as he leaned over the railing toward the musician's bald head, consisted of a shouted repetition of the singer's words.

"A thousand thanks, oh, a thousand thanks!" the singer trilled between smiles and looks, igniting Reyes' heart with sparks of glory. He saw fireworks for a quarter of an hour afterwards. His ears were ringing. He thought that if at any moment that woman had proposed that they run away to the ends of the earth, he would have started off immediately without any baggage whatsoever, without even his slippers—this from the very man who was unable to conceive that any decent person could get out of bed in the morning and jump into his boots right away. When he read adventure stories about long journeys and the great hardships endured by castaways, missionaries or conquistadors, he always pitied them most for having to go without house slippers.

As a result of his attendance at every single rehearsal and at the regular nightly performances, as well as whenever he could steal a little time from his domestic tasks, Bonifacio became fairly intimate with the members, as he called them, and his friends in Cascos' shop even began to believe that he was having an affair with La Gorgheggi.

"I tell you that he is courting her," the prosecutor assured them.

"I maintain that he is not courting her," the dandy replied, jealous.

If truth be told, the relationship, indeed, after a few days, the cordial friendship between Mochi and Bonifacio had become so strong that one afternoon when they had been drinking coffee together, the tenor did not hesitate to ask his "nuovo ma gia carissimo amico"* for the sum of *duocente lire*, or forty *duros* in the coinage Bonifacio understood. The Italian asked for these eight hundred *reales* with such simplicity and facility—the request was actually the continuation of a story about a Neapolitan adventure which had cost him almost two thousand *duros*—that Bonifacio could not help but think: forty *duros* are no more to this man than a mere cigarette is to me. He asked me for this money as though he were asking me for a light. Surely he must have more than enough money, even if he doesn't have it here just now; the problem is, neither do I. But I'll have to find some immediately. There's no alternative. God knows where I'll find it, and even if I should give it to him, I suppose he won't appreciate it. What is such a sum to this man? On the other hand, if I don't produce the money soon, he will despise me and look down upon me as a miserable wretch. I'd rather die first.

Turning as red as a pepper, the Spaniard explained that, by an unfortunate chance, he did not have that insignificant sum with him just then, but that he could run to his house, which was very close by, and be back with the money in a trice.

And Bonifacio rushed away before he could hear the words with which Mochi then refused the loan for fear of inconveniencing him. Emma's house actually was not very far away, but the simple process of getting there and going in was far easier than returning to the

* "new but very dear friend"

34

tenor's room with the forty *duros*. How could he, his wife's unfortunate slave, get hold of that sum? Ay! For the first time, he contemplated with bitterness his sad dependency, his absolute poverty. He did not even own the trousers he wore, despite the fact that he seemed to have been born wearing them, they fitted so well. He did not have two *reales* to call his own. What should he do—renounce his ideals forever? Mochi would be waiting for him with mocking, even malicious eyes. And it was Mochi who stood between Bonis and La Gorgheggi, his protégé, his ward. Very well, then, given the fact that he neither had nor could obtain the forty *duros*, why not steal the silver candelabra shining on the table before him in the late Don Diego's office, which was now used by everyone. No, since he did not have forty *duros* or any way to obtain them, he would renounce his happiness and never again present himself before his dear Italian friends, before those sublime artists; he would sacrifice himself silently, anything rather than return with empty hands.

At that very minute, Don Juan Nepomuceno entered the office with a little bag of coins in his hands. He greeted Reyes solemnly and began counting out silver coins on the table. It was the rent from La Comuña, a country estate which gave a clear profit of forty thousand *reales* a year. Paying no attention to the importunate fellow, Don Juan was piling coins into an ordered formation which reminded Bonifacio of the ruins of a Greek temple. That poor dilettante thought, I should be the one making these silver columns. I should be the administrator of my wife's goods.

A feeling of dignity made him flush and gave him courage enough to say, "Don Juan, I need one thousand *reales*."

Years later, recalling that audacious act, that brave request made possible only by the power of love, what he found most astonishing was the extra bit of nerve: the two hundred *reales* by which his demand exceeded his needs. Why did he ask for one thousand *reales* instead of eight hundred? He never quite understood it himself.

Without answering, Don Juan Nepomuceno looked at his in-law. One thousand *reales*! That crackbrain had gone mad!

"Yes, sir. One thousand *reales*—and my wife need not know

a thing about it. I shall return the sum to you tomorrow. I'm lending it to a childhood friend who is in bad straits. It's a safe debt."

"Childhood friend? Safe debt? I don't understand." This was all the administering uncle said. What childhood friend of that milksop could be expected to repay promptly? He wanted to make this understood. Bonifacio, following him, qualified his words somewhat:

"He's not exactly a . . . childhood friend. No, rather he's one of the friends . . . of Cascos' widow." He blushed.

Don Juan, with a penetrating look, fixed on his in-law's troubled eyes. Although he suspected something, he checked through his accounts in a flash and, taking two heaps of silver, put them into the hands of the stunned Bonis, without saying more than "Take this. One thousand exactly."

"Excellent, thank you! Tomorrow first thing."

"It's up to you."

"And Emma must not know."

"For the time being it's not necessary for Emma to know anything."

"What do you mean, for the time being?"

"Reimburse the cash box soon," said the uncle, who often spoke in this way, "and Emma will never know."

"Fine, fine, first thing tomorrow."

But it was neither tomorrow nor the next day nor any other day. Mochi received his two hundred *lire* with a greater display of appreciation than his "nuovo amico" ever expected, but of repayment not a word.

What emotions crowded into the poor flutist's head in those days! Most of the time, he did not so much as think of the debt or of his promise to "reimburse the cash box" or of the danger of Emma's discovering anything or even of Nepomuceno's existence, for that matter. By pure chance, Serafina Gorgheggi's increasing friendliness coincided with the loan. Though a privilege enjoyed by few, the impressario consented to let Bonifacio remain in the wings during the performances. The good flutist would choose his position very carefully and wait, as if by coincidence, at the entrances and exits where, thanks to the rehearsals and the prompter, he knew the soprano had to pass. Serafina always became flustered as she walked on stage, but he encouraged her with smiles for which she seemed to thank him with her tender, *maternal* eyes. When she left the stage to applause, no matter how light it was, she would see Reyes clapping enthusiastically; then she would smile, acknowledge him with a nod of her head and pass quite close to the unhappy lover. What perfumes trailed behind that woman! To Bonifacio it was a spiritual vapor, not to be detected by the gross nostrils, but rather by the soul.

On the night which corresponded to the day of the loan, Serafina received an ovation in the second act. She withdrew from the stage by a side door set in a piece of scenery which was put up in such a way that the wings formed a sort of vestibule, closed on all sides. There Bonifacio had taken his customary position. One could only escape from that canvas chamber by lifting a heavy curtain which was used for the backdrop in other sets. La Gorgheggi and her idolater found themselves alone in that hidden spot. Radiant with the great satisfaction of the applause that still resounded from without, she smiled and greeted her gallant admirer as usual, but then she hesitated for an instant, feeling with an unsure hand as if she were blind for the exit from that trap. She did not find it.

Bonifacio was generally incapable of taking advantage of a situation, but now he began to tremble as though he *were* capable, as though he had, in fact, actually taken advantage and had already repented of his bravado. He began to look for the exit, but he too failed to lift the heavy curtain on the first try. While this movement was going on, their fingers brushed. Since he did not know what to say and she understood as much, in order to break the silence, the soprano remarked, "Il Mochi m'a detto. . . . Ah! Siete un galantuomo,"* alluding vaguely, delicately, to the loan.

Serafina, an Englishwoman, spoke Italian at solemn moments when she wanted to give a certain amount of importance to her words. Ordinarily, she jabbered on in a Spanish filled with charming little absurdities. She only spoke English with Mochi.

* Mochi told me. . . . Ah! You are a gentleman."

"Señorita, that is nothing . . . between friends. You were sublime, as always. You are an angel, Serafina."

His words made him grow tender. They sounded like a declaration to him. He thought of his wife and the poor treatment she meted out. Suddenly, two tears big as fists, transparent and slow to fall, rose to his clear and handsome eyes. He grew pale. His teeth chattered.

"O, amico caro!" she breathed in her sweet, tremulous voice. "Come siete buono."*

And she took his hand, which was fumbling in the curtain, pressing it with open cordiality.

"Serafina, I don't know what I'm doing. You must think . . ."

She did not answer him. She found the exit, raised the curtain and, with an intense look filled with kindness and solicitude, indicated that he follow her. But Bonis did not dare to interpret the soprano's look, and he did not follow. As soon as he was left alone in that hidden corner, he felt as though his legs were strangers to him; he dropped to a sitting position on the stage. He almost lost consciousness, and as though in the midst of a dream, he heard a murmur of voices and blasphemies which seemed to come from above. A curtain fell, missing his head by the breadth of a hand, and part of the wings were dragged down. Reyes found himself in the middle of a group of ladies and stagehands who were shouting:

"A wounded man, a wounded man! A curtain has bowled over a gentleman!"

"Ay! Señor Reyes!"

"Reyes wounded!"

"How terrible!"

Before he could put an end to the alarm, it had reached the dressing rooms of Mochi and La Gorgheggi. Both of them came running, anxious, even frightened. Serafina rushed to the front. Taken aback at seeing himself surrounded by that mob, along with his previous emotions and the shame of confessing the truth, Bonifacio could

* "O, dear friend!"   "How good you are."

38

not manage to speak. They thought he had a concussion or that he was the victim of a fainting fit, he looked so pale. The beautiful hands whose touch from a few minutes earlier he still felt, Serafina's hands, now applied essences to his nostrils and dampened his temples. A moment later, he was seated on the blue satin love seat in the soprano's dressing room. Bonifacio let himself be taken care of, consoled and fondled almost like a child, and he did not have the courage to deny the accident. How could he say that he had fallen to the floor from pleasure, from love, rather than crushed by that thick forest of scenery?

Serafina seemed to divine the truth in her lover's eyes. The curious left them alone after a while. Mochi ran in and out congratulating himself that a terrible misfortune had not taken place; then, finally, he had to answer the prompter's call. La Gorgheggi's maid, who was also a bit player, had to appear on stage too. The soprano was not to sing until the end of the act.

In order to prepare him for the dangerous operation of making a declaration, as this ardent Englishwoman had resolved to do, she had to anesthetize the patient with electric gazes and emanations of her body, which had drawn very close to his. Half-dreaming, Reyes indeed opened himself up and, stupefied and dissolving into a sea of tears, talked without any idea of what he was saying. If La Gorgheggi had been more perceptive, she could have learned from that confession both what the Valcárcels were and exactly where ill-matched marriages led. In his condition, Bonis was responsible for neither his words nor his deeds; one could not say that he had, as it were, bitten the hand that fed him. He spoke of Emma, called her by name and complained of the life with which she had saddled him, but although stunned and half-crazed, he did not really malign her. He related the facts as they were, and yet the commentaries were not unkind. Serafina was told that Emma had talent, imagination and the energies of a superior man; she would have made a great commander or dictator, but as fate would have it, she did not have anyone to whom she could dictate except himself, Don Diego Valcárcel's miserable clerk.

Eight days passed without Mochi's asking Reyes for more money. For a week, the latter regarded himself as the happiest man on earth, in spite of the fact that he had never before lived so dangerous a life, now accompanied by periodic but intolerable pangs of conscience. It was on one of those days of anguish that he realized for the first time that a strong passion eclipses everything else, just as he had read and heard a thousand times but without real understanding. Sometimes he looked upon himself as a reprobate, the most wretched of ordinarily docile husbands; at other times he saw himself as a hero, worthy to be the protagonist in a novel.

Mochi had failed to remember the forty *duros*. Reyes did not dare to ask him for them; however, after those initial days of his blind passion he returned home every night trembling for a number of reasons, but especially because of the thousand *reales*, the rent from La Comuña. Yet how could he reclaim that loan for which his idol had called him *galantuomo*? Ultimately, when he could think again with some measure of tranquility, two things seemed strange: first, that Serafina was aware of the small favor he had done Mochi, or "Julio," as he called him; second, that she had given such importance to an insignificant service. Had it been a pretext for provoking his declaration? Reyes' doubts went no further than that.

A week after the declaration of love, when Julio had once again worked up the nerve to ask Bonifacio for money, the lover's amours with La Gorgheggi had gone no further than a few sweet preliminaries which, due to the nature of the gentleman involved, threatened to be prolonged indefinitely.

As to the second loan, Bonifacio had to admit that it shocked him like the blast of a shotgun, the very phrase he used.

Julio asked for five thousand *reales* to pay off the basso profundo, who had fallen out of favor with the public, which preferred, in his place, the basso cantante. The basso profundo then left the company out of petulance and, it was said in private, at the insistence of the patrons. Of course, the wages owed to him did not approach the sum of five thousand *reales*, but it was also necessary to finance the "star" who was going to replace him with an advance in salary.

In short, the necessary amount came to five thousand *reales*. The management did not have the money at that moment, but with the renewal of the subscription series, a good profit was forthcoming. Here again, a safe debt. And Mochi smiled with the communicative tranquility of the fat, healthy puppeteer who makes the weak, disjointed child, usually listed in the program as his son, perform on top of a pole. That smile, thought Bonis, is the equivalent of a mortgage; it's not trust I lack, but money.

It did not occur to Bonifacio to reason that refusing the loan to the tenor was not tantamount to rebuffing the soprano. A hidden sense of disquiet, which he tried to ignore, constantly reminded him that there was a mysterious solidarity between La Gorgheggi's interests and her maestro's. To deny him this sum is to deny it to her, he could not but feel, and, as well, to repudiate her myself. In these circumstances, I can't deny her anything, not even those things I don't possess.

He thought of Don Juan Nepomuceno, and he even went back to the house one evening with the intention of asking him for five thousand *reales*. Yes, there was no doubt about it; this would have been the height of heroism. Didn't I promise to return the one thousand *reales* twenty-four hours after borrowing them, eh?, he might say. Isn't that true? Very well, here I am eight days later, not to return that sum, but instead to ask for five times as much. Insane! The height of heroism, yes, but insane!

And he went to bed and turned out the light, giving himself over to his remorse; this custom had become virtually necessary to put him to sleep. That night before dozing off, he made the following resolution: he, Bonifacio Reyes, would not ask his wife's uncle, no matter what happened, for even one coin more. But since he had promised to deliver five thousand *reales* to the theater the next day—and he had offered to do so without hesitating and with the nonchalance of a man who has thousands of *reales* to spare—they would never forgive him if he failed.

Since he had to pick up the money—he had not said look for it, but pick it up—he awoke early and directed his steps towards the

Plaza de la Constitución, a popular gathering place for carriers in town. What am I doing here? he wondered. It's not likely that one of those Galicians is going to give me five thousand *reales* for my handsome face. The sweepers raised clouds of dust, which an orange sky tinted the color of the mist that hung over the rooftops. I doubt if one of these gentlemen with a broom will give me what I need either, he continued. What am I doing here?

Just then he saw coming up a narrow walk, the Calle de Santiago, Don Benito Major, a thin, small clerk, who was blowing on his hands; under his left arm he carried a roll of paper. He was called Don Benito Major to distinguish him from another clerk, Don Benito Minor, a handsome man who, like Benito Major, was surnamed García y García. Either because he was older or because he was richer, the tiny one was called Major. He lent money to prominent persons, he was not very strict about interest rates or terms, and his discretion and prudence were proverbial throughout the province.

As soon as Bonifacio recognized Don Benito, he felt a surge of sudden joy flow through him, a feeling afforded by the consciousness of a strong and atypical resolution. This is my man, he whispered to himself. Providence made me get up early this morning; I knew that I had come to this square for some reason.

Half an hour later, Reyes received three hundred *duros* in gold from Don Benito, in the latter's office and without any witness other than the books of judicial records which always inspired in Bonis a sort of superstitious terror.

Don Benito Major had the custom of grasping his customers by the ear, whether he knew them or not.

"Let's see," he said, tweaking Bonifacio's left ear lobe. "Now that you have the money without any security except a simple receipt, now that you won't suspect me of trying to deny you this simple little favor, will you permit me to ask, without the least intention of offending you—I cross my heart, I cross my heart a million times—why the head of the Valcárcel household has come to borrow six thousand *reales* from me."

"I am not the head of the Valcárcel household."

"You are the husband of Valcárcel's only heir. Why, not four days ago I notarized the sale of the famous Valdiniello mill, and you're well aware of that because you signed every document that your uncle, Don Juan, brought here."

"Don Juan is niether my uncle nor . . ."

"All right, your wife's. Yours by marriage."

Nor have I signed anything, Bonis was going to add, but he checked himself, remembering that he had, in fact, signed the documents; he had, however, signed as usual—without reading, without even vaguely understanding. He could hardly confess this humiliation to the clerk.

Without finishing the sentence and without giving further explanations, he departed, shamed and disturbed, as if he had actually stolen that money from Don Benito. He went directly to the theater.

Observing his departure and having second thoughts, the notary repented having given those coins to such a bungler. Don Benito knew a little, more than a little, of the tune that Reyes whistled in his own home, but what he had just heard, added to what he had already suspected, made the melody even clearer. In the light of this new understanding, he began to worry about his money, but his new fears were soon allayed by the thought that he could exact serious guaranties from the uncle, Don Juan, who, as every sign indicated, was the director of the household.

On that glorious day, Bonifacio's sense of remorse went. He handed over the five thousand *reales* to Mochi, retaining the extra one thousand to meet any extraordinary expenses which might crop up; and he allowed himself to be morally smothered, as he was to remark later, by the incense with which the tenor was quick to repay his largesse.

That night the company sang a patched-up version of *Don Juan.* Even at midnight, after receiving an ovation, the tenor's enthusiasm and gratitude were still very much in evidence. He shut himself in his dressing room with the benevolent Reyes and pressed his "savior" to his breast. Mochi was in his shirt-sleeves and stocking feet, with very tight breeches of lilac colored silk; without either of them noticing, he had covered Bonifacio's face and hair with rice powder.

At twelve-thirty, by moonlight, in the middle of the Plaza del Teatro, Serafina, Julio Mochi and Bonifacio conversed in voices low and confidential. Julio swore that Reyes had the soul of an artist, that if fate had been otherwise, he without a doubt could have ventured to live by his art and would be at that very hour an illustrious musician, a composer, a great instrumentalist, God knew what. . . .

"Non è vero, mia figlia?" Mochi demanded. "Con quel cuore ch'a questo uomo, chi sa cosa sarebbe diventato!"*

La Gorgheggi replied with contained enthusiasm, "Ma si, babbo, ma si!"† And she tapped Bonifacio's foot, which was near her own.

Babbo, figlia! thought the flutist. So, in fact, the relation between this pair is filial. Art, in a spiritual way, has made them father and daughter. And he began to value Mochi as a sort of father-in-law, artistic and, why not admit it, adulterous.

All that was sheer felicity! He a poor provincial, an ex-clerk, a dishrag in his wife's house, the last citizen in the most backward town in the world, was out at the late hours of the night, speaking intimately of the great emotions aroused by art with two stars of the theater, with two persons who had just received a standing ovation on stage—and *she*, the diva, loved him. Yes, she had conveyed it to him in a thousand ways, and the tenor himself admired him and had sworn his eternal gratitude.

Suddenly Mochi decided to return to the box office, where he had left some money; he explained that he did not have much faith in the lock. "Go along. I'll catch up," he said, breaking into a run. The lodging house where La Gorgheggi and Mochi had rooms was a good distance away, at the far end of the Paseo de los Alamos. Serafina and Bonis continued walking. After several steps, near the shadow of a tower, she grasped her friend's arm without saying a word. He allowed it, just as he had allowed Emma to elope with

---

* "Isn't it true, dear daughter?"   "With the heart this man has, he could have become anything."
† "O, yes, papa, o, yes!"

him. La Gorgheggi spoke of Italy, of how happy she would be living there in a green corner of the Lombardy she knew and loved with a man she adored, a spiritual man capable of understanding the soul of an artist.

There was a silence. They were in the middle of the Paseo de los Alamos, which was now deserted. The moon was pursued by thin clouds pushed along by the wind.

"Serafina," said Bonifacio in a trembling voice, but a voice in which sounded a metallic note of energy new to him. "Serafina, you must think I'm a fool."

"Why, Bonifacio?"

"Oh, a thousand reasons." He paused. "Well, this may be respect or love. I am married, you know, so every time I draw near to ask you to love me, I am afraid of offending you. I am afraid that you will misunderstand me. I don't know how to speak well; I never have, but I'm mad about you. Yes, actually mad! I don't want to offend you. What I've done for your sake, I never thought I would dare to do. You don't know what it is, nor perhaps will you ever know, because I am ashamed to tell you. I am very unhappy. No one has ever loved me, and I find nothing of true substance in anything in this world—except love. If I enjoy music so much, it is only because of this: it is tender; it caresses my soul. I have already told you that your voice is not like other voices. I have never heard, *never*, a voice quite like it. There may be better voices, but they can't reach into my soul like yours does. Others say that it is cloudy. I understand nothing about cloudy voices, but that quality must be what I call a mother's tone, a tone which lulls me, consoles me, gives me hope, encourages me, speaks to me of my memories of the cradle! I don't know, I don't know, Serafina! I have always been very fond of my memories, of the most distant—those of my childhood. I take my mind off all my sorrows by remembering my early years, and I become very melancholy. But I relish this; such sadness is sweet. I recall the day when I was vaccinated. You'll ask, what does that have to do with this? Granted. But I have already told you that I am completely unable to speak. Simply, Serafina, I adore you—married and everything! No, I swear to God; no, I have never tempted Fate until now, but the fault is yours. You have sympathized with me, looked at me, smiled and sung to me in such a way! Oh, yes, if you could read my innermost feelings! I have heard of passions before.

"This, this is a passion—a terrible thing! What will happen to me when you go away? But it doesn't matter. This feeling frightens me, and yet for all the world I would not have wanted to die without experiencing it, come what may. Ay, Serafina, my soul, love me for God's sake. I am alone, forlorn in this world, and I am dying for you!"

He was unable to go on. Tears and sobs choked him. He was almost senseless as he stood there in the middle of the paseo. For a moment, the moon and the soprano seemed one, like two bodies intimately united. He felt again, as on that night of the first loan, that his feet could not support him. He felt ill; he needed assistance, affection, the warm bosom that would provide an enduring assurance that he was not dying. He was going to drown in tenderness, he felt. That was obvious.

La Gorgheggi glanced about her, making sure there were no witnesses. Her eyes warmed with a dream-like sensuality. Holding between her fine, white hands the handsome head of that quixotic and romantic Apollo, grown tired by the strain of a prosaic life, of years of humiliation, she drew his forehead to her breast and pressed him to her forcefully. Directly, she searched for his trembling lips with her own.

"Un baccio, un baccio,"* she murmured, whimpering in a low, passionate voice. Sinking, Bonifacio saw her between the half-dreams of his insensible and feverish desire. He neither heard nor felt anything. Suffering from convulsions, he fell senseless.

When he regained consciousness, he found himself stretched out on a wooden bench. At his side appeared three shadows, three phantoms. From the direction of one of them the light of a small sun burst forth, blinding him with a reddish glare. It resolved itself

* "A kiss, a kiss"

46

into the night watchman's lantern. The two remaining shadows assumed the forms of La Gorgheggi and Mochi, who together were sprinkling their friend's face with water from the basin of a nearby fountain.

Chapter Six

The next day at eight o'clock, Bonifacio was awakened and told that a priest wished to see him.

"A priest to see me! Tell him to come in." Bonis jumped out of bed and walked into the sitting room that adjoined his bedroom; it could not be called his own sitting room, since everyone in the house used it. Tying the sash of his robe, he greeted an old man who entered the room bowing and sweeping off his greasy, high-crowned hat. He was a poor curate, humble, even miserable in aspect, from a mountain hamlet.

He looked around, and after the usual formal greetings in which neither of the parties demonstrated great originality, the clergyman accepted an invitation to sit down, resting his body on the very edge of an armchair.

"Well," he said, "since you are actually the legitimate spouse of Doña Emma Valcárcel, sole and universal heir of Don Diego, may he rest in peace, there is no doubt that you are the person who should hear what, in the secrecy of the confessional, someone has charged me to tell you. Yes, sir, 'Tell her or her husband,' the person said. And, to tell the truth, I prefer to come to an understanding with fellows, with other *men* shall we say. But of course if you had been out, I would not have hesitated, believe me, sir, to have spoken with—if she were at hand that is—Doña Emma Valcárcel herself, the universal and sole heir of . . ."

"Fine, fine, Father, but let's find out what this is all about," interrupted Reyes with some impatience. His superstitious custom of always fearing bad news in the unexpected and the mysterious was exacerbated that morning because of the remorse he felt.

"I urge, that is, I wish—not for myself but to maintain the confidence of confession—the delicate nature of the message . . ."

The priest did not know how to conclude, but he looked toward the door, which remained wide open. As his wife was still asleep at that hour, Bonifacio saw nothing to prevent his rising and closing the door to the room; no one but she could bring him to account for these subterfuges.

"That was what you wanted, wasn't it?" Bonis said with an air of triumph, like a man who gives the orders in his house and who can have the door of *his* sitting room opened or closed just as he pleases.

"Exactly so, yes sir. Secrecy, secrecy. I ask nothing more of you. Afterwards, you can tell your wife what has happened or not tell her, as you see fit. I don't interfere in private matters. In fine, you must, as is natural, be the administrator of your wife's goods, and although I don't know if this counts as the wife's property or not, because I don't understand—of course, it doesn't concern me, and, in fine, the husband usually handles everything—that is, I understand that it is customary, and a law doesn't oppose it."

"Look, Father, you must realize that I don't understand a word you are telling me. Begin at the beginning, please."

The clergyman smiled and said, "Be patient, sir, be patient. The beginning comes afterwards. I've said all this so my conscience may be clear. I consulted the boy from Bernueces who is an apothecary and a lawyer—without giving him any details, of course—and the truth is that I have decided to give you the money without scruples of conscience. Yes, you, the husband, are the person legally and morally designated—that's it—to receive this sum."

"What! A sum?"

"Yes, sir, seven thousand *reales*."

And the curate put his hand into the inner pocket of his long, grimy alpaca coat and drew out of that cavity which smelled of tobacco, along with bread crumbs and cigar stubs, a roll of paper that must have contained doubloons.

Bonifacio stood up and, without realizing it, reached for the roll of paper. The curate smiled as he handed over the packet, not in the least surprised by the involuntary gesture of Emma's husband, who took the doubloons with no idea why they were given to him. Bonifacio, however, regained his senses and exclaimed, "But in the name of what saint do you bring me *this?*"

"Seven thousand *reales*, exactly."

"But why? I'm not the one who . . ."

He was about to confess that the person who took care of the accounts was Don Juan Nepomuceno, but he restrained himself because he was very much ashamed that strangers should be privy to that abdication of his rights.

"This must be an old debt?" he said at last.

"No . . . well, yes and no. I shall explain."

"Yes, indeed, let's bring this to a close."

"These seven thousand *reales* constitute a restitution; yes, sir, a restitution made in the secrecy of confession, ah, *in articulo mortis.* The person who has returned these seven thousand *reales* to the heirs, to the sole and universal heiress, of Don Diego Valcárcel, this person—do you understand me?—did not want to depart for the other world with such a quantity on his conscience, a quantity which he owed and which he did not owe; that is, I cannot speak more clearly . . . because . . . confession, you see, is a very delicate thing."

"Yes, it is," exclaimed Bonifacio, who had turned very pale and was thinking of something which the curate from the mountain could not even remotely suspect.

"Nevertheless, I absolutely must not . . . omit the circumstances which explain, in a way, this affair. This, I told myself, is indispensable in order that the heirs or, rather, the heiress, or whoever takes her place, accept this quantity without any doubts, with the clear conscience of somebody who takes what belongs to him by right. Yes, indeed, it belongs to you people without a doubt. You will see. It is a case of . . . it is necessary here to omit certain specific details which do not favor the memory of . . ."

"The deceased."

"Which deceased?"

"The one who is making restitution."

"No, sir, of the deceased . . . of the other deceased. Don't pump me; that won't do!"

"I am not, God help me! It must be that the Valcárcel estate lent this money without guaranties and now . . ."

The curate had been woefully shaking his head ever since Bonifacio had mentioned the word *estate.*

"No, sir, it was no loan; it was a donation *inter vivos.*"

"And so?"

"So, don't pump me. I have already said that the matter is not favorable to the memory of the deceased, "X"; we will call him "X," God rest his soul. Fine, now, I have not exactly explained. It is favorable, and it is not favorable. Strictly speaking, he is . . . innocent, in this particular case at least; and furthermore, even if he were not, he who breaks something must pay. He wanted to pay; only . . . he had not broken anything. Do I make myself clear now?"

"Not a whit, but it doesn't matter. Don't bother."

The curate had begun to think that Doña Emma Valcárcel's husband was a blockhead. He tried again.

"Did you know, or did you have anything to do with, the deceased, Don Diego?"

"Yes, sir, since he was my father-in-law, or, I should say, my employer."

Is this gentleman mad or stupid? thought the clergyman. Suddenly a fortunate idea occurred to him.

"Listen," he cried, "I can explain everything to you by means of a simile. In this way, I say it—and I don't say it, eh? Do you understand?"

"Let's see," said Bonifacio, who scarcely heard because he was engaged in a terrible battle with his conscience.

"Imagine that you are a hunter, and you pass through an estate of mine. Let's suppose that I am another hunter. Good. Now, you see on the ground of my estate a deer, a wild boar, whatever you like, say, a rabbit."

"A rabbit," repeated Reyes automatically.

"It's running and—bang!"

The gun blast, executed with great verisimilitude on the part of the priest, made Bonis, who was extremely nervous, jump.

"You fire your shotgun and—no, no, not a rabbit; big game is better for this case—and what you think is a wild goat or a stag falls; however, it's neither a stag nor a wild goat, but instead you have killed one of my cows who was peacefully grazing in the meadow. What do you do? In my example, in my case, you pay me for the cow by means of a donation *inter vivos* of seven thousand *reales*. I keep the seven thousand *reales* and the boy. Sorry, I mean the cow. But the best part comes now: you were not the killer. Your shot missed the target; your shot was off the mark, up in the clouds. Now, before you, a good while before, as a matter of fact, another hunter, carefully hidden, had also fired. He was the one who killed the cow. He kept both the cow and your seven thousand *reales*. Time passes. You die, so to speak, and the other hunter dies as well. But before dying, he repents of his trickery, and he wants to return to your heirs the money which, strictly speaking, was, of course, not his, although you gave it to him *inter vivos*." The curate placed great importance on the Latin without which he did not believe the donation was clearly explained. "Now, what are you thinking? Have you followed me?"

Not a word. Bonifacio did not understand that all this had reference to one of those gaps in his honor which Don Diego had stopped with money. In that specific case, as the curate said, an offense of honor did not exist, or at least, Don Diego was not responsible, and he had been forced to pay when he did not owe. The person who gained, thanks to the excessively timid conscience of that jurisconsult, always afraid of scandal, had made a restitution at the hour of his death, doubtless from fear of hell.

The priest felt that his explanations were more than sufficient, and very satisfied with the analogy, the exposition of which had made him sweat, he rubbed the back of his neck with a green and white striped handkerchief. He did not really care now whether that gentleman who seemed so stupid had understood or not; the secrecy of confession, as well as the good name of Don Diego, did not permit him to go on at greater length or to be more explicit.

He spoke further but without adding anything more substantial. He insisted that the matter should not be spread abroad, demanding that Bonifacio give his word of honor to this effect. No one but he and his wife, if he thought fit to tell her, should know what had happened.

"And that means *no one*," he emphasized. "As you can see, it is a delicate matter, and if malicious people, especially in town, should learn that I came here—and gave—they will immediately make certain deductions. Prudence is the word. Especially, the young lady herself—I mean your wife—should know as little as possible. She might think about it over much, and women, particularly married women, are very quick to comprehend. She might understand it all too well." No doubt, even better than you, so far as I can see, he mumbled to himself.

And the mountain priest left, satisfied with himself and even confident in the word of his dull, almost half-witted host, who, despite everything, had an honorable, serious face. Competent or not, a man can still keep his bond, the curate remarked to himself descending the stairs.

It occurred to Bonifacio, before anything else, that in what he had called Chance he now saw the hand of Providence—or maybe the Devil, he added to himself. The very first thing he thought of doing with the money, no matter whether it came from heaven or hell, was to take it to Don Benito Major to fill that wide cavern of debt, that black hole from which all the Furies of Avernus poured forth, screeching at him, "Infamous man, adulterer, what have you done with your wife's money?" (Bonifacio's imaginative excursions assumed a rather high style.) Reason told him in vain, "You have not committed adultery yet, except for the exchange of vows; nor has your wife's fortune been compromised by this loan of six thousand *reales*, even if *she* should have to repay it." But it made no difference, for remorse, or rather his fear of Emma and Don Juan Nepomuceno would not let him sleep that night. With the help of sophistries, he might find a way to excuse that illegitimate love in his own eyes, but the question of the money did not admit of excuses. Simply, he had borrowed six thousand *reales* from a usurer and abused his wife's credit. It was unjust and, worse, it might involve him in a domestic tragedy. Imagination, that domestic mad thing, created for him a terrifying tableau: Emma leaped out of bed in her night cap, pale and bony, with sparks flying from her eyes. She began to advance in silence towards him. In her trembling hand, she clutched the receipt of the loan which Don Juan Nepomuceno, impassive as always and wrapped up in the dignity of his side whiskers, had just given her. She knew everything! She knew about the *fifty* duros, about the six thousand *reales* and about the nocturnal walk along the paseo. The night watchman and Nepomuceno had put her in the know. How horrible! What fantasy does! Bonifacio thought, shaking from head to toe. Fortunately, that was no more than an imaginary picture, and yet reality could easily approach it. On the other hand, that priest had actually presented him with seven thousand *reales*, so that he, Bonifacio, could spend it in any way he pleased, without another born soul to obstruct him or even to know about it. Furthermore, the priest had insisted that secrecy was of prime importance. But how could he guard the secret if he returned those thousands to what Don Juan called the "cash box"?

Neither the curate nor the honest penitent knew that he, Bonis, had no power whatsoever in his own house, that he did not even administer the funds, in spite of his legal rights. Truth to tell, for all the laws in the world, he did not have a single coin to call his own, and his only legal function was automatically to sign any and all papers which the man with the devilish side whiskers presented to him. Very well, things being what they were, how could he return that money to his wife's coffers without anyone's knowing? Impossible. His conscience told him, "That's up to you." But if he used that money to his own advantage, would he not be robbing his wife? Well, yes and no. No, because that sum would cover up a breach in the Valcárcel credit. As we know, he did not have a single coin to call his own, nor any way to earn one. Don Benito Major had lent him the money depending on Emma's capital. Too, Reyes himself fully realized that he had always planned to pay Don Benito back with his wife's money, although it shocked him to think of the when and the how. In one respect, then, he did not mean to steal, but in another, yes, he *did* mean to steal. This was appropriation, fraud, larceny or whatever you want to call it—it *was* stealing.

In a strange way, however, he was satisfied with himself. For in the middle of his moral desolation, he stood in awe of a new rectitude found in his conscience, which rejected casuistry and instead shouted, "Thief, thief!" This inner remonstrance did not impede Bonis from washing and dressing as quickly as possible and leaving the house, without being seen or heard, with the intention of returning before Emma awakened.

It is necessary, he thought as he made his way along the street, to do things like this. If I vacillate, if I spend days worrying myself sick with the idea that this is a crime, the storm of a scandal will probably break. Don Benito will grow tired of waiting for his money. Nepomunceno will find out about the whole business. No, I'd rather die first. I'd prefer death or hell a hundred times to scandal. I'll pay. I'll pay. Didn't the curate demand secrecy? Well, he will see just how secretive I can be. True, I am a thief; there can be no doubt. A thief, yes, but for love. This expression pleased him and calmed him somewhat. A thief for love: it was well put, wasn't it? he mused as he reached the doorway of the clerk's house. Should he enter? Of course. In the final analysis, he was convinced that if what he had in mind was a real crime, family honor, the force of honest blood, his own instinct for good deeds, would prevent him from carrying out his plan. Wouldn't his tongue turn to felt or his legs fold as they had in recent incidents? If nothing of that nature happened, it would stand as a clear indication that there had been no crime and, hence, no need for guilt.

Don Benito was standing in the middle of the dark, low-ceilinged office. He was surrounded by clerks, working at ancient desks covered with green swanskin. The judicial records were stacked up high.

Those solid, ponderous volumes bound in dusky brown conveyed a sense of mysterious solemnity which inspired a superstitious fear in the romantic and unforensic Bonifacio.

The notary stepped over to his friend, Señor Reyes, and began to rub his ears with both hands almost as if to warm them—an unnecessary stimulation; the air in the office was already burning, Reyes felt.

"How goes it, you sly fellow? What brings you here? To steal more of my time, no? Well, you shall pay for it, don't worry, because time is gold," and Don Benito laughed, enchanted with his own wit.

"Señor García, I would like to have two words with you," Bonifacio said, making a gesture which implied his desire for a private interview.

Catching hold of the debtor by the lapels of his overcoat, Don Benito pushed him into an adjacent office. Here the walls were darkened by more bookcases filled with more legal records, these the books from centuries past. *Dios mío*, Bonis could not help thinking, how old these bundles of paper neatly covered with clerical inventions must be! Without knowing exactly why, he suddenly recalled a description of the *bodegas* in Jerez, stocked with ancient wine barrels that ostentatiously displayed sacred, age-old inscriptions on their bellies. But what a great difference, he thought, between that place and this!

Don Benito brought him back to reality. "Let's see now, old friend; what new secrets do you have to tell me? 'We two are all alone. Alone in the face of heaven. . . .' Heh, heh."

After declaiming these two verses from an amateur comedy, popular in town because it was for men only, the notary gave Reyes a slap on the stomach and suddenly turned very serious without saying a word. The implication was clear: I am all ears. Enough jokes. Here you have either the representative of public trust or the heartless usurer. The choice is yours.

"Señor García, I have come to settle that little matter."

"What little matter?"

"The six thousand *reales* which you had the goodness . . ."

"*What* goodness? I mean, what six thousand *reales*? You owe me nothing."

"What kind of prank is this?" gasped Bonis, better prepared to receive the Last Sacrament than to listen to jokes. He fell back into a chair and began to count out doubloons on the table.

The money seemed to scorch his fingers or, he thought, *should* have scorched them. The truth is that he performed the actual operation of counting with sufficient calm, intent only on making no errors, since he had a normal tendency to do so, and to divide that amount into so many thousands of *reales* appeared to him a calculation far beyond his ordinary resources.

Don Benito let him continue, either from stupefaction or an amateur's pleasure. It was an undeniable fact that the spectacle of gold always dispelled any desire on his part to joke. Under any conditions, money was a most serious matter.

"Here are six thousand. Change this."

"But . . ." Don Benito seemed to choke on something else, also very important. "Really, what are you doing here, young man? Didn't I tell you that you owe me absolutely nothing?"

"Señor García, please. I would be delighted to go along with you if I were in a good mood, but . . ."

"What the devil! I tell you that just yesterday that insignificant sum was returned to me."

"Yesterday? What? Who?" Whatever had stuck in the clerk's throat seemed to have entered Reyes' windpipe, for the poor fellow choked as well. "By the nails of Christ, Don Benito, explain yourself."

"Very simple, my friend. Yesterday afternoon, in the casino, Don Juan Nepomuceno, your uncle . . ."

"He is not my uncle."

"Well, then your . . ."

"Never mind, go on, this uncle *what*?"

"But, my boy, what is the matter with you? You're quite pale. You must be catching something. Is it the heat? Let me open this, and . . ."

"Don't open anything. Speak up. The uncle *what*?"

57

"Nothing, really. We were talking about business. We stopped to consider the possible results of this industry which you people are going to establish with the proceeds from the last bit of property you sold."

"An industry? That we are going to establish? Ourselves?"

"Precisely, my good fellow. The factory for chemical products."

"Yes, yes, yes and so?" Bonifacio had, in fact, heard something at home from his wife's relatives about chemical products, though he had no concrete information. "Come to the point," he entreated, more dead than alive.

"With the greatest innocence in the world, I asked your . . . relative if the money which you had just borrowed, when you honored me with your confidence, wasn't perhaps for the initial expenses, for some test, some collateral, for—oh, I don't know. In short, I had gotten the idea into my head that it was for the factory. Don Juan looked at me with those eyes. He did not respond immediately. This I noticed. Yes, he was slow to answer. At last, shrugging his shoulders, he said to me, 'Yes, as a matter of fact, it was for some preliminary expenses, some preparations, but I've been informed, now that I think about it, to repay you immediately.' To tell the truth, I was rather surprised at this, since you had walked off with the loan only a few hours before. But, why should I pry? Agreed? So, we made an appointment to meet at my house at ten o'clock that night and at ten-fifteen, Don Juan Nepomuceno was there with the six thousand *reales* in silver. This is the story."

That was the story, thought Reyes, from the depths of his humiliation. It was incredible. He was annihilated. The uncle knew everything—and he had paid! And Emma? Remembering his wife, he experienced that weakness in his legs, an insupportable sensation that always attended his moments of great anguish.

Neither of them said a word. The notary understood that something was fishy. A family mystery, he thought. But as he had collected his money and been sufficiently reimbursed (the last made him very happy), he was able to contain his curiosity in favor of the most exquisite prudence. That is their affair, he said to himself. So he remained silent.

Bonis broke the silence, intoning in a sepulchral voice, "Could you please send for a glass of water?"

"Overjoyed."

A serving woman, dirty and very fat, presented him with a glass of water, which had a lump of sugar on top.

"Thank you, without sugar. I never take sugar with water. Thank you." Bonis said this with his blank eyes riveted on the maid's coarse, silly face. He said it in the tone of a player who takes his leave of the vile world at the end of Act Three, with his soul in his mouth and a dagger in his entrails.

The water calmed him somewhat and gave him a certain strength. He managed to get up and say good-bye, but without giving a single explanation or excuse. His silence, of course, appeared ridiculous. What must this clerk think of him? At the very least, that he was mad. It scarcely mattered. At that very moment, Bonis did not care a jot whether the whole world laughed at him or not. So, Nepomuceno had paid the six thousand *reales*. That was the worst that could happen. Should he return home? Should he run away?

Seeing him so disturbed, Don Benito Major did not venture one word more on the subject of the inscrutable affair. Without pulling Bonifacio's ears or cracking a joke, he saw him out with a serious, mournful face as though sympathizing over a source of grief as respectable as it was unknown. After accompanying Reyes to the first landing of the stairway, he returned to his office. It was not until then that a perverse idea occurred to him: Something is fishy here. I don't care, but if—it's a hypothesis—if I could have found a convincing . . . legal way to collect the six thousand *reales* first from the uncle, then another six thousand from the nephew! Nonsense, absurd, perhaps not even very original. But wouldn't it have been amusing?

With a pathetic sigh, he rubbed his hands, and renouncing the idea of collecting twice, he thought no more of it and returned to his business.

As to Reyes, when he reached the doorway where an old-time cobbler worked and ate, he had several random thoughts and then fainted. The ideas: That prankster up there has deceived me, and I should have had the courage to break his neck or, at least, to show him a thing or two. He lies like a real rogue. Uncle Nepomuceno paid him because that traitor had no confidence in me. García knew from my face that I couldn't get six thousand *reales* anywhere, so he went to Nepomuceno and sang his little song. It is true that I did not specifically charge him to keep it secret. He knew that I needed the money desperately; he must have seen it in my face. And, of course, I turned to him because of his reputation for discretion, for being a man of known secrecy. I shall go upstairs with the express purpose of killing him! With that resolution, Bonifacio immediately felt the absolute necessity of letting himself fall. He dropped to a sitting position in the doorway. The shoemaker hurried to help him. When Reyes recovered his senses somewhat, he felt, as on the previous night, that someone was dampening his face with water, and half-delirious, he said, "Thank you, plain, without sugar."

Chapter Seven

With deep expressions of gratitude to the shoemaker, who even offered to accompany him home, Bonifacio drew himself together as best he could and started off, moving quickly without knowing precisely where. I should throw myself into the river, he thought, but he quickly reflected that no river passed through the city and, further, that he had no vocation for suicide. He came near the Café de la Oliva, where he often ate biscuits and drank sherry on Sundays after high mass. He yearned with all his soul for a friendly sort of shelter. He went in and walked up to the first floor, where the regular customers were served. He sat down in a dark corner, but there were no other customers to be seen. The waiter for that particular room, who had been tuning a guitar, wiped the table and asked Reyes if he wanted the usual sherry and sweet wafers.

"Away with your wafers. *Botillería* is just what I need. My throat feels like a grate full of coals."

The waiter smiled, pitying the gentleman's ignorance. *Botillería* at that hour!

"But, sir, *botillería* this early?"

"You're right, I suppose. It is a strange request. Instead, bring me a glass of water and, wait, put a little sarsaparilla in it, all right?"

It should be pointed out that when Bonifacio and the waiter spoke of *botillería*, they were referring to the strawberry ice cream in the Café de la Oliva, which according to the townspeople was better than that in heaven itself.

After serving Reyes, the waiter returned to his guitar, and having tuned it to his satisfaction, he began playing the funeral march of Louis XVI.

Without consciously listening to the music, Bonis drank his mild sarsaparilla. But music had been his first love, and in a few moments he felt, as he would put it, "at one" with the guitar. For Reyes, the guitar was to musical instruments what the cat was to domestic animals: the softest, most discreet and most indolently tender friend. The guitar touched the strings of his spirit like the softness of a cat's fur when its back is scratched.

The sound of trumpets and drums, imitated by the strings as they were plucked and released, caused Reyes to imagine himself in the position of the martyred king, and he remembered a confessor's phrase, "Grandson of Saint Louis, rise to heaven." He had read it in Miñano's translation of Thiers. He felt very pleased to see himself so moved, realizing that only sentimentality could impart an energy sufficient, or almost sufficient, to confront face-to-face the terrible situation with all his family, that is, all his wife's family.

He saw that it would be necessary to muster his courage, to march to the place of execution with the spirit of resolve he ascribed to the martyred king. For him, the execution would take place in the presence of Emma and Nepomuceno. The guitarist buried Louis XVI and broke into an Aragonese dance. This pleased Bonifacio because it edified. It was a hymn celebrating patriotic valor. *He* would be bold, not as a patriot, but as a civilian or a family man or—he did not know what. He would be brave. Why not? Moreover, he considered his passion for Serafina as respectable and as worthy of defense as the independence of nations. He would die at the base of the cannon, at the feet of his soprano, over the rubble of his passion—his own Saragossa!

We won't talk nonsense; we'll be positive, he remarked to himself. Suddenly, he thrust his hands into his pockets with a nervous gesture of uncertainty. Had he left his doubloons in that scoundrel's house? No, they were in the inner pocket of his overcoat. Instinct is strange! He did not even remember how or when he had gathered them together and wrapped them up again in the paper.

Reaching for his little treasure, touching it, he began to delight in the sweet weight against his chest. Peculiar it may seem, but money gave that romantic individual a warm feeling. Seven thousand *reales*! He felt consoled and, as much as anything else, was stirred by a sense of *civic* righteousness that sprang from the pressure of those doubloons. True, what the professor of economy and geography had once said in Cascos' shop was indisputable: "Riches are a guaranty of the independence of nations." If those seven thousand *reales* were mine, he reasoned, I could cope with my embarrassing situation with far less fear. I would flee to foreign parts; yes, sir, I would escape. And if Serafina were to accompany me? Oh, what joy! Together, in that corner of Tuscany or Lombardy of which she spoke. And yet, seven thousand *reales* are such a paltry amount to share with so great a companion. How poor he had been all his life! He lived on charity when, in fact, he wanted to be the lover of a great artist, a woman who would need luxuries and gifts. Oh, unfortunate man! He flushed, thinking of certain malicious silences and scornful allusions, as veiled as they were venomous, on the part of his envious friends. The preceding day as a matter of fact, the dandy, who had tried in vain to make a conquest of La Gorgheggi, had remarked in Cascos' shop: "These gentlemen believe that you have reached an understanding with the soprano, Señor Reyes, but I defend your virtue. I'll help you in your campaign to explode these calumnies. My argument is this: Señor Reyes knows that a woman of this sort is very expensive, and he would certainly not want to ruin either himself or his wife for the sake of an actress. Without presents—expensive ones—it is ridiculous to court an artist of such pretensions. You are far too discreet for such things."

Actually, up to the present, Bonis had needed no more money than he had loaned to Mochi; as to the future, if his relations with Serafina were formalized . . . It was indispensable now to have a little money on hand. No matter how disinterested Serafina might be, and he imagined her to be every bit as disinterested as his Beautiful Ideal could be, there was still no doubt that if they continued seeing each other, if their intimacy grew, occasions would arise in which one of the two would have to pay *something*, to make a few expenditures. And his "ideal" could not be stretched so far as to allow the woman to pay. So, of course, he would pay. How? The voice of temptation prompted: "The money is in your pocket." The voice of honor, disagreeable to be sure, responded: "That money is not yours." The guitar seduced Bonis with the temptation of soft music; the music gave him energy, and the energy suggested ideas of rebellion: the irrevocable exhortation to emancipate himself. From what? From whom? From everyone! From his wife, from Nepomuceno, from everyday morality, from whatever offered an obstacle to his passion. He had fallen in love; that was evident. Then, he was no poor fool, at least not such a fool as he had thought for so many years. He left the café with a thrust of activity generated also by the music, and ready to confront the situation with the added determination to keep hold of the coins for the moment, he took the road to his house. Clearly, he would eventually have to return the seven thousand *reales* to the "cash box." But when? There was no rush, no rush at all.

Once in the street, he no longer heard the waiter's guitar, and immediately his courage abated. Without quite realizing where he was going, he found himself, instead of entering his house, in the vestibule of the theater. It was rehearsal time. Serafina was certain to be there. That instinctive change of direction was only further proof that he was very much in love. He had always read that true lovers, in similar cases, did just what he had done: instinctively follow the mysterious attraction of love. Furthermore, what he was sorely in need of was the absolute assurance that he experienced an ungovernable, even fatal, passion. Once assured, he could then consider all the consequences, also fatal, as necessary.

A week after this day, Bonifacio did not even recognize himself. He was glad of it, and moreover he did not even care to recognize himself.

Serafina was his, and he—insofar as Emma's lackey could be—was Serafina's. Reyes had never conceived of caresses so intoxicating as those of the Anglo-Italian. I had never dreamed that the ecstasy of physical pleasure could reach such heights, he told himself, savoring in private the extraordinary delights of the artist's love. She had proved it to him: artistic love was extreme, madly voluptuous; from an ideal, almost mystical ecstasy it passed ineffably into unrestrained sensuality.

In a word, he had visions—beautiful, bewitching visions. Now he had to confess that the animal part, the beast, the brute, was much more developed in him than he had realized. Bonis surely would not have thought that the once harmless flutist who smelled of almond extract had within him the untamed *Turk* who could love so richly and with such artistic, even Oriental style. Simultaneously, his soul, his pure spirit, kept vigil, yes. And Serafina was the first to kindle that sacred fire of poetry. Kisses and music. To have never known such things is to have never known anything. No moralist has the right to reprimand me for my passion if he has never enjoyed that delight, he thought. Kisses and music. But the greatest enchantment, the height of fortune resided here—in the intimate happiness of satisfied pride.

Serafina loves me; she loves me! I am certain! She sobs with pleasure in my arms. She is not pretending. She is not even able to convey passion so well on stage. She truly loves me. I please her. I please her physically and spiritually too. What source of greater glory than pleasing her, the woman of his dreams, the woman he loved as Lover, Mother and Muse all in one.

The truth of the matter was this: La Gorgheggi had been corrupted at a very early age by Mochi, her maestro, her protector. She revenged herself on both her seducer and her bad fortune and she knew not what else by flinging herself with the greatest lasciviousness and wildest abandon into the short-lived love affairs which her infamous corruptor and lover suggested and then exploited.

Mochi, it should be made clear, had seduced the girl in order to dominate her. For a long time, he thought he had found in her a glorious future and an income of many thousands of *lira*, which he felt would soon begin rolling in. He corrupted her in order that he might unite her with her destiny. Afterwards, when the disenchantment set in, the cold lessons of reality made him see that he had been mistaken, that his beautiful possession lacked something, would always lack something necessary to becoming a great star. She lacked timbre and the necessary pliancy of the throat. She sang with great taste and infinite feeling, but there was this strange cloudiness, what Bonis called the mother's tone. That quality reflected wholesomeness, a hint of honesty and feminine discretion, a sort of domestic sweetness, but it was hardly a voice to prevail in the grand theaters. Her throat seemed inflexible. Just as an oversized virgin resembles a matron although yet very young, La Gorgheggi's voice manifested a certain *embonpoint*, as Mochi used to point out, which deprived it of its agility and its elegance. In short, despite Mochi's certainty that there resided in her the heart of a great artist and a very unusual, seductive tone, he did not have a star of the first magnitude. Serafina finally became aware of Mochi's conviction, although it remained a mutual secret, if one can call it that, which they never mentioned. Their common sadness united them more than their feckless relationship or their business interests, but it also formed the cause of hidden resentments and bitter grudges. Mochi, because of self-love and professional vanity, refused to be cajoled into confessing that he had been mistaken in taking up Serafina. She was not a great artist? Well, she was not a bad one either, and moreover she was a very beautiful woman and, more than beautiful, seductive. Realizing that, because he had not married her, he could, in fact, drop this "enterprise" as soon as it became burdensome, he ventured to trade on her beauty, and he himself put temptation before her.

The first time she fell, Serafina fell like so many others, seduced by vanity, giving way naturally to the grandiose excesses of a woman of the theater, and by self-interest. Her first lover, for whom she actually felt some measure of affection, and of whom she had been very proud, was a French general, a duke, a millionaire. For revenge, in order to make his protégé pay for the spontaneous infidelity which he himself had provoked but which pained him, Mochi let her see that he knew all about the affair and that the duke, in fact, was his own good friend and benefactor. The gifts which Serafina hid for herself did not equal half the profit which the company had drawn from her romance. Always serene, always smiling, Mochi made his mistress understand that his tolerance would continue and that it was actually indispensable for keeping the company's budget balanced. It was unnecessary to explain all this directly. What, by his lights, would have been repugnant to discuss became an implicit fact. Mochi continued to be Serafina's lover, and on occasions a real love filled him, a love to which she was expected to correspond or, at least, pretend to. But business was business, and when a profitable match came along, Mochi shrank into the role of the complacent husband. In front of any new gallant, he was neither more nor less than what he appeared to be before the public: the maestro, the adopted *babbo*.

Serafina's second flirtation, in Milan, was not spontaneous as the first had been. She accepted this new lover just as she accepted a theater contract, because Mochi demanded it. Then, too, she believed it was in good taste to maintain established forms. She acted as though she were deceiving Mochi, her "artistic director." And she did deceive him to some extent, because taking revenge in her turn for the sordid trade to which he had condemned her, she gave him to understand that she submitted to those advantageous intrigues only for profit, out of obedience, and that at heart she loved no one but her maestro. Mochi believed her in part. "She still loves me, and she loves only me," he would assure himself. "If that were not so, she would run away. With the other men she only feigns love."

In fact, La Gorgheggi did not love this dictator, and she had thrown herself wholeheartedly into being unfaithful to him from the first. Her pride was hurt because she had believed that Mochi was mad about her. When she realized that he was an accomplice to her improprieties, a discovery which demonstrated no great passion on the tenor's part, she felt even more alone in the world, far more unhappy, and she experienced the despair of the coquette who wants everyone to adore her. Already inured to vice when she entered the theater, she had had scant opportunity to acquire even the slightest notion of dignity or pure love. The strange combination of love and gain appeared to her as a product of her position. She readily admitted that beauty was the necessary complement to art, a way to further progress, especially since she herself was convinced that she would never reach the stature of a *prima donna assolutissima* in the great theaters. However, Mochi's complicity stung her. I would have done the same thing on my own, she often thought, and he would have retained my respect and my friendship, even my caresses whenever he wanted them. I would have shared the profit of my infidelities with him as well. How could he do such a thing? He doesn't say a word to me about it, but he thrusts me into the arms of those men whom he should rightfully regard as rivals.

It was because of this ruthless interference that La Gorgheggi wanted him to suffer. How? She assumed that although Mochi was no longer in love with her, he still believed himself to be loved. She deceived him further by throwing herself happily into her affairs. To give freely the kisses she sold was her revenge, and she did so without even realizing that her own nature was being corrupted in the process. She had begun to enjoy these amours.

When her solid, shapely, soft and palpitating body fell into Bonifacio's arms, she was growing tired of her revenge, but her sexuality was still very strong wine for the weak stomach of Don Diego's miserable clerk, so long sobered by indifference. He was overcome, for living in a state of perpetual drunkenness, he seemed to feel those undefined caresses (how describe them?) at every hour, everywhere. It appeared to him that all day long he was locked in Serafina's embraces. He sensed that he saw her, heard her, smelled her, touched her everywhere, even among the medicine bottles and malodorous intimacies of his sickly, unclean wife. At times he was surprised that his wife did not realize that another woman stood between them, closer to him than she herself was. The power of that woman! Bonifacio exclaimed to himself everywhere he went. Who could imagine that women like her exist? Oh, all of this is art, for only an artist could push love to such delicious extremes.

The most piquant of all, that which added the final touch to his felicity, resided in the contrast between the tired, pensive Serafina and the ecstatic, inviting Serafina: a captivating creature, all fire, who startled him with her cries and gestures of furious love, who spoke when she caressed him in a harsh, guttural voice which seemed to leap from her throat without passing through her lips, saying things so strange, words that even further inflamed him— although that hardly seemed possible—in the midst of his lust. When inevitable physical fatigue overtook them, and the moment of silent calm and inert repose fell, Serafina, no longer a sensual witch, assumed the attitude, the posture, the expression, of a sweet young mother who sleeps beside her child. The sleepy kisses in those final hours of Bacchic transport appeared to be innocent lullabies which united in holy tenderness the mother and the child. Bonifacio drowned in remembrances of childhood, intensified by a nostalgia for the maternal breast.

After they drew apart, Serafina rearranged her hair with light, confident gestures, raising her Junoesque arms to her head. She looked upon him in a quiet way, the trace of a smile playing about her mouth, her cheeks cool and radiant like a becalmed sea. Brooding over the pale face of her impulsive lover, left more dead than alive by his intense passion, she considered Mochi and thought to herself: if that wretch could only be told how happy this poor creature has just been! He believes that this unfortunate man has to do at best with half-hearted embraces; he hardly suspects that I am glutting him with so much pleasure he may die from joy!

Bonis, too, believed that this sort of life could lead to an early death, but in spite of those vague fears of consumption, he was highly satisfied with it all. He compared himself to the heroes of those novels he read before going to sleep or when he kept vigil in his wife's room, and he saw with pride that from now on he could match profiles with the authors who invented those marvelous tales. He had always envied those privileged beings who, in addition to having an ardent imagination, as he felt he himself had, were able to articulate their ideas, to transpose each dream to paper in their own vivid words and in intricate plots. But if he were unable to write books, he knew how to live them, and he felt that now his life was as novelesque as the best of novels. Often such a mode of life cost him no small amount of worry, simply because there were times when his economic situation, his regrets and, above all, his anxiety carried him to the verge of what he thought was insanity. It did not matter; for the most part of the time he was satisfied with himself. The absence of literary genius, which, as he saw it, was the only thing he lacked to be a writer, was compensated for now by the reality of his deeds. He was a hero. All of his acts and adventures became the embodiment of that which other imaginations could only scribble about. Reviewing his life, he focused on its startling contrasts: the risks his passion forced him to run and the quality and quantity of that passion.

While her husband was thus preoccupied, Emma, increasingly apprehensive and irascible, exigent and capricious, managed to complicate her infirmities, both real and imaginary, to the point that, in spite of his singular efficiency and experience, Bonifacio had to resort to a memorandum book in which he noted down the medicines, dosages and the hours they should be administered, as well as many other details related to his incumbency. Since the sick woman complained of more ills than she really suffered, she was terrified that the prescribed draughts might actually *harm* her stomach. Generally, she preferred medicines for "external use"; so the tasks prepared for her husband *cum* medicine man were often doubled, in that all this involved annointing and rubbing down the thin, frail body of grumbling Emma Valcárcel, whom Bonis referred to privately as his "better half"; unlike his wife's medicines, *his* consolations were for internal use. The one-time clerk believed himself to be an authority on every inch of the surface of that worn body, for he had many times applied his rubdowns to it with both force and delicacy, just as the patient demanded. He could pass a brush, dipped in iodine, around the region of the breast as easily as over the shoulder or the flanks. And yet, this unlovely conjunction of bone, hide and troublesome curves made him think somehow of a ruined building which the owner is shielding from the municipal pickax by means of whitewash, coats of paint and roof repairs. Oh, in vain do I rub her, anoint her, massage her and paint her, he would sigh. This woman of mine leaks all over, and the waters of destruction drip through a thousand holes, and the winds of bad temper enter through a thousand gaps. This broken-down machine, useless to me as a legitimate wife, only serves, doubtless will continue to serve many years, as a shelter for the subtle spirit of discord and contradiction. The bad angel would need little excuse to perch on her like a buzzard on a gibbet or an owl in a solitary and abandoned round tower, and from his ghastly lurking place wait to attack me.

In point of fact, Bonis exaggerated both his own language and his wife's infirmities. Emma, who had been in real danger of death some months before, was now recuperating little by little, and she put to use her increasing energy in inventing more pressing needs and new complaints and in demanding other ointments which would not actually jeopardize her improved health. All this had become second nature to her. She could not feel well unless her body was lathered with liniments and raw cotton was applied to every area; the burning sensation caused by the iodine and the sweep of the brush had become one of her greatest entertainments.

Her growing exactions served to multiply Reyes' duties, responsibilities and patience. The husband's air of resignation became so extreme that it finally struck Emma as being almost supernatural, and it annoyed her immensely. She could not say why absolute submission created suspicions. A short time ago, when subjected to any dreadful humiliations, he had protested timidly, but now— not even that! He only held his tongue and rubbed. He responded to insult, to all provocation, with the kind of charity that immortalizes saints. In certain cases not only was sacrifice of the heart necessary, but also sacrifice of the stomach; well, now he sacrificed everything. With this new attitude, Bonis was neither proud nor easily nauseated; his sense of smell seemed to have disappeared with his self-esteem. What *was* this? What before had been for the autocratic wife her husband's only virtue suddenly became a source of suspicions and nagging doubts. Why is he so quiet? Why does he obey so blindly? Does he despise me? Is he finding compensation elsewhere for these miseries? One day, Emma, on all fours on the bed, was enjoying the touch of her husband's gentle and solicitous hands on her shoulders as though he were trying to bring that brittle torso to life by removing a coat of varnish. "More, more!" she shouted, knitting her eyebrows and compressing her lips, savoring, even though she feigned exquisite pain, a bizarre sense of the voluptuous which she alone could understand.

Sweating drops big as fists, Bonis rubbed and rubbed indefatigably, a smile little short of seraphic fixed on his peaceful face. His eyes, blue, clear and wide, seemed to smile, too, at sweet images and delicious memories. Emma cursed and hectored him. She reproached and insulted him. In vain. He did not even hear her. He finished his duty and was on his way. She raised her head, glaring at that expression of enigmatic beatitude on his face. That look of patience and absolute humility stunned her. Something is going on, something very odd, Emma thought. He seems even more cow-like than usual, and at the same time, there is an expression on that face which I have never seen.

"You seem distracted, young man," she offered. That expression "young man" carried the tremendous irony of a woman who, seeing *herself* drooping and sickly, would remind her tender spouse that he was growing old as well, not only from the passage of years, but also thanks to the hardships of domestic servitude.

The "young man" made no substantial reply. She looked him over from head to toe and slowly circled him in order to see perhaps if she could detect the secret which he must have hidden in his heart. She smelled him. Her instinct told her that her discoveries might begin with her sense of smell. Of what did he smell? Of lavender and camphor, naturally, the unguents with which he massaged her. He must be smelled when he comes in from the street, she reasoned. Then she dismissed him, as she almost always did, with a curse.

Although Emma slept a great deal, even awake she wanted to be alone most of the time, since aside from the little intimacies which Bonifacio could, no, *must*, attend, there were other more hidden ones at which not even he could be present. A few of these belonged to her dressing room, the *sanctum sanctorum*, and others involved mysterious whims which she wanted to keep secret. Add to this the fact that she had developed the habitual quirk of daydreaming hour after hour in bed. Emma sometimes awoke to bouts of extreme laziness, so much so that, as in her fits of spleen, she could not tolerate anyone's presence. For these reasons and despite his strict attention to his duties as husband *cum* nurse, Reyes had a great amount of free time. Although it was essential for him to be punctual at the required hours at the bedside, his tyrant did not inquire as to anything else. All the hours which Bonis had spent forgotten by the whole world in years past, hours for which he had to account to no one by virtue of his insignificance, were now devoted to his love. He saw Serafina in the theater, in her lodgings and during the long walks they took together through areas which were either very secluded or very remote from the city.

That day after washing himself very carefully with large, fine sponges, a method he had learned from observing La Gorgheggi in her dressing room, he rushed out taking the steps two by two. What difference does it make, he murmured to himself, if here I am a slave and smell like a foul apothecary shop, when elsewhere I am lord of the loveliest domain, arbiter of a will worthy to be subdued, and am awaited in a bed of roses and exotic, almost Oriental aromas that madden the senses.

Bonis knew very well that he was living on the edge of the abyss, that all of this could not end well, but "in for a little, in for a lot." Furthermore, in the romantic novels of which he had become increasingly fond, he had learned that "you do not catch trout with a dry line," that a passionate man engaged in extraordinary adventure, as he undoubtedly was, always wound up in hell or, at the very least, in his wife's clutches. In this case, maybe even in Don Juan Nepomuceno's bad graces for nonpayment of debts! Thinking of Don Juan, he shivered with cold because he remembered that the seven thousand *reales* of providential restitution had evaporated, leaving at the present date only two thousand. The rest of the money had filtered through Serafina's hands in the form of either gifts or just plain cash, since he often had not the courage to make various loving purchases himself, fearing that the secret of his love affair would become known and spread abroad by the local merchants. In what manner could he enter a shop in his town and baldly request the finest rice powder, silk garters, lace stockings or women's panties tucked this way or that way?

Mochi did nothing whatsoever about his financial situation, neither asking for more money nor returning what he owed. Reyes did not even want to think of the question of precise sums. He imagined that the entire state debt was his, that he alone owed it. First one thousand *reales*, then six thousand, now the seven thousand of restitution: the world, the entire world appeared as a mass of digits. No, he did not count that way; he did not count in increasing amounts or, even less, in sum totals. He remembered that first he had lent what he did not have, then afterwards much, much more, and finally that he had committed the sacrilege of profaning a sacred quantity, money related to the secrecy of the confessional, by spending it on a tight corset, on vases painted with figures of Chinamen, on rings, flowers and panties. How horrible! Yes, horrible, but what could be done about it? In for a little. . . . It was atrocious, yet the very deed, the expenditure of so much money not his own, demonstrated the intensity and irresistible force of his passion. Well, on with it! It was certain that the worst was still to come; Don Juan Nepomuceno had him by the nose and could do whatever he wanted with him.

Little by little the figure of Nepomuceno, of the hated and hateful Nepomuceno, had grown ever more menacing in Bonifacio's eyes. Especially hated were the ash-gray side whiskers, which the poor fellow saw as the symbol of all the repulsive calculations attached to the estate, the symbol of abhorrent material interests, of business, of foresight and savings—even embezzlement if the opportunity arose. Those whiskers! They seemed to extend from the highest heaven to the deepest abyss! Let them be damned!

Loving the art of belles lettres, Bonis could not bear numerals, and as to arithmetic, he said that he understood everything except division; the problem of calculating how much of one number goes into so much of another number had always made insignificant even the best of his resources. Upon arriving at the point where so much of one number does not go (or "fit," as he said) into so much of another number, he perspired, his mind fogged and he felt nauseous. So too, with his presence, or even the *thought* of his presence, Nepomuceno produced the same effect on Bonifacio as a problem of division when something was left over. Nepomuceno did not "fit." Add to that the fact that this sly dodger always kept as quiet as a mouse. He never said so much as one word after discovering and repaying Don Benito's famous loan. Bonis certainly would not be the one to broach the question. In the matter of the uncle, Reyes was like someone condemned to death who, his eyes covered, awaits the executioner's blow and with great surprise, but without losing his fear, realizes that time is passing and the blow has not yet been struck. Ready with allegories and fanciful analogies of every type, Reyes also pictured his situation in another way. He imagined that there was a mine at his feet. He was sure the fuse was lighted. Why, then, was there no explosion? Was the powder wet? Was the fuse damp? (Actually, he was convinced that Nepomuceno was dry, very dry). The fuse must be longer than he imagined. The spark was following a roundabout course, but the explosion must take place; it could not do otherwise. Even in this condition, Bonifacio thanked God for that extra time which permitted him to abandon himself to his great passion without the economic complications that would have ruined everything utterly.

Reyes arrived at the rehearsal smelling of cologne, smiling and, insofar as he could manage, looking almost arrogant. There came the sound of applause from the stage. It must be one of the "sunny days" inside. Very little light ever penetrated far enough through the doors of the boxes and vents in the roof to reach the stage and the auditorium; the sun Bonifacio saw there was an emotional lighting; that is to say, everyone was happy. Mochi had paid the company some of their salaries, and the past grudges appeared ended. At least, they were hidden. The baritone joked with the contralto, the director of the orchestra with the bass, Mochi with a lady in the chorus, and La Gorgheggi came and went, distributing smiles and greetings in her canary tones. She flirted innocently with everyone, beamed on them with voice and gesture—the singers, the season-ticket holders and even one or another musician who had played out of tune or whose timing was out of kilter. Radiant, Serafina forgave each one with an interjection or a nod, assuming the responsibility herself. If, for instance, the director said "Christ" and looked with feigned anger at the French horn, then she would look petulant and bite the top of her tongue like a mischievous school-girl, only to say immediately, filled with a kind of self-effacement, "Maestro, maestro . . . senti, non è colpevole, questo signore; sono io."*

What music in her voice, what heart! thought Bonis, who was just entering his friends' box.

* "Maestro, maestro . . . listen. It is not this gentleman's fault; it is mine."

Chapter Eight

On a certain night a supper for twelve was prepared in the upstairs dining room of the Café de la Oliva, a dark chamber which the local playboys and the owners of the establishment thought very confidential, very mysterious and perfectly suited for "orgies," as they said. The waiter with the guitar and two other colleagues took great pains attending to the table, simply because those who would come to dine were opera people, and that night, *mirabile dictu*, the actresses were expected as well: the soprano, the contralto, her sister and even Serafina's maid, who was listed on the posters in the dubious category of "second soprano." The only lay person invited was Bonifacio. Filled with "artistic" pride, though aware that the supper would take place at the same hour which his wife had appointed for the nightly rubdown, he agreed to attend for dessert and coffee, reserving for himself the right to be off when the time came. He was unaware, however, that he had been invited solely in order to pay. He learned this afterwards when, drunk on love and a little *non sancto* Benedictine, he felt himself enveloped in a sense of universal love, giving way to all the bottled up enthusiasm of a creature more impoverished than his smart appearance suggested.

He arrived just as the musicians and singers were sampling the Roman punch which Mochi had insisted upon for the supper menu. Bonifacio was welcomed with a cheer, which even the ladies joined in. Excited and somewhat confused by all this approbation, he then found himself, without knowing precisely how, seated next to his idol, Serafina, who herself had eaten quite heavily and drunk proportionate quantities. Her face was flushed, and her eyes were sparkling. As soon as she had Bonis beside her, she coyly nudged his foot with her own, which was shoeless and covered with a fine silk stocking.

"Little one," she said, drawing her face close to his ear, "you reek of cologne."

She prodded his ankle with her dainty foot, and Bonis blushed, not because of the foot, but because of the cologne. That smell was the mark of his domestic servitude. If I did not smell of cologne, what *would* I smell of? he thought. Rubbing alcohol, to be sure. But he quickly forgot his embarrassment as he heard Serafina, with the slightly hoarse voice which she used for intimacies, whisper in his ear, "Come closer. No one will see anything here. They are all drunk now anyway."

Without waiting for a reply and without getting up, she thrust her chair next to her lover's, and both bodies remained in very close contact. The odor of cologne seemed to dissolve, dispelled by a more piquant, exotic aroma, the almost spiritual atmosphere through which Serafina moved. That odor of distinct, yet delicate perfume, coupled with the "natural" aroma of the singer, was what effected in Reyes the most violent amorous crises. He forgot his apprehensions, stupefied by the fervent, fragrant presence of his love. And as though that were not drunkenness enough, he allowed himself to be further seduced by the propositions of Mochi, who invited him repeatedly to try a bit of everything. So, Reyes drank punch, champagne and afterwards Benedictine. His conscience too far dulled to disapprove of the liberties which the baritone and the contralto and another couple were taking, he consented finally to drinking a toast while exhortations went up from every side, inviting him to open his heart in the name of artistic friendship, which, he reflected, was no less firm and deep for being so new.

Bonifacio had never been totally drunk—light-headed, yes, but only occasionally. In such situations, however, his tongue loosened, and he would confess matters close to those which stirred so deeply in his heart. His candid eyes upon her, he asked his loving Serafina if he should indeed propose a toast. La Gorgheggi approved with a surreptitious squeeze of his hand, and the flutist rose to his feet. There was applause.

"Ladies and gentlemen," he offered with a glass of water in his hand, "my gratitude is so great, so strong, that an overpowering emotion grips me. Now, I say it and I won't repent. I, Bonifacio Reyes, will pay the entire cost of the dinner, all the food and all the drink—the ice cream too. Benito here (to the waiter) will testify to it; *all* of it is to be charged to my account." Bravos followed upon exclamations. Mochi smiled with satisfaction, a prophet seeing his prophecy fulfilled.

"I will pay for everything," Bonis continued, "and you don't have to ask where the money for *this* Mass comes from! 'In for a little, in for a lot.' Let no one mention my private life. That hurts. A person's private life, as we all know, is a sacred refuge, the sacred ark, ark *sanctorum* . . ."

"Sancta sanctorum!" interrupted a prompter who had been a seminarian. Cries were heard: "Silence! Get out!"

"Very well then, *sanctorum omnium*. Gentlemen, I cannot, I do not know how to say—nor should I, nor can I, nor do I want to— all that your affection means to me. I love art, yes, but I do not know how to express it. I cannot find a form, and yet I have an artist's heart. Art and love are two sides of the same coin, the face and reverse of that medal we call Beauty, let us say." Exclamations, amazement. "I read novels. I am aware of the dog's life I lead in this godforsaken town. I abhor it! Here everyone despises me! They look upon me as they would a useless mongrel, old and toothless. Why? Only because I am gentle-natured and detest worldly things: vile gold and, above all, industry and commerce. I know nothing of trading, scheming or exhibiting myself in society. Therefore, I am called a louse. Absurd! I understand, I feel, I know that there is something inside me, something . . . You artists, whom these sedentary shopkeepers, these barnacles, these provincial oysters ridicule, you understand me, tolerate me, accept my company, take me in, even applaud me, you . . ."

Bonifacio was pale. His words stuck fast in his throat. He was on the verge of tears. Yet he did not appear ridiculous to the now still, silent guests, who, eventually realizing the depth of his emotion, were stunned. They began to listen to the sorely distressed man with serious attention, and that unhappy soul, that spendthrift, touched their hearts, both flattering them and moving them to compassion. The speaker did not run out of words, but his tears rushed to replace them. Then his unfortunate legs crumpled again; he felt himself topple, and his beard almost touched the tablecloth when he recovered his balance and went on to say, "Ah, my comrades! My dear friend Mochi, dear Gaetano (this to the baritone), you have no idea how deeply it affects me to know that artists such as you sympathize with and even love this poor Reyes, otherwise abandoned, despised, humiliated. If I had the courage, I would actually join you. I would, of course, be the least of you, but an artist nonetheless: independent, free, indifferent to my income, dedicated to music alone. Do you think I don't understand you? How often have I read in your faces the nagging preoccupations which afflict you, the worries about an uncertain future! But little by little, art draws you back to your peace of mind, to your carefree existence. Applause is your opium. The pure love of song beautifies you and shuts out the wretchedness of your real lives. Oh yes! And the least of you, Cornelio, who has nothing but a thin summer suit to wear in the winter, casts aside and scorns those hardships, growing ever more enthusiastic at that moment when, filled with artistic inspiration, even in his modest role of chorister, he is able to shout that oh so poetic 'Lucrezia, Viva il Madera!' "

At this juncture, wild applause interrupted Bonifacio. The chorister to whom he had just alluded was present and, in point of fact, sported a very worn suit appropriate only for the tropics. He embraced Reyes, who kissed him through his tears.

Bonis wanted to continue but was unable. He collapsed in his chair like an old sack. Proud of the spontaneous delivery as well as the discretion with which he avoided mentioning her, Serafina congratulated him by squeezing his hands and, more energetically, pressing her foot against his.

Mochi sidled up to the hero, embraced him, their faces touching and whispered in his ear, "Bonifacio, this humble artist, unknown and ignored, will never forget what he owes you and just how much you are truly worth." Mochi's tears, mingling with the rice powder that had not all been rubbed off that night, touched the cheeks of the improvised host. Reyes scarcely had strength enough for any reaction. But suddenly livid, his arm rigid, he started! He pointed with his index finger to the face of the clock in front of him. "The time!" he screamed, and leaping from the table, he rushed about.

"What time?" everyone asked him, perplexed.

"The time for . . ." Bonis looked at Serafina with eyes which pleaded for compassion. Serafina understood. She knew something about his domestic servitude, though she could never have suspected quite how humiliating it was.

"Let him pass; let him pass," she said. "He has something he must do now, and it cannot be left undone. I do not know what it is, but it must be important. Let him pass."

Bonis kissed his idol with a melancholy look of longing; he could kiss her no other way here. Moved by their gratitude, he descended the stairs. The players let him pass, though they cast questioning looks at Mochi, who remained smiling and tranquil. Pulling his waxed moustache, he urged, "Gentlemen, please, don't be afraid. Word of honor, they know him here, and they know that there is no debt safer than Señor Reyes'. If he failed to pay just now, then he simply forgot, or perhaps he did not want to embarrass us."

"Of course," said the baritone. "That would mean limiting our expenses."

"Yes, it's well known that he is a gentleman."

Everyone agreed that Bonis would underwrite all the expenses incurred that night.

As to Bonifacio, he realized with great relief that, as he walked, his drunkenness was gradually disappearing. Too, he was sure that the process which the cool air had initiated would be completed by the fear that his wife roused in him. I am calm, he thought. I must be calm. When I enter her room the "instinct for survival," we may call it, will automatically help me to recover the use of all my faculties, and Emma will know nothing. Besides, she may have fallen asleep anyway, and if that is the case, there will be no complaints about my late arrival until tomorrow morning. Let tomorrow come; I shall be as clear of wine then as the Koran.

He arrived home, opened the door with his key, lighted a lamp, mounted the stairs to his wife's suite on tiptoe. One melancholy lamp, the flame squat within panes of dull rose-tinted crystal, shone from a corner of the sitting room. The room where Emma slept was suffused in shadows. The frayed rays of light that reached the spot served to impart absurd, terrifying qualities to the most innocent of objects.

Feeling his way, Bonis approached the bed, opening his eyes wide, craning his neck and stepping in a special way he had discovered that kept his boots from squeaking, as they tended to do. This was one of the misfortunes to which he was subjected by a cruel fate: the soles of his shoes always made noise.

As he drew closer to his wife, he thought of the Moor of Venice, whose tragedy he knew through Rossini's opera. Yes, he was Othello; his wife, Desdemona—only the roles were reversed. He was Desdemona; his wife, Othello—she certainly had the temper for it. The most important thing just then, however, was to see whether she was sleeping. At least she is quiet, he thought. With luck, asleep. He begged it of the Supreme Maker with all his heart. From the time assigned for the last rubdown, a quarter of an hour had passed. His feet bumped against the bed, and he stood still.

Unfortunately, her silence was no accurate proof of sleep, no more than her closed eyes were, for on many occasions just to mortify him, to castigate him, she would lie quiet like this with her eyes closed and would not respond even if he called her. She would not respond unless (it was horrible to think of, but why deny it?) with a vicious slap! "Take that," she would say. "Go frighten your grandmother! Infamous man, traitor, idiot husband!" And so forth and so on.

All of that was history, true, and Bonis knew that if he ever had the idea to write his memoirs, he would have to forego it. Why? Simple. He would have to omit incidents such as the slaps, because certain particularly distasteful misfortunes to be found in daily life are not suitable for the realm of art. Either memoirs should not exist, or they should be artistic. But whether omitted or not, these blows were historical facts; there had not been many, but there had been enough. Further, he had to confess to himself that strictly speaking they did not offend him. He even preferred her blows, perhaps, to her screams. Noise was by far the most painful torture, for when Emma insulted him, she always repeated herself a hundred times. That could be positively nauseating. It is true that when she hit him she also repeated herself, but not so often.

At any rate, Emma's eyes were closed. But Bonifacio did not trust her. He put his ear to her mouth. Her breathing showed the regular rhythm of sleep. She could be pretending, of course. One simply could not tell.

As to the matter of calling aloud to her, he had renounced that type of thing some time ago. No, he preferred to stay there a while with his head arched over the face of this supposedly sick woman. He would make it clear that he had tried to do his duty. After three or four minutes had passed, he would conclude that Emma had forfeited, and then retire, satisfied with having done his best. The next day, she could prate about his neglect, nag about being abandoned and so on. As for now, he felt sure that she had no reason to complain, for, he told himself, if she is awake, she knows very well that I have not forgotten my post; if she is asleep, then she does not need me. It all seemed logical.

The four minutes of waiting passed, and Bonifacio thought to prolong the experiment because of the unusual circumstances. At the end of five minutes, Emma opened her eyes wide. After a short, inscrutable stare, she said in a pathologically calm voice that horrified Bonis, "You smell of rice powder."

In the romantic novels of that period, the authors used an expressive phrase to describe critical situations: "If a thunderbolt had fallen at his feet, it could not have frightened him more." Immediately, Bonis applied the expression to himself and added, this miserable bolt has cut me in two, curse my luck!

"You smell of rice powder," Emma repeated.

Bonifacio was mute. He thought, what luck is this; even fate is against me. I'm punished at the strangest moments. I must have smelled of rice powder a hundred times and nothing happened, but tonight, when I was innocent . . . Suddenly, he remembered Mochi, his embrace and the tears that caused this smell of powder. The damned fop, he thought. So it was he! What a conflict! What torture! Who could ever try to tell this one, "Look, I smell of rice powder because I was embraced and kissed by . . . the tenor of an Italian opera company."

"You smell of rice powder," the vigilant wife pointed out for the third time.

Then to her husband's great surprise, an arm slipped from the bedclothes, not in a show of aggression, but rather to embrace him and press him to her. Close to him, Emma then sniffed Bonifacio's neck, in such a curious way that he began to believe that she no longer smelled with her nose, but with her teeth. He suspected a kind of vampirism, and so he steadied himself, God save him, for a tremendous bite into his jugular vein, already envisioning the jet of blood; but as he pulled away nervously, he felt the weight of two arms around his neck squeezing him with an insistence that was hardly hostile. He now began to understand, with great surprise, what it was all about. He heard the hoarse but affectionate moan of sleepy desire, a muffled cry with which he was now perfectly familiar and which could not be mistaken for anything else. What could this signify but the reclaiming of a conjugal initiative long relinquished? In this most intimate of intimacies, Bonis had not had any more authority than in his other domestic occupations. Nothing was expected or even accepted regarding *his* initiative. "If a thunderbolt had fallen at his feet" and suddenly become a shower of flowers, it could not have amazed Serafina's lover so much as the attitude on the part of his sleepy and capricious wife. But without investigating either immediate or remote causes, he decided, as he sized up the situation, to let things take care of themselves. His wife's invitation, undisguisedly clear, filled his soul with clouds of memories: his long ago honeymoon, his bygone love for her.

He answered the invitation with equally clear signals. This is not infidelity, thought Bonis, but rather a situation of *sauve qui peut*. His conscience, the conscience of a man who has fallen in love in order to be in love, this false conscience accused him now. It told him that his recent elation at the party had created in him a fire which was not extinguished. Whether due to the last traces of drunkenness, gratitude or nostalgia, the truth was that the pantheist of the feast felt no repugnance whatsoever this night in fulfilling the most basic duty of a husband. The surprise occasioned by Emma's strange attitude was followed by a succession of other surprises, all, let us say, of an unmentionable nature, surprises which revealed to Reyes as he lay there half-asleep that he who believes he knows the most, knows nothing, that appearances are deceptive, that apprehension often makes us see what does not exist—and vice versa: either he was seeing visions, he was spellbound, or his wife was not quite so close to death's door as she had led him to believe. Evidently the chicken and chops, which she swore she could not digest, and the fine wines, which she insisted poisoned her, had ultimately had a good effect on her health. Apparently the wads of cotton and ointments had brought about . . . what? Regeneration. She was like a plant that grows in the dark, pale but not puny.

Bonis was in a dilemma. He had been an unfaithful husband, and *now* he was an unfaithful lover. He was confused, and his conscience—also confused—troubled him. Sophisms offered no help. Only half-awake, he surrendered himself readily enough, partially through fear, in order to "disorient" her, as he said to himself, but also through a new source of sensuality, a new and frightening lust. He reacted to Emma's insistent invitation with no great originality, yet with a kind of spontaneity that caused his bitter remorse, for he regarded it as a betrayal of Serafina. There was no originality, no; the words, the stifled moans, and the intimate playfulness which Emma received with weak protests and finally savored with great delight and a quick instinct for common sin—all of this seemed a parody of his other passion. Every touch, every word revealed La Gorgheggi's style. That very night, in the excitement of love (which he always referred to in his innermost thoughts as "physical," to distinguish it from the other kind), Bonis heard Emma utter exclamations and vocatives which might have come from his mistress' amorous dictionary, and he felt her give him caresses much like Serafina's. Oh, this was like a contagious disease; Emma, his wife before God and man, had "caught" Serafina's habit of loving.

The conscience which protested here was that of the husband, of the head of the family (theoretical, to be sure), of Bonifacio Reyes. I am contaminating my marriage bed with a kind of secret moral sickness, he remarked to himself, and I am failing in my duties as a romantic and artistic lover as well. A weight of chronic remorse settled at the bottom of his poor brain, along with the fumes of drink, which he thought had vanished and which instead had simply assumed another form. On one side, his head was weighted with lead; on the other, with concupiscence. Both threatened to overwhelm him. Lying in Emma's arms, Bonis heard exploding within his head random cries of Bonifacio! Reyes! Bonifacio! He recognized the voices of the baritone and the bass and the one who sang "Lucrezia, Viva il Madera!"

Morning came. The sad couple dozed. At ten o'clock, Emma woke up, remembered everything, coyly smiled as a cat might if it could, and kicked her husband on the shin. "Bonis, get up," she demanded. "Eufemia is going to come."

Eufemia was the maid who was responsible for bringing Emma her chocolate at ten-fifteen on the dot. She did not want the girl to find out that she and her husband had slept together.

When Reyes "opened his eyes to reality," as he put it, the first thing he did was yawn. The second was to feel again a burning thirst for his Ideal, the Infinite, for regeneration through love and, even stronger, a physical thirst for water and a great desire to sleep longer. He did not want to think about his situation. It horrified him for a number of reasons. "Sideo," he murmured, recalling one of the Seven Last Words of the Martyr of Golgotha, his own name for Jesus Christ. Emma repeated the kick with her bare foot on the bone of his right leg, and Bonis, translating the Latin, explained, "I'm thirsty. Give me something to drink for the love of God, even if it's syrup."

"Listen, you," Emma barked. "Do you hear what I said? Get up before the girl comes. If you have no sense of shame, at least I do."

With a burst of energy, the sort that had often made Bonifacio think his wife would have made an impressive man of action, a politician, a captain, Emma kicked him out of the bed quickly and efficiently. Reyes had no alternative other than to dress himself quickly and "provisionally" and leave his better half's chamber without further protest.

Half-naked, shoeless, his boots in his hand (how could he put on boots first thing, instead of slippers?) he bumped against everything in the hallways, crossing the dining room, drank a glass of water forgotten there the previous night, reached his room, undressed hurriedly and awkwardly, breaking buttons in the process, and flung himself into bed, his own bed. He planned to reflect about many things, all within the wide, wide range of painful contradictions that generated feelings of guilt. But soon he felt that his physical nature could face no more. The freshness of the smooth bed and the softness of the carefully plumped mattress drew him, like triumphant sirens, into the deepest sea of sleep imaginable, where waves of tranquility and oblivion rolled over him.

Chapter Nine

Bonifacio slept like a dead man, but not for very long. As though brought back to life, he blinked at the crude light of the noonday sun, which stole in through the slit of a half-closed window and painfully touched the point of his nose and a spot between his eyebrows. That ray of light reminded Bonis of religious prints he had seen in which mystic rays, not unlike the one annoying him now, fell over the heads of imprisoned saints or saints who were simply out in the middle of open fields. If he were a pagan (which he felt he certainly was not), he would have seen the hand of Providence in that light. He was not a pagan, no; he believed in a Supreme Being and His justice, which had conscience as its principal agent. Undoubtedly, his situation had become more complicated overnight. "You smell of rice powder," the deceived wife had said. She said it three times, but instead of becoming angry, of choking him or poisoning him . . . the strangest things had happened.

In arriving at this point, he envisaged his wife's flesh just as it had been caught in a fleeting glimpse when he leaped out of the conjugal bed. The reality with which he had been presented in the morning was not quite the same which he believed he had found in the exaltation of drunkenness on the night before, but even this reality greatly exceeded the condition one could believably have attributed to what he referred to as the veiled—and probably withered—charms of his wife. When applying the ointments and various other necessities to Emma's body, he saw a great deal of her flesh, but due to her excessive show of prudery, he himself could never really observe those hidden regions which always held so much charm in the anatomical and poetical preoccupations of Bonis. It was, then, in these zones that he had found surprises, unexpected gifts, a kind of Indian summer of which even the greatest optimist could never have dreamed. Why? Bonifacio could not explain it to himself.

Although he was of a philosophical turn, very fond of slowly reflecting on all the events in life, whether they affected him or not, he was one of those thinkers (of whom there are more than enough and to spare) who only turn over well-known ideas. Bonifacio never made discoveries or penetrated into new regions. As to finding out the whys and wherefores of natural or sociological phenomena, he was as obtuse as so many celebrated philosophers today—men who have never managed to extract any of the useful secrets from sly reality. So Bonifacio deliberated at length but never succeeded in determining the *quid* of his wife, always posing as half-defunct, whose hidden recesses were by no means contemptible although pale and so synthetically soft that her skin was almost like gauze, lacking certain qualities of viable material. It would seem that the cotton wads, the unguents and the warm atmosphere of the perfumed sheets had produced a kind of artifical robustness, almost false flesh! Bonifacio lost himself in such conjectures and absurdities, but he always ended by rejecting his own wild hypotheses, hypotheses against which all the textbooks of secondary school (which he had read some years before when, inspired by a newspaper editorial on progress and the wisdom of the middle class, he had tried to make himself a son worthy of his century by advancing through science) protested vehemently. No, it was impossible. All the physical and mathematical laws opposed the proposition that raw cotton was assimilable and could convert itself into the fibers of human flesh.

There is no reason to follow Reyes through the rest of his conjectures. Certainties alone matter, and it was certain, very certain, that Emma had been subject to various corrosions, that her flesh had slowly wasted away because of disorders originating in the misfortunes of the frustrated mother, her nerves, apprehensions, extreme pseudohygienic measures, cavillations, fits of temper and the lack of light and fresh air, but it was also true that the tough body of that Eumenidae did not lack *some* fiber. Her constitution had, in fact, stood up to life with a fury, so that finally her stomach, assimilating good meat and drink, showed a great improvement. Her health returned with a rush, filling her spirit and keeping intact what could so easily have collapsed. She saw herself reborn into a pale youth. But Emma had always thought of herself as a hothouse plant whom her beast of a husband and those other brutes in the house might want to transplant into the open air as soon as they became aware of that rebirth. Now her principal crotchet, among many others, was this: she had been given new life, which she very much enjoyed, but she must remain in her hothouse, she felt, and still be treated like a sick woman (although, of course, she no longer was one). Now sickness became perversely delightful. She found satisfaction, for instance, in textures, odors and flavors—all inanimate, all abstracted from the vital. She derived no little pleasure from the batiste sheets, the warm bed, the feather pillows, the air enclosed in silk hangings, the carpeted floor, the crevices in the hermetically sealed door, the sweet hay, apples and satchets packed into her clothing, the camphor and the hundred odors which Celestina already knew.* Emma savored all the delights of the three senses that earlier she had ignored as means of either pleasure or new discovery. In her methodic "imprisonment," neither sight nor hearing could impart much enjoyment. In contrast, however, the new sensations were highly refined—the sense of taste, of smell, of touch. Her whole body stretched and turned languorously within her soft, white gowns, like a drowsy, pampered cat.

During those days when her apprehensions, coupled with her very real nervous afflictions—weaknesses to which she gave way—had placed her in danger of death, she had begun to feel a horrible loneliness, the solitude of the egoist who, left alone, foresees the end of his life. Everything and everyone conspired in letting her

---

* *Celestina* refers to the central character in the *Comedia de Calisto y Melibea* (1499), a celebrated work of prose fiction that is popularly known as *La Celestina*. She is a formidable bawd who knows many tricks for attracting lovers.

die alone and make her way to God on her own! With sharpened vision lent by serious illness, she was able to perceive to just what extent general indifference to the impending danger prevailed. The realization was bitter.

You die alone, completely alone, she reflected. The others are smug; they stay behind in the world, well satisfied with themselves. They do not even offer to die with you out of courtesy! No one did anything to ease her death. No one said, "Well then, Emma, I shall accompany you!"

Emma was an absolute atheist. She had never given a thought to God, not even to deny His existence. She neither believed, nor ceased to believe, in religion. She fulfilled her obligation to the Church grudgingly, automatically. In her time and her country, it was not customary to discuss religious matters. Those who were not really devoted enjoyed complete tolerance. And since they, like Emma, were not *un*believers, they did not have to go out of their way to neglect pious customs; they simply maintained appearances. They bothered no one. "I am no saint," Emma remarked and thought no more about the matter. The Church and the curates were not objectionable. Everything was acceptable. No, she was not fond of novenas, but all of that was part of the general order, like having kings, taxes and the Civil Guard. She did not question herself about those things; she could hardly care less. Why? "I am no saint," she said. Enough. She was a perfect atheist.

She lived with total unconcern. Never had she meditated on affairs beyond the tomb. She pictured hell, perhaps, as an oven, but to her what did that matter? Hell was reserved for the great sinners who killed a father, a mother or a priest, who trampled on the host or did not go to confession. No one knew anything for certain about such things. But dying—yes, that was horrible, not because of hell, but because of the pain of death, the pain of coming to an end.

Coming to an end! Without considering the conflict between her private beliefs and the dogma of heaven and hell, Emma saw only the utter terror—and this with a deep conviction, with the awareness of her own fears—of the finality of the grave. No master of fine logic, Emma did not stop to separate matters rational from matters imaginary. So, in this way, she did feel *something* of death, made all the more graphic by her vision of the shovelfuls of lime, the damp earth, the closed coffin, the lonely cemetery and a dark eternity. Unaware of her contradictions, she suffered from the whole idea of annihilation and the image of the sepulcher. She thought about death in terms of life—the ordinary, daily round of her uninspired existence—and the horror of the contrast increased with these thoughts.

It never occurred to her to commit herself to the protection of a saint. Nor did she offer anything to the Virgin or Jesus to regain her health. The first sign of successful convalescence was only a smile—and a bitter one. The newly resurrected Emma's intentions took a demonic turn. Petulant and convinced of abuses, like so many other convalescents, she fixed on one immovable resolution: to take revenge on those miserable relatives who would have allowed her to die alone.

Like the majority of people of her century, Emma had only enough intellectual vigor and willpower to cope with the immediate interests of the petty prose of life. She referred to everything else as "poetry," regarding as serious nothing other than her vulgar, run-of-the-mill egoism; it was only this that she was able to understand or consider with any strength. This spirit was far more compatible with the self-conscious romanticism and the outrageous fantasies of her youth than she herself could have imagined, even if she had been capable of comparing the present squalor of her soul with those extravagant dreams cultivated in her spring days.

The rebirth of her flesh she guarded as a secret. She was naturally hypocritical when it came to health. She continued to feign bodily indispositions as if having them constituted a virtue. Eufemia, her maid, was partially confidante to her deceptions, the mean little games she played on her relatives. Alone with her maid, Emma savored the details of these pretenses. Valcárcel's daughter squandered her inheritance in secret with the help of Eufemia, who brought home from the shops and plazas the finest brocades and the most expensive trifles in the way of fashionable underwear, perfumes and dainty morsels. In every commercial establishment and food stall, Emma began to run up enormous accounts. Neither Uncle Nepomuceno nor Bonis nor Sebastian suspected the existence of that hole she was scratching into the fortune that they perhaps hoped someday to inherit. So she thought, and she took a voluptuous delight in the little "surprise" she had reserved for her expectant relatives. To enjoy the best partridge and sea lamprey from the plaza, to use carelessly the finest batiste, to twine her fingers through the daintiest laces, to spill the most expensive powders profusely among her sheet, shifts and stockings, astonishing Eufemia all the while with her prodigality, this was the very quintessence of delight, augmented by the knowledge that she was playing quite a trick on those relations, in particular Bonis and her uncle. Don Nepo, she would say quietly to herself, rob me, go ahead, but I can look after myself too.

Although wholly engrossed in the material life, she gave not the slightest thought to preserving her fortune, nor did she even give a thought to the source of her money. She vaguely believed that the capital of which she was mistress was inexhaustible, located perhaps in some mysterious spot. There was no need to enter into a tiresome investigation of its whereabouts. There, somewhere between her uncle's papers, lay the mine. He would, of course, keep a great part of the treasure, but what difference did that make? It was not worth the trouble to reckon the accounts, to waste time being suspicious, to administer for herself. Bah! Absurd! There seemed to be enough money for everything. He stole; she stole too. He deceived her? Well and good, for one fine day a swatch of bills would arrive at the house and leave the good Don Nepo dumbfounded, since it was, of course, clear that he and he alone would have to pay them.

In fact, the bills had already come; some had been paid. Don Juan Nepomuceno pursued the same line of behavior with Emma as he did with Bonifacio, given that each of them, as he put it, had "surrendered to prodigality." Actually, Emma's extravagance was real enough; she well knew it and actually relished, as though it were a great luxury, the opportunity of undercutting her uncle. She realized that he was feathering his own nest with her money, that a great part of the administered capital was passing directly into the administrator's hands. It was perfectly clear that each time Don Juan spoke of his own income (which "thanks to miracles of luck or a benevolent Providence" was prospering), on the very same day he also spoke of the countless calamities that befell the Valcárcel estate and their property, which was invested in various industries in Spain and in foreign countries. The iron and coal mines being developed in the provinces at that time became the constant source of disappointments, and not a few of those disappointments devalued the stocks purchased for Emma by Nepomuceno, always solicitous for his one-time ward's financial interests. But—oh remarkable coincidence and consistency of Fate—the mines in which this same Don Juan invested his own wretched savings did not fail, but rather yielded a healthy and reliable profit. Emma, then, understood well enough that her uncle robbed her, but here her sense of refined indulgence came in. It did not matter to her; she let him do it, refusing to tire herself by calculating prices, demanding accounts or quarreling over a question of *ochavos*—this very woman who went into a screaming fit over a bowl of overheated broth!

With a strange sense of amusement and a certain vanity springing from the conviction that hers was a singular, even unique spirit, Emma tolerated and, more, encouraged her uncle's weaknesses, even though they actually endangered her own position. She indulged herself in this savage whim with a delight not unlike that she took in being tickled until she was almost made sick with giggles. The discovery of evil in somebody else charmed her, fed her pride and inspired her to even greater capriciousness. In evil she discovered a peculiar beauty, the product of energy and cunning. Any artful rogue, shrewd and bold in his misdeeds, was a hero in her eyes. She dreamed of Luis Candelas as he appeared in popular books of adventure. She read about scandals avidly, reserving all her compassion for criminals awaiting the executioner. Her tolerance toward crimes of passion was infinite. When really sick, she had looked with contempt, repugnance, even anger, at everything which tended to foster love; as soon as she felt a breath of life within that pale, soft, almost spongy hide, she regained her limitless respect for amorous frailties, and she again began to admire all the great romantic feats of audacity—especially if the deeds of daring were carried out by women.

As a result of rumors spread by Sebastian and Eufemia, she knew that Nepomuceno had developed an old man's passion for a German girl, the daughter of M. Körner, an industrial engineer and a noteworthy chemist who had come to town to deal with some metallurgic business. Without a doubt, Emma said to herself, this uncle of mine wants to make himself rich by hook or by crook, and fast. He wants to seduce the German's daughter with his fortune, since he certainly can't do it with his ash-gray side whiskers! And with a delight so palpable that she could almost taste it, a delight akin to her prediliction for salacious literature, Emma pictured this good gentleman of more than fifty leaping about like a young colt, pierced to the quick by the demon of love.

She spent long hours meditating on the contingencies of that oh-so-entertaining love affair until she reached the point of vividly imagining the wedding day itself. She thought of the likelihood of a charivari, since the uncle was a widower; she herself would join in, disguised—after first presenting the bride with a magnificent set of jewels. Afterwards, she and the German girl would become good friends, take promenades together, and together begin to make fun of the ridiculous old gentleman with the side whiskers, who was uncle of one, husband of the other. How amusing! She began to consider, further, just how her aunt-in-law would cuckold the unfaithful administrator. With whom? Why not Cousin Sebastian? Emma finally tangled the skein of fantasy so that in her imagination she herself would be partly to blame for her uncle's unhappiness. So? All the better. Had he not deceived her? Had he not robbed her? Well then, he would surely pay.

Yes, Emma reserved for herself the right to take revenge for the old thefts she had tolerated. She would reveal Don Nepo's depredations as soon as his marriage went awry. What a laugh! What a chance to embarrass him! In this matter and in the case of anyone else whose weaknesses represented a potential injury, Emma determined that her revenge would be both refined and cruel. She did not know how or when, but one day, one day! And with the consciousness of these postponed retaliations, these vengeful punishments and torments conceived and projected in the mists of her voluptuous contemplation, she experienced a sense of joy and excitement much like that others felt at the expectation of being happy.

To explain fully her conduct towards her uncle and Bonis as well, it is necessary to add to this examination of her distorted sentiments her penchant for the unusual and the unexpected. It irritated her when someone foresaw her vexations, her fits of temper and her spiteful ways of getting back at them all. She preferred to lose her temper for reasons nobody could understand, to baffle the most expert observer by remaining cold and impassive in the face of offenses they thought would have goaded her beyond endurance. With Eufemia, her confidante, she exercised this whim for contrariness—sometimes in their personal relations, sometimes in regard to a third person—continually.

Nothing that the uncle and Bonis could do to her would ever again cause in her so much rancor, however, as the fact that they had left her at death's door without offering to accompany her to the grave. That was what she could not forgive. Yes, she had to dissemble now, but what a shock she was going to give them one day, say, when her uncle discovered that the fortune he had reserved for any unexpected expenses (at a time, perhaps, when the German presented him with Sebastian's little ones) had passed according to law into the hands of her creditors, the shopkeeper on the corner, the merchant in the portico, and all the others.

Life held an interesting future for her. She began to realize that she had not been selfish *enough* in the past. To force others to kneel and simultaneously to divert herself in a thousand as yet undiscovered ways—ah! these were the twin springs of pleasure from which she wanted to drink great draughts forever.

96

With the arrival of new health, Emma entertained wild hopes for pleasure. This liberating force finally became so strong that the secret luxuries of her voluntary retreat began to seem insufficient. They did not gratify her thirst for stronger emotions. Finally, breaking through the cocoon, she decided to go out into the world in search of newer adventures, but not without caution, not without cunning. The relatives needed to know nothing. Mystery would add zest to her outing.

One night Eufemia was dozing in her mistress' bedroom, nodding against the wall; she was awakened with a start by a blow on her shoulder. It was Emma, dressed in her nightgown, paler than ever, breathing heavily, her nostrils distended and wide as bellows.

"What time is it?" she asked in a hoarse voice.

"It must be about ten, miss."

"And it is raining?"

A pause. Eufemia listened to the noise in the street.

"Yes, it is raining."

"We are going out."

"Going out!"

"Shut up. Hurry and bring me one of your own dresses, the percale one, and one of your shawls, too, and a kerchief. We are both going to the theater as 'artisans.' We'll sit in the area reserved for women. Tonight they are putting on . . . what? I don't remember the name. It's a new opera, very good. I read about it on a poster at the corner by the town hall when I came back from mass. Be off now. Go get those things. Wait, bring me one of your hairpins as well, the one with the silver-plated head that cost you two *reales*. Bonis and Nepomuceno have both gone; no one's at home. *We* are going out on the town tonight. Now then, hurry—we're on our way!"

Chapter Ten

Very early one morning, Eufemia entered her master's bedroom and awakened him saying, "The mistress is calling. She wants you to rush and bring Don Basilio."

"The doctor!" exclaimed Bonis, rapidly sitting up in bed and rubbing his eyes, which were swollen with sleep. "The doctor so early? What is wrong? What has happened?"

It did not really occur to him that Emma might want the doctor for reasons physical. Experience had made him skeptical in this regard, for he knew now that his wife was not actually sick. God knows what hidden caprice made her demand the doctor at such an hour, or what misfortunes would almost certainly befall him due to his wife's new and unexpected deviltry this morning.

"What is the matter? What does she want?" he groaned in an anguished voice as though pleading for lights and help and courage, while he groped uncertainly under the mattress for his socks. Eufemia shrugged her shoulders; then, recalling her sense of modesty, she left the bedroom so that the master could dress.

After two minutes, shuffling along in his slippers of fake tiger skin and buttoning up to his beard a lightweight, well-worn, gray overcoat that served him as a bathrobe during moderate weather, Bonis approached his wife's bed. He shook, less from the morning chill than from frightening incertitude. Nothing in the world made him tremble more than undefined anxiety in the face of what he took to be an approaching evil, an evil not even remotely conceived of a short time before, especially if the announcement caught him

98

totally unprepared, to say nothing of undressed, at a bad hour, cutting off his sleep, ruining his digestion, his pleasure in listening to music or his imaginative reveries.

How the imagination exaggerates danger, he thought. I would prefer eight misfortunes with which I am precisely acquainted to four at which I can only guess but which I picture as forty times more horrible.

His relations with Emma and with the uncle had been for some time the occasion for quickly sprung surprises. From both of them he began to fear and expect new and ghastly discoveries, complaints, then concrete accusations and finally cruel recriminations, particularly from his wife. What did she know? What did she not know? What diabolical truce (it could not possibly be divine) was she maintaining? Why was she doing it? How long would it last? Why, since she had caught him in flagrant odor of rice powder and could hardly have seen he was innocent that time, had she not yet exacted from him the consequences of her damned observation? What must she be preparing for him! The "moment of truth," as he named the scene which he so clearly foresaw, horrified him, yes, but he preferred it, or so he believed, to the state of perpetual suspense, of rabbit-like nervousness in which he now lived day and night. Every time Emma spoke to him or looked at him or summoned him, he imagined the time had arrived.

"What has happened, my dear?" he asked with all the forbearance in the world, his teeth chattering as he leaned over the pillow of her bed.

"I want you personally to fetch Don Basilio now, right away, before he sets out on his calls. I want to see him *immediately*."

"But, do you feel sick? You've been so much better lately."

"Exactly. And I understand my needs. Go on, go on. Run and bring Don Basilio!"

Bonifacio did not argue. Better to leave it alone, he thought. The matter of the rice powder could spring up from *any* direction. He returned to his room, quickly washed and dressed and stepped into the street, a little braver now, thanks to the slaps of cold water with which he had cooled the back of his neck. He had noted before that cold water splashed on the neck gave him a great deal of courage and reconciled him to life. The dependence of the psychological state on the physical was repugnant to him, but he was forced to recognize it as a truth.

Fortunately, the doctor's house was not very far, so there was little time for further painful hypotheses about the connection between Don Basilio's visit and the conjugal drama at his own house, the plot of which was reaching its climax or Bonis knew nothing of domestic theater and his wife's talent for histrionics. What role did Don Basilio play, this unexpected actor who appeared so late? He could not guess.

The unexpected actor was a man of about forty, who managed to conceal at least ten of those years. Not very tall, thin, he was well-built in his own way. He wore a long, narrow-waisted, cream-colored frock coat, as well as gold spectacles and a high silk hat with a broad brim. His face was pale, almost anemic, his eyes dark blue, lively and very penetrating when they remained fixed on someone. He had long, black whiskers, possibly dyed, thin lips and neat hands; his small feet were always elegantly shod. He was a homeopathist, and a very sentimental one. In addition to homeopathy, which he practiced largely because it was fashionable with the common run of women, he was a specialist in matters of childbirth and feminine illnesses, both real ones and ones brought on by the lack of education that made the married as well as the single ladies apprehensive and capricious. Yes, he recognized the therapeutic effect of prayer, faith and vigil lights, but notwithstanding, he insisted that credit be given to the mysteries of his homeopathic pills as well. All in all, he believed strongly, or said he believed strongly, in the influence of the psychological over the organic, and he employed a singular smile, at the same time melancholy, resigned and intelligent, in order to communicate this belief to the beautiful women he treated.

Don Basilio Aguado divided his patients or "customers" into two classes: those who called him Don Basilio and those who called him

Aguado. The latter understood him; the others were usually foolish or malicious. Emma never made this mistake; she always called him by his surname. Bonis called him Don Basilio. In spite of his efforts, he gave way to the local custom of calling the doctor by his first name behind his back. The title "Don Basilio" this physician interpreted as a symbol of his unhappy destiny, of his father's sins, of the stupid fate which relegated him to the post of an obscure, provincial doctor. That "Aguado," he felt, represented his ambitious dreams, his penchant for refinement, his triumphs among the ladies, his professionalism, and other ideals which are not important here.

The homeopathist was an early riser, and he began his housecalls very early indeed. Bonifacio found him nattily attired, as though he were going to pay a visit to an ambassador. That was the way he always dressed for his bedside visits.

While he buttoned his gloves, he listened to Bonis' stammered explanations, and by means of nods of understanding and assent he gave an air of great importance to all that was said. Actually, Reyes had nothing really to explain, but it made no difference; the doctor seemed interested, and smiling courteously, he followed the worried husband through the streets. With gestures and steps aside, they disputed as to who would leave the sidewalk to whom. Bonis finally won, for his insistences were much more vehement and his humility much more in evidence than the doctor's. Don Basilio continued to ask questions, believing that to be his duty. Bonis continued to say a great deal about nothing. As to the rest, Aguado knew Doña Emma Valcárcel's case by heart. He was her favorite doctor, but only on a temporary basis, because she did not want one sole and permanent doctor. She changed physicians as she would have changed lovers had she been a Christina of Sweden or a Catherine of Russia. She loved having a ministry of physicians in attendance. Aguado was one of those most in evidence, since he specialized in infirmities of the womb, in hysteria, in flatulence, in anxieties, in disorders of that nature.

Bonis respected science in spite of a kind of instinctive antipathy toward the exact and physical sciences, which "speak only of material things." He believed in medicine, not for any reason, but in cases of illness, if one did not have recourse to doctors, then where would one turn? It was necessary to have faith in something. In times of tribulation his weak spirit required some source of hope, something he could hold on to. He remembered that during the illnesses of his parents and his brothers, all dead now, he had regarded the doctor as a sort of Supreme Providence. When everyone was in good health at the house, he had joined in the general skepticism suspecting that physicians only wanted to make a big show, but no sooner had a family member fallen ill than Bonifacio once again began to believe in medicine.

He had read a little about the human organism, and he had always planned to read much more if he ever had a family in order to take good care of his son or, now that he knew he would never have a son on account of Emma's damaged womb, then to become more philosophical, to prepare for that time when his relations with Serafina would come to an end and when he would begin to grow old. (That was his plan, by the way, for his solitary old age—to become a philosopher.) In spite of his reading, actual and intended, he pictured the human organism as having a certain consciousness in each finger and in each visceral organ and in each vein. He took literally, for example, the saying that some medicines "gratify the stomach." Moreover, Bonis saw the relation between medication and sickness as a kind of magic; the idea of venoms and elixirs was in his eyes a complete and miraculous mythology wherein only one drop more or less of each liquid would, according to him, absolutely annihilate the patient or heal him in a trice. He had learned this from his wife who, because of one drop too little or one too much poured by him with trembling pulse into a coffee spoon, had berated him soundly on infinite occasions.

In short, Reyes respected in Señor Aguado the occult sciences. And also, to his wife's favorite doctor, homeopathist and *accoucheur* he had pinned his earlier, now deceased hopes of one day having a son.

They arrived at Emma's bedroom together. Don Basilio smiled

with his thin lips compressed professionally. If a Sagasta or Cánovas, fallen from favor, had been called by the queen at dawn, it would not, of course, have occurred to either of them to ask her why he had to get up so early; instead, he would appear in front of her posthaste. Thus Don Basilio, who had been neglected by Doña Emma for months, refrained now from asking why there had been such a rush in calling him. No, he came to the point immediately and asked only for the medical facts and antecedents.

"Let's see what has happened since I last saw you," he said, referring to the precise date of his ultimate visit. It seemed that Don Venancio, the allopathist, an older man and a specialist in childbirth, too, had been called in. Why? No reason; he had simply been called in. He had recommended a diet. Bad! Don Venancio, the story went, was a tremendous glutton; he always suffered from indigestion, such as a loaded cannon might if it could feel, which he cured with diets worthy of the *Thebaid*. For no other reason, he prescribed strict diets for all his patients. Aguado, who had a weak stomach and hardly ate a bit, abhorred this idea of diets, especially when delicate people like Emma were concerned. Clearly he thought that the problem of which this lady had not yet spoken was due to her lack of nutrition, to the other's diet. Emma remained silent; she did not dare to tell him how well or how much, in fact, she had been eating of late. Finally, Don Basilio let her explain her case, and she complained of the following:

Nothing actually *hurt*, but she had suffered from insomnia, long periods of depression, the anguish of suffocation and sudden fits of terrible anxiety about what she did not know. The room she slept in, the entire house, seemed narrow to her, like tombs, like caves filled with chittering crickets. She longed to fly out over the balconies and far away, to drink in great quantities of air and expose herself to great quantities of light. At times her melancholy seemed to have its foundation in the sorrow of always living in the same town, of always watching the same horizon. She said that she felt a nostalgia (she did not call it that, of course) for countries which she had never seen and could not even picture in any vivid way. The extravagant longing sometimes reached the really absurd point of her deeply desiring to be in many places at the same time, in many towns, near the sea and inland, in sunlight and in shade, in a country like her own where there were many green plains, but also in dry regions, under transparent skies, without rain clouds or dark showers. But, more than anything, she begged to be free of suffocation, of the oppression of ceilings and walls.

To Bonis, there was nothing new in this except for the form; his wife had spent almost her whole life asking him for the moon. However, when he heard the part about her longing to go flying out over the balcony, he was unable to help thinking of the witches who go through the air to Seville on Saturdays, mounted on broomsticks; and he regarded this new inclination, which offered a suspicious novelty, with a certain superstitious fear. He flinched, ashamed of his thoughts. He did not even dare to offend Emma in his mind for fear that she might be able to see through him.

Don Basilio finally interrupted Emma and extended his hand as a signal that he wanted to take her pulse. He smiled pompously as if to say that his wisdom had foreseen all that the señora had expressed and that it was all described in his books back home. Then, as was his custom in such critical moments, he completely ignored all the little phenomena Emma had described so that he might concentrate upon the "primary cause." He said, "Hysteria is a kind of Proteus."

"Who?" asked Emma.

"The one," Bonis informed everyone, proudly displaying his knowledge of the classics, "who stole fire from the gods."

"Precisely," agreed the doctor, who knew no more about the story of Proteus than the jumbled facts he had assembled in his own mind. "Hysteria," he added, "like Proteus, has a variety of forms."

"Oh, no," Bonis interrupted. "Excuse me, Don Basilio. The one who stole fire from the gods was someone else; it was Prometheus. I was mistaken."

The doctor's face reddened slightly and, tapping his forehead as though he had merely made a slip of the tongue, he muffled his anger, double for being called Don Basilio and for revealing how inadequate was his classical education. What a perfect toad, this Reyes! he thought. He continued.

"It is necessary for us to get to the root of the problem. Your particular ailment lies within, in what we call the 'spirit,' and let me tell you"—he said this turning to Bonis that he might dazzle him and revenge himself—"that I am a vitalist, and not only a vitalist, but a spiritualist, although that is not particularly fashionable now."

Reyes was not really swept off his feet by this announcement, as the physician thought he might be. In those periods of time when he put away his flute, on those days when he could not see Serafina or when his wife had not called him, especially when he was in bed, before going to sleep, he himself had spent no small amount of time considering the great problem of what, in fact, *is* inside everything; and in relation to the reality of the soul, he felt he had very daring ideas, ideas which he believed to be extremely original. *He* was also a spiritualist. Yes, indeed!

"The malady here lies in the spirit, and the spirit, let me add, simply cannot be cured with potions," continued Aguado.

"But didn't you say this is hysteria?" asked Emma coyly.

"Yes, señora, of course; but there is a very mysterious relationship between the soul and the body, and I am not one of those who say," as he turned again to Bonifacio, "post hoc, ergo propter hoc."

Decidely, he wanted to flabbergast Reyes and make him pay dearly for having corrected him as to Proteus and Prometheus. Don Basilio was not as a rule accustomed to making shows of erudition; at the bedside of the sick he usually wanted to appear as a moralist of the sophisticated and urbane type rather than as a doctor of philosophy with his yellow tassel.

Bonis started to translate the Latin in his head. He only stumbled over the word *propter*, the meaning of which he could not recall. He would have to look it up later in the dictionary. It was obviously a preposition. As a young man, he had studied the liberal arts in the Provincial Institute but without taking a degree. However, his learning did not have its source there, but rather in what has already been mentioned: his great desire, now that he had grown older, to teach himself. Not only did he want to "complete his education," but in those days, still recent, when he had dreamed of becoming a father, the great dignity he attributed to that very "priesthood" seemed to necessitate a plan, a total program of absolutely serious study that would, one day, have served as the spiritual nourishment for this son who might have sprung from his own loins.

Emma, who knew nothing of the trivium or the quadrivium, began to grow somewhat impatient seeing that Aguado had not yet prescribed anything for her. The doctor must have seen her impatience, for he proceeded with his résumé: none of his colleague's ridiculous draughts were needed. A few doses of those pills which he kept in a pretty little box would suffice and, added to that, a great deal of walking, a great deal of exercise, distractions, diversions, the open air and a lot of English-style meat—all this would suffice. With the mention of the meat, Don Basilio began to discourse on a theme which was almost unheard-of at that time in that town. It was a great novelty, anyway. He loathed stew. He imputed the lack of national vigor to stewed meat, which is eaten instead of fried meat in this poor country, Spain. He rambled on and on.

After all that was said and done this day, there was a revolution in Emma's house. Soon all of the Valcárcels in the province, even those in the most remote mountains, knew that because of certain medical advice, Emma had changed her whole life. She had resolved, overcoming her previous repugnance, to go out as often as possible, to frequent the promenades, the *romerías* and the crowded, solemn functions of the Church. Perhaps she would go so far as to attend the theater.

Don Juan Nepomuceno saw it all without comment. Emma presented him with her dressmaker's bill, which amounted to no small sum, but he paid it without grumbling. Too, it was indispensable to have new clothes made for Bonifacio, as his wife had firm opinions relating to her husband's dignity on this, if on no other, point. He was expected to accompany her on excursions, but she would display her best fabrics and most expensive hats in vain if Bonifacio ruined the elegance of the tableau with the sleazy materials and foul garments which the local tailor cut for him; so he returned to English wool and the work of the famous *artistes* in Madrid. Now, however, Bonis allowed himself to be dressed well with the greatest pleasure; Serafina had noticed the change and liked it. Yet, there was a drawback; Emma's new habits had created problems for the lovers. They had little free time together, and sometimes they were even forced to dissemble on the promenades and in other public places when they caught sight of each other in Emma's presence. She appeared to notice nothing, but God alone knew. . . .

His defenses down, Reyes feared at every hour that the "moment of truth" would arrive, but Emma never returned to the matter of the rice powder. She never alluded to what had taken place on the strange night, nor did she ever have initiatives of that nature again. She did, however, speak a great deal about the theater, asking her husband if he knew the tenor, the baritone or the soprano; and she pleaded for information about their "lives and miracles" once he had admitted knowing something about them. By hearsay, he was quick to add.

One afternoon after a meal in the French style (a great novelty in a town where the classic dish, plain meat and vegetable stew, was served in almost every house from twelve until two), Emma began to stare fixedly at her spouse. Her eyes seemed to question and mock him, simultaneously. She was drinking, with her dessert, a glass of excellent sherry ordered directly from the *bodegas* at Jerez. She drank a mouthful, pushed her chair away from the table, stretched out her leg and then, as if she could not speak because she was still savoring that wine, she began to interrogate Bonifacio with signs, conveyed by the prominently displayed foot and a raised finger which she moved in time with her head, pointing toward some faraway place.

Except for Don Juan Nepomuceno, the married couple was eating alone, for by a rare accident, no relative was visiting the house at that time. (Don Juan, of course, lived with his niece and nephew.) Reyes felt himself lost in confusion. At first he understood nothing of his wife's signals, nor did he ascribe much importance to them.

"What are you saying, woman? Explain it to me," he demanded.

"Mmm, mmm!" Emma murmured and continued with the pantomine, exaggerating the gestures now. Nepomuceno concentrated on the sherry, which he had filled with pastry crumbs, as if it were not his function to notice the pranks of his niece, who from the first moment of her new liberation had played the young coquette, permitting herself alarming little jokes and allusions which he did not want to take into consideration, at least just then.

"But, speak up woman. I don't understand this foot business, . . ." repeated Reyes.

Emma swallowed her mouthful of sherry, but instead of saying anything, she filled her mouth once again and then renewed her pantomime with even greater relish. Bonifacio began to pay close attention. First she showed him her foot; then, with an outstretched finger and her head, she tried to indicate something, or someone, who was not present.

Bonis could not understand. Suddenly, his heart flipped over twice; cold sweat began to run down his back, and his legs, playing the same vile trick to which they always resorted in such perilous situations, jumped as if they were about to flee on their own from danger. His physique announced to him an evil his brain was as yet unable to realize. Something very serious was happening. What was it? What could it possibly be? Bonis cast an anguished glance at Nepomuceno to see if he could detect a hint of complicity between uncle and niece. Nothing. It was as if Don Juan were not there.

"Oh, my sweet dear, for Christ's sake!"

Emma spat the sherry onto the floor, stretched her foot out even farther toward her husband, showed him even more of her calf. Then, she shouted as though she were speaking to a deaf man.

"For goodness' sake, *this* is what I mean. It is perfectly clear. What do you think of *this*, fool, what I am showing you?"

"Exquisite, my dear." Bonifacio was dumbfounded.

"I am not talking about the foot, you moron. I already know what the foot is worth. I am talking about the *boots*! I ask you, who has a pair just like them?"

"How should I know?" He paused.

"Only this pair and one other like it have been sold. Fuejos, the shoemaker himself, told me. Your friend, Fuejos. He sold this pair to me and another pair to the soprano. This is why I asked, you blockhead. You have a memory like a bird's. *Now*, do you remember? Are they, or are they not, like the soprano's? Exactly the same, exactly the same, aren't they? Look! Look at them carefully!"

And Emma raised her foot high enough to rest it on her husband's knees. The uncle was on the other side of the table. He could not see her raised foot, and he did not try.

Bonis reached instinctively for a glass of water. He put it to his mouth, and there he sat, first drinking and then pretending to drink. Unable to help himself in the middle of his indescribable agonies, he thought, this is what is known as the "catastrophe" in tragedies and operas. His situation brought to mind *Norma*, with his wife singing the title role, the soprano the part of Adalgisa, and he himself Polion. Further, he recalled that it was the "priest," now Nepomuceno, who gave the order to behead Polion.

"But come on, you silly man, say something. Are these, or are they not the same as the soprano's? Did that fellow deceive me? Out with it!"

Reyes gathered his strength, from where he never quite knew, and speaking like a ventriloquist's dummy with the little bit of voice at his command, he finally uttered, "But Emma, how should I recognize . . . this señorita's boots?"

Suddenly, Don Juan Nepomuceno stood up and stared intently at his nephew-in-law; then, just when Bonifacio believed that he was about to be knifed, the uncle declared. "Bonifacio is right. How should he know what kind of boots the soprano buys? He is not the one who has to pay for them."

"That's silly, uncle. Excuse me," said Emma. "The one who buys boots for these señoritas does not usually recognize them. If La

Gorgheggi has a lover who buys her boots, well, he, *whoever* he is, would always notice other things, things other than boots and, least of all, these I'm speaking of, since she herself purchased them only this morning. But this *ninny* has seen them, and that is why I asked him; only, he has a head like a stone and forgets everything. Let's see. Weren't you in Fuejos' shop this morning around twelve o'clock when that soprano came in to pick out some boots, and after she asked for the latest style, didn't Fuejos show her a pair like this? And didn't the soprano ask for your opinion, and didn't you say they were lovely? And didn't she try them on there in front of both you and the hypothecary, Salmón the Cripple? Well, dearest, the shoemaker *told* me all this; that is why I bought them. The only other pair sold was sold to the soprano, who dresses very well."

"All of this story, insomuch as it relates to me, is absolutely false," Bonis asserted in a voice as composed as possible. He turned to the uncle. "I did not go into Fuejos' shop today, and I can prove my alibi. At twelve o'clock, I was . . . somewhere else."

He had a point. At twelve he was in Serafina's room. The whole yarn was a lie, a piddling little scheme on the part of Fuejos to pressure Emma into buying the shoes. But, as Fuejos was Bonifacio's friend and a trustworthy person, how could he have committed such a calumny? Didn't he know that there were rumors in town to the effect that he, Reyes, had a relationship with the soprano? And knowing this, as he must have, would he have told Emma? Impossible. No, the shoemaker had not invented the lie—Emma had! The situation was as grave as the perspiration running over his body signaled. Emma must be preparing some acute form of revenge, and in the interim she was merely toying with him as a cat does with a mouse, all at his expense. Perhaps she regarded him with so much contempt, thought the unhappy man, that she did not even want to concede him the dignity of showing jealousy, but jealous or not, she would not abandon her revenge. That much was certain.

Yet, in spite of these last reflections, the perplexity of the Unfaithful Husband was not entirely dispelled. He grasped the idea, as a source of hope, that Fuejos had, in fact, lied. As soon as we have finished our coffee, he determined, I shall go to the shoe shop to see what went on.

But Bonis proposed, and Emma disposed. As soon as they had had their coffee, Emma, who was in high spirits, got up and said in a tone of comic solemnity, "Now, both of you stay seated. I have a great surprise for you." She paused. "What time is it?"

"Eight," said the uncle, who in spite of his formerly easy manner, was somewhat anxious.

"Eight? Magnificent. Wait here a quarter of an hour."

Emma disappeared. Uncle-in-law and nephew-in-law fell mute. Between them, Reyes envisioned a wide abyss, or rather a vast ocean of silver and gold coins which swelled to at least . . . God knew how many *reales*. His terror in respect to what he owed the Valcárcels had reached such proportions that he had not even taken the trouble to add up the quantities which he owed the "cash box." Including the seven thousand *reales* which the mountain priest had given him, it all seemed like a fortune great as Croesus' to Bonifacio. In fact, it seemed so much that from time to time, reading in the newspapers discussions about the national debt, he grew disturbed thinking of his own. He experienced similar sensations when he heard or read about enormous embezzlements, about treasurers who fled with cash boxes, and anything in that line.

Luckily, Emma actually returned in a quarter of an hour, and when she appeared, her table companions exclaimed in unison, "What is this?" Both rose to their feet automatically, stupefied. The situation demanded no weaker a reaction. Emma was wearing a magnificent dress which neither of them had ever seen. Her face was covered with rice powder. Her hair had been combed by a hairdresser (she had never before allowed anyone to touch her hair). Last of all, around her neck was clasped a diamond necklace, with a bracelet and earrings in the same style, all very expensive, all new, all displayed for the first time.

"What you see, it is." She held before her husband's eyes a slip of yellow paper on which was written MAIN THEATER, MAIN BOX, NO. 7. "We are going to the theater," she continued implacably.

111

"We have places in the military governor's box. Since he has no family, he seldom occupies it. On your way, Uncle. Put on your glad rags. And you, Bonis, come here. I shall dress you myself in a matter of seconds."

Emma did not even give her subordinates time to recover from her remarks, her resolution. She, who had indulged in so many whims throughout her life, had *never* shown interest in the theater, and even less in music. From the hour of her miscarriage up to the present (and a lot of water had passed under the bridge since that time), she had not been in the playhouse four times. She had not so much as seen the present company, who were finishing the third subscription series. And, suddenly, zip! without telling a soul, she had taken a box and was bundling everyone off to the opera. This, anyway, is what Bonifacio thought, making a mistake about one small detail as we shall see. The uncle, too, thought the same thing, but unlike Bonis, he rapidly added up the situation in order to work out the plan most conducive to his well-being. Without uttering a syllable, he disappeared, to return shortly, dressed in a black frock coat with a greatcoat over it which suited him like a pearl.

My uncle looks very presentable, thought Emma, but I will still make him pay for everything, like everyone else.

Reyes' preparations were more complicated, directed as they were by his wife, who made him shave in about the time one could say Jack Spratt, with a result of only three slight wounds which she herself covered with sticking plaster. She insisted that he "premier" a dark suit cut in the latest style, of English wool, of course. At moments Reyes imagined that he was being prepared for the stake and that the extremely elegant suit of clothing which Emma had taken out of a box sent by the *artistes* of Madrid was a shroud—of English wool to be sure—for his remains.

Eufemia, who evidently had been commanded not to register any surprise, lighted their way to the front door, where there was no lamp. She watched them go out into the street, Emma on Bonifacio's arm and Don Juan following, as if the same thing happened every night of their lives.

The maid, in truth, had her reasons for not being so astonished as the other two: first, the señora's eccentricities (some of them intimate secrets only the two of them shared) formed part of her daily bread; further, she knew of antecedents—a few days ago, they had gone together to the theater, sitting in the highest balcony, dressed as artesans.

This was what Bonis did not know, this and also what his wife had seen, heard and felt on the night of her excursion; nor did he know what she had dreamed, desired and plotted afterwards.

When they arrived at the theater, Emma's entrance produced a much greater effect than she could have imagined. She had not gone to create an impression, but once she realized that she had done so, it was honey on her palate. She had discovered a new sin—that of making less resplendent women envious of her fine attire. Beforehand she had overlooked the fact that it was one thing for her, who never went to the theater, to appear dressed in extreme luxury and seated in the main box, the brigadier's box, and quite another for her to enter disguised and take a seat in the gods, hidden from the public who did not so much as dream of her presence. She had gone in a mood to enjoy herself enormously, and it was not exactly from the public that she expected the strong emotions for which she had prepared. The already well considered expectations which she was about to realize related to her own domestic affairs. Yet, to this complicated and bizarre program was suddenly added a new, keen pleasure on which Emma had not counted; this revealed to her a new world of intense delight, heretofore undreamed of but which she now saw quite clearly from the first moment she stepped into her box. Leaving her coat to her uncle and turning around before seating herself, she noticed gazes fixed upon her. In the nearby boxes, she heard murmurs of approval, and in the air, so to speak, she caught the general effect of her presence. Even after she had sat down and began to take in all that lay before her, the admiration did not cease.

The choristers were alone on the stage, like the Galicians in the story, incompetently led by a bit player distinguished only by a pair of boots made of artificial chamois and the fact that he sang more off-key than all the rest put together. In vain, they shouted like people possessed; no one paid any attention to them. The distinguished theatergoers in the stalls and the boxes attended to the civil spectacle that Emma presented. The season-ticket holders in the proscenium boxes, who could not see the auditorium without leaning far over the rail, peered out in groups to see Reyes' wife, and the ones in the box reserved for the habitués of Cascos' shop happily saluted Bonis and Emma.

The brigadier general was among them, and he, too, nodded his head in approval. Emma came out of her self-imposed solitude as if from a prison. The emotions aroused by the walks and *romerías* could not compare with this; *this* was sheer glory. How she was going to amuse herself! With her new-found celebrity, she had not lost sight of her plan. Nothing would induce her to change that.

Lawyer Valcárcel's daughter understood quite well that it was not her beauty which attracted so much attention; it was, she knew, principally her trappings, her new dress, her jewels and, of course, the novelty of seeing her in the theater after so long an absence. She realized that many of those ladies who were devouring her with their eyes from the stalls and the boxes must be saying, "So! This one is launching herself into the world again." Yes, she reflected, I am launching myself headfirst, and why not? She had discovered just how to thwart her uncle's schemes for robbing her.

For many of the ladies present, those who were very young or who came from other regions, Emma's entrance into the "world," if that was, indeed, the world, was unique, because they could not recall, as could others, that years ago this very lady, whose luxurious outfit did not hide her worn features, nervous tenseness and sour expression, had been the public's favorite topic of conversation: a spoiled, rich and extravagant young girl who gave full reign to her caprices.

Emma well understood all of this. She had no illusions as to the effect she caused, the curiosity and near amazement and the motives which prompted those reactions. No, she had no illusions, yet nonetheless she was closely observed, even studied, and the stage was forgotten because of her presence; no matter what prompted it, the sensation was for a woman of her nature intense and memorable. She relished more than anything else the envy; of this she was confident. Not only the poor envied her, but also those two or three rich women who could have worn outfits as fine as hers or even finer. Yet they, too, were jealous. Persons of this type live like animals for the immediate sensation, and in this moment Emma outshone them; she was easily the most richly dressed and adorned woman in the theater. The public did not care who *could* outdo her. Actions alone tell. Perhaps the most envious of all was the wife of the South American, Sariegos, the richest man in the province; he could outstrip all the Valcárcels in the world, parceling them away in government bonds and bank stocks and a thousand other grand things. Sariegos, however, did not allow waste (although he could hardly have felt the pinch), and his wife had to content herself with a mediocre sort of luxury. His wife was furious, and Sariegos himself, seated behind his wife, soon began to despise Emma too because it was her fault that his wife was silently cursing and detesting *him* for his greed just then. Improbable though it seems, he too observed the "little lawyer's" finery with envy, but then he forced himself to overcome sentiments so base, and thanks to his crematistic or plutonic philosophy, he reached higher spheres, finally mumbling in a low voice, from the summit of his heartfelt contempt, "That girl is going to lose her shirt within a very few years." He could see clearly enough that Emma was no longer a girl, but that fact was not at issue. The reference indicated his contempt—thus, that "girl," the "little lawyer."

Emma, however, did not hear any of the impudent remarks. She saw the envy; she did not hear it. She saw the burning eyes, the sad smiles, the sincere and melancholic faces of those who could not manage to dissemble and so were left like Saint Theresas, entranced in mystic contemplation, but of a far different sort.

A few girls, real girls, who minutes before had been flirting vivaciously, happily indifferent to the bits and pieces they were wearing, now languished, forgetting their admirers in the stalls as though something much more important were taking place; with faces from which every touch of grace, poetry and idealism had disappeared, they consecrated themselves to the cult of envy, venerating the jewels and the silk, hiding their bitterness toward the priestess who displayed on her body those pagan splendors.

A rustle of starched petticoats on stage attracted Emma's attention, drawing her out of that ecstasy of contented *amour propre*. From the rear stage door, an elegant lady entered with sprightly steps, her long train sweeping the boards. Her whole body seemed to sparkle. She was dressed in costume brocade, covered with false jewels and even a false diadem.

"Who is that?" Reyes' wife demanded.

Seeing that Nepomuceno had ignored the question, Bonifacio answered, not without swallowing hard beforehand, "It is the queen, who is coming hastily to learn that the prince . . ."

"No, I did not ask about that," interrupted Emma, turning to look at Bonis, who was seated behind her in the penumbra. "I asked if it is the soprano."

"I believe . . . that it is, yes, exactly, the protagonist."

"The one with the boots. Will she be wearing them now?"

Bonis was quiet.

"Well, husband, do you think she is wearing them now?"

"It would be . . . an anachronism."

"Shhh! She is mounting the throne. Let us see—bah!—one cannot see her feet. Perhaps when she steps down . . ."

Emma first aimed her opera glasses at the soprano's underskirts, but since she made no move, Emma raised her gaze to Serafina's face.

"How pretty she is! I've already seen this face. What is her name?"

"Serafina Gorgheggi, I believe."

"You believe! But, you don't know for sure?"

"I may have confused her with the contralto."

"You may have, yes."

"But, no. Yes, it is the soprano. Exactly, La Gorgheggi."

"You are certain now, eh?"

"Yes, certain."

Bonifacio admired his poise. This was to grow in the face of danger. He understood everything. There was the matter of the rice powder. His wife was making fun of him. She knew about his love affair, and that unexpected trip to the theater was a confrontation—yes, a confrontation of criminals. He was a criminal, of course. It did not matter. Whatever happened, he would have to defend himself like a cat with its claws outstretched. He had to sit down, there behind his wife, because his legs were trembling as was usual in these situations (although he had never found himself in a situation quite like this one). He was prepared to dissemble, to "lie like a trooper" if necessary, since the Lord had endowed him with the gift of parrying, of which he would never have believed himself capable if he had not heard his own words. What the instinct for survival can do, he thought.

"Ah!" Emma choked back a scream, for she had just seen one of La Gorgheggi's feet as the soprano descended majestically from the brightly painted wooden throne. Whether it was an anachronism or not, "her highness'" boots were identical to those Emma herself had purchased that afternoon. Fuejos had not lied.

"Exactly like mine! That Fuejos is a person whose word can be trusted. Do you see, Bonifacio? This lady is wearing the other pair, just as the shoemaker told me. Why do you accuse him of lying? Why do you deny having seen this lady's foot? Do you believe that I am going to get jealous, you unfaithful husband?"

Bonis was deathly quiet. No matter how brave he was, and he believed himself to be very brave, that could not last long now. Where would his wife stop?

"Do you know if this Doña Serafina has a lover? If she has, he must have paid for the boots," Emma went on.

This frank use of words did not surprise Nepomuceno, who from the moment he had seen his niece with a little flesh on her and a better color had expected any form of madness in speech or deed.

As to the husband, he did not see in such great effrontery more than the terrible sarcasm of an outraged woman. To him, it seemed fairly natural that a deceived partner would amuse herself with ironic warning signals before taking the most terrible vengeance. It happened in tragedies, and it happened in operas.

Absorbed in anxiety, his face turned toward the rear of the box, Bonis could not see why Emma did not persist in her jokes, if those capricious questions were, in fact, jokes. He had flushed and afterwards turned very pale when Serafina made her entrance on stage; now it was Emma who turned scarlet. She riveted her opera glasses on the person who had just arrived from the land of the Moors—a peerless conqueror who found himself confronted with the fact that the queen had arranged the marriage of his fiancée to the king of France so that she would have no rivals for the hero's affection. The conqueror of the infidels was played by the baritone, Minghetti, who was wearing two spurs that shone like suns and who had a tremendous voice, fairly sonorous and full of energy. The "throne room" was cleared of the chorus singers, vile courtiers all. When they were alone, the queen threw herself upon his neck, begging his pardon, but the baritone refused to compromise; he escaped from her arms and called to his fiancée in a loud voice.

He is very handsome like that, thought Emma, but I preferred him in the barber costume.

When the commander could shout no longer, the soprano began to lament her ill luck and to sing of her passion in high trills, accompanied by the crook-backed flutist. As disdainful lovers tend to do in such cases, instead of listening to the laments and the complaints of the queen, the baritone took advantage of his respite and started unobtrusively to cough and spit; then he began to scan the boxes with an air of insolence. His gaze reached Emma's box. She felt his sweet, blue eyes shining through the lens of her opera glasses and smiling at her as if they had known each other all their lives, as if there were something between them. Emma smiled too without thinking, and the baritone, who had an eagle's eye, noticed her smile and smiled again, not only with his eyes this time, but with his whole face. La Valcárcel's response to all this was even more intense than her earlier reaction to the admiration her presence had produced in the auditorium. This, she thought, is more serious. It is a richer experience; it fills more desires and has more substance, *and* it can become part of my plan.

Her plan was to make fun of her uncle and her husband, to toy with them, to try to discover even newer ways to deceive and ruin them, ways that might offer her great entertainment. For some time she had known what methods to use against the uncle. She planned to throw, as it were, the whole house out the window by spending money wildly on herself. Bonifacio was another matter. Strictly speaking, she did not dislike him nearly so much as she disliked the uncle, nor until this moment had she decided on any specific form of punishment for him. She had only thought of keeping him on the rack for the rest of his days, of treating him like a slave subject to unknown torments; but when Minghetti's smile, his look, smote her with a lightning flash, then she suddenly saw how she might punish her unfaithful spouse. Yes, she had guessed that he was unfaithful long before; yet when she would meditate in her bedroom alone (with hysteria for a sybil), Emma had reached the same conclusions about all men: in her eyes, they were animals with only gross and cruel instincts. She could not conceive of a husband who was totally faithful to his wife. Further, the very existence of such a creature seemed ridiculous, and she freely admitted to herself that if she were a married man, she would not be satisfied with just a wife. She would not admit that women had the same right, except in extraordinary cases, because "it would appear ugly," because "a woman is different." However, once a husband's infidelity was discovered, the case changed. *Then* there was a right to reprisal. This was true, too, if the husband were brutal. If Bonis hit me as I hit him, he would pay for it, Emma thought. This much was evident. And if he deceives me . . . Here Emma hesitated and returned to her considerations for excusable feminine infidelity. If he deceives me, I would deceive him as well, she mused . . . if anyone inspired great passion in me.

Emma's moral excesses had little to do with the decadent literary romanticism of her town and her time; she was original in her temperament. She hardly read verses or novels, using only a few phrases that she picked up from the neighbors like a disease; this vague idea of the Great Passion which sanctifies everything was one of those diseases. For the rest, she alone could make a clean slate of a hundred commandments. According to her whim, she would do away with any rules of conduct which stood in her way. But in the "pure region of ideas," as Bonis might say, another rule was to be found: Emma's sixth sense told her that there is a long distance between word and deed, that she would not betray Bonis unless it were in a moment of madness aroused, say, by a Russian prince or another person of exceptional merit, for such abandonment would require great changes on her part. Her flesh was tranquil; the extravagant tastes in which she indulged were sensual but not, strictly speaking, erotic. Moreover, in the end, Bonis was what could be called a good-looking man, and she was very satisfied with his physical appearance. But the baritone's looks and smile were something else again. For the present, Emma forgot everything in order to concentrate on the pleasure of intercepting through her opera glasses those eyes and that smiling mouth under the dark chestnut-colored moustache. Every time Minghetti returned to the scene, Emma tried to repeat the incident which had tasted so sweet to her, and generally her efforts met with success. Whether it was purely a matter of chance, or because the singer was simply in the habit of often looking at the boxes, flirting, directing his attention to those who admired him no matter the role or the dramatic circumstance, the fact was that the pleasure, so hungrily solicited through Emma's opera glasses, was renewed with interest even during some of the most solemn and critical moments in the opera; and all the while, in despair because of his fiancée's flight to France, the baritone did not stop quarreling with the queen.

Bonis was amazed to observe that, to his great relief, Emma no longer mentioned either the soprano or her anachronistic boots. Now, anything which remotely touched on the "rice powder business" had been dropped. The opera ended, the Valcárcels returned home, or the Reyeses, if you prefer, although it is perhaps more correct to say the Valcárcels, since Bonifacio was hardly the master of the house. Nepomuceno took his leave of the couple and went to bed, trying to think out his plans for the future which, if he did not misjudge, would be subject to a change not exempt from danger. When Reyes asked his wife's permission to return to his own room, it occurred to Emma to put to use what in that marriage relationship could be called the Royal Prerogative.

"Look, Bonis, I'm not sleepy. The noise of the music has made my head feel like a bass drum. I can tell I am going to be wide-awake and nervous; I shall be afraid." There was a moment of silence; then she added, "Stay here."

They were already in Emma's bedroom. She stripped off her jewels in front of her dressing-table mirror, which was illuminated by two rose-colored candles. Bonifacio saw her mirrored in the crystal with mysterious depths and shifting shadows. Without realizing how or why, that "stay here" caused him to look at his wife with the eyes of a judge of beauty. A strange thing! Until that moment, he had not noticed that Emma seemed years younger that night, especially just then. True, she did not appear to be a beautiful, fresh woman. There was neither perfection of features nor of figure, but there was a great deal of "expression." Her cheek seemed to sing an elegy for her youth; the wrinkles sketched around her temples and under her eyes told a complicated and sentimental story; the contrast between her sorrowful, cautious, even profound gaze and her dry cheeks and inert lips, spoke worlds. These qualities exercised a romantic attraction for Bonis, there in her room, in the half-light, and the imperative "stay here" flattered him after so long a time since Emma had last made use of her initiative.

For the second time, Serafina's lover felt remorse for his infidelity in sin. In Bonis' eyes, the intensity of his passion whitewashed those illicit relations with the player; but from the very moment that he had been "unfaithful" to Serafina, letting himself become devilishly interested in the faded but melancholy and expressive charms of his legitimate partner, it had automatically been proven that the Great

Passion he claimed he was experiencing was not so great and, for that reason, less excusable. However it came about, Bonifacio began to unbutton his English suit in his wife's bedroom. He stood there, without his frock coat or his waistcoat, displaying the silk suspenders and the front of a starched white shirt with three coral buttons. In this prosaic but familiar dress he smilingly turned toward Emma, who wet her dry lips, her eyes sparkling, and, serious and quiet, looked at her husband's robust neck and his milk-white complexion. Bonis felt that she desired him. The scene which took place on that night of the rice powder became very clear to him. In his wife's face, he read a periodic debility, a feminine weakness, the submission of the female to the male. He also divined a strange and nameless corruption, seeing all of this only by chance and confusedly. He felt mounting in himself a sense of superiority, fugitive and passing. Fired by his own caprice or Emma's sunset beauty or more, perhaps, by the desire which shone clearly in her face, Bonifacio suddenly fell on his knees in front of his wife and embraced the starched, white linen undergarments which rustled against his chest, and in a voice muffled by emotion, he stuttered a thousand mad things, lascivious words in amorous jargon, diminutives, just as La Gorgheggi was wont to do.

Instead of lifting her husband from his prostrate position, Emma screamed, the same scream with which she always entered her bath of tepid water. Then she began leaning further and further over until her mouth reached the level of Bonis' mouth. With both hands she seized him by his beard, drawing his head back, and as if his lips were an ear, she said in a loud whisper, "Swear that you are not unfaithful to me."

"I swear it to you, my soul, my richest possession, my jewel! I swear it to you, and I swear it to you again! Look in my eyes, deep in my eyes, in the eyes of my soul. . . . I swear again and again that I adore you, with this and this and this, I whom you see here, beneath you, beneath you . . . but, look, you are going to break my neck; I mean, the back of my neck is breaking!"

"Does it matter? Let me, let me. Like this, and more. . . . Let it hurt. Let it hurt, and enjoy it."

There was a silence which was put to no other use than to their staring at each other, and all the while, Bonis' neck was bent backwards. Emma finally released him, and standing up, she said, "Look, look, I am La Gorgheggi, La Gorgoritos,* the one who sang a little while ago, Queen Micomicona. Yes, dear man, the one you like so much, and in order to keep up the illusion, look at me, here, here, here, stupid, rogue. *Here* I tell you, at the boots just like hers. Clutch one of La Gorgoritos' feet, go on. Clutch one. The stockings will not be the same color, but these are quite pretty. Go on; now sing; tell her, yes, that you love her, that you have forgotten the girl from France and that you will marry her. . . . Your name is . . . what is your name? Yes, dear fellow, the baritone, who is he?"

"Minghetti?"

"Exactly, Minghetti. You are Minghetti and I, La Gorgoritos. Minghetti of my soul, here is the queen of your heart, your little queen. Take me, take me. Love me, pet me, Minghetti of my life, Bonis, Minghetti of my heart." She paused. "But listen, Moorslayer, if you want your lady-queen with the new boots to be yours forever, put out the lights by the dressing table and come with me on tiptoe or else Eufemia will hear you; she is sleeping just outside."

* "the triller"

Chapter Eleven

Bonifacio Reyes was an admirer of art in all its manifestations, but music remained his favorite form because it entered more deeply than all others into his soul, and, too, it had a vagueness which charmed him and which did not require that he study the multitude of details which trip through the books of divinity, law and medicine. Music, furthermore, was the art in which he had achieved most, thanks to his studies of solfeggio and the flute; yet, despite this bias, at various times in his life and in the capacity of mere amateur, of course, he had practiced other means of expressing beauty. He regarded poetry as respectable, and he had put many verses to memory, but the difficulties of rhyme had always dissuaded him from serious cultivation of that muse. He avoided meaningless words and facile rhymes because his sincerity as a man of sentiment and conviction gave him no alternative, and so, whenever he attempted to write poetry, he headed straight into the danger zone of difficult rhyme scheme. The last time he had flung away his pen with the resolution to give up verse had been the result of his trying to write a sonnet in honor of a certain Señor Menéndez who had founded a charitable fund.

According to the books of rhetoric and poetics Bonifacio had consulted on that occasion, the principal word is the one that should terminate the verse. But in this case, he pondered, biting his fingernails, the most important word is the name of the founder of the fund. There are thousands of rhymes for the word *charitable*, but I cannot find one for Menéndez. So, rather than relegate Menéndez to a place in the verse unworthy of his philanthropy, he preferred to put aside the sonnet.

This lack of poetic inspiration and of rhymes ending in *éndez* did not diminish one whit Bonifacio's artistic pride, moderate though it was. After all, if one looks closely, poetry is subsumed in music, anyway.

The art of drawing was something else again, and in this matter, the skillful penman felt confident of his ability to create, if not works of genius, at least very attractive arabesques. The arabesque was his favorite type of drawing, because it was related to his abilities as a clerk, and more important, it shared with music an intentional vagueness and power of suggestion. The arabesque approached allegory and fantasy on one hand and, on the other, the calligraphy of Iturzaeta.

Reyes was ruminating on things of this nature one afternoon toward twilight in the neither luxurious nor spacious room which Serafina Gorgheggi occupied on the third floor of the lodging house connected with the Café de la Oliva. Mochi and his protégée had decided some time ago to change hostels, which in that town only signified a change of evils. In the Hotel Principal, at the far end of the Alameda Vieja, they had lost credit because of their delays in paying for their board. The opera company had just been dissolved due to straitened finances and the general incompatibility of the singers, but the impresario, the soprano and the baritone had remained in the city—according to some sources because at present, having no contract or any place to go, they would be better off where they were, and according to other sources, because they were waiting to launch the new company which Mochi was busy forming. But, no matter what reason lay behind their prolonged stay, they were forced to pinch pennies. Minghetti himself stayed on at the Hotel Principal, tolerated for some mysterious reason although he was a bad risk, but Serafina and Julio were compelled to transfer themselves and their luggage to a mediocre lodging down the way, the Fonda de la Oliva, which the owner of that ancient café maintained with great difficulty.

That afternoon Reyes watched over the sleeping Serafina, who was stretched out nearby in the bedchamber, victim of an acute toothache. Happily, the pain had abated little by little, enough to allow her to fall into a heavy and semipeaceful sleep, which was somewhat feverish but not too disagreeable. Reyes kept vigil. He had gone there for other reasons, but the sight of his Anglo-Italian and the odor of anticonvulsive medicines, added to the decline of the day, had made him change his mind. He was now disposed only to melancholy and poetic reflection, to spiritual and pious abnegation.

Watching over the sleep of someone dear is not an occupation which requires the hands; so Bonis, seated beside a dirty papier-mâché night table, which was covered with coffee stains and traces of silver nitrate resembling a blue and pink Venetian scene, began to sketch idly with a quill pen on a scrap of untrimmed paper. As usual, he drew calligraphic fantasies with borders made up of bizarre flora and fauna. After the change which circumstances had just wrought in him, he felt as if his soul were filled with music; his heart, rather than his ears, heard the song.

If he had had his flute there and Serafina had not been asleep, he would have expressed aloud those interior melodies, languid, vaporous, filled with a soft, crepuscular sadness: half resignation, half extraterrestrial expectation—feelings that the young cannot know—the peculiar sadness of maturity that still feels on its lips the traces of illusion and savors its memory.

But the flute was not really necessary; he had his quill pen which made only faint sounds as he covered the paper with energetic strokes, flourishes and outlines, a chiaroscuro which suggested a piece of string or a sheet of metal. Little by little Bonis began to feel the music in his soul descend into his fingers. The curves of his lines became more graceful, the symmetrical complications and decorations each more elegant and expressive than the last. Undelineated tracery began to merge into concrete, representative forms, and finally, from the union of whites and blacks, the image of a moon in a grey sky, a crescent moon surrounded by sinister clouds, appeared. Half of the clouds were devils or witches mounted on broomsticks, half were fantastically formed beehives, but quite clearly beehives, from which a multitude of insects poured forth. Dots united with other dots were transformed into the bodies of bees, but with the feet, tails and claws of infernal furies. Some of those diabolical bees or wasps flew in formation around the moon; others covered its face, which, seen in profile, assumed the features of Satan himself, eyebrows arched, mouth and eyes flaming. Above this grotesque scene of confusion Bonis drew symmetrical beams like the reflection of a calm sea; over the highest line, the line of the horizon, he traced another image of night, but a serene night, a sky crossed by five threads of weblike mist, the lines of the musical staff. The full moon rose, soft, majestic and poetic; there within its disk, a series of elegant and sinuous curves formed the word: Serafina.

This symbolic composition cost the dreamer a long half-hour, but his inspiration and his ability earned him the noble pride of the satisfied artist, a sensation soon joined by a tenderness voluptuously austere, which made him bow his head down, rest his forehead on his hands and meditate, sobbing while large tears welled in his eyes. What a strange life! What things can happen to the soul of a poor devil such as I, thought Bonis.

The allegory, which the pen seemed to have drawn of its own will, was more than clear. It was the synthesis of his present life. In the upper sky, the serene region over the ocean of his becalmed passions, shone the full moon, the satisfied, ideal love of his Serafina. These were no longer the days of stormy sensuality in which physical love mingled strongly with platonic in an arabesque of headstrong, chaotic passion. Here the soul had won its mastery. It set the standard for their affection, which, now that it had become almost a habit, a peaceful convergence, had taken a more spiritual direction. Well enough, yet from the lower half of the picture, that mysterious region of the abyss inhabited by the enemy, issued subterranean voices, threats of punishment. In a stormy sky, another moon appeared like an unfaithful reflection of the first—the satanic moon of *Walpurgisnacht* which his wife, Emma Valcárcel, had decreed shine during those nights of unexpected and almost desperate lovemaking.

Bonis got up and contemplated La Gorgheggi sleeping. This beloved woman does not know that I am unfaithful to her, he reflected, that there are hours of the night when I taste a love philter made up of fears, of bitter memories, of duty, of bodily habit, of the remnants of almost forgotten pleasures, of the aroma of withered roses, of pity and even of black philosophies. This woman does not know that I let myself be kissed and that I kiss like someone giving alms to death, kisses which I want to arrest quickly to stop the rush of time passing through my mouth. Yes, Serafina, in these hours I feel *pity* toward my wife, whose slave I am. Her awkward caresses are reflections of my own; her caresses, perhaps innocent in her, represent my crimes. Her cries of love terminate in sighs of sad old age, in the creaking of decaying bodies, alive with I know not what terror and suffocation, the embalmer's salts and oils. I am the lover of a sick and lascivious woman who, yes, has the right to my lovemaking, but a right which is not like yours, like yours which men do not recognize but which seems much, oh much, stronger to me: subtle, invisible. It is your right . . . and mine, the right of my weary soul. He began to weep again.

Bonis had been thinking in other words and, in part, without words. He was not even aware of the meaning of some of those words which it has been necessary to use, for example, *ultrateluric*. What did Bonifacio know of ultrateluric? But for all that, he was always thinking along such lines, and he commingled that awareness with all his cavillations and with all the anxieties of his stifling existence. In his time, men did not speak as they do now, and even less so in his town, where for forceful, yet intricate effects, the style of Larrañaga and Don Heriberto García de Quevedo dominated. We must also realize that, had he intended to, Reyes, who was even less educated than this biographer, would have been absolutely incapable of finding some of the expressions used here to interpret or at least approximate the tribulations of his spirit.

For whatever reason, La Gorgheggi was not awakened by these psychological rumblings. Her lover tiptoed about without bumping into anything and even managed to cover, without her feeling it, a part of her white shoulder which was, he feared, becoming cold. In Serafina's room, he was the same refined, thoughtful, gentle and dexterous gallant who took care of his wife, like the black servants in the enchanted palaces of his novels.

He was acquainted with every nook in Serafina's room and, also, Mochi's. He was the one who had found the new lodging house and settled them in it, the one who endeavored to introduce the spirit and practice of order and economy into the domestic affairs of these artists, bringing to them a little of the saving influences of his own home, which in the final account was a home, although it could hardly have served as a model—less so every day. Reyes imagined that he had two houses, his wife's and his mistress'; just as he himself had unintentionally introduced into the Valcárcel estate an atmosphere of libertinage and corruption for which the terrain of Emma's soul was well prepared, in the very same unreflecting manner, he had sown the seeds of sedentary ways, of provincial order and of domestic discipline into his relationship with the singers. Perhaps even more evident than in his own house, this influence was generated and inspired by reminiscences of times long past, the habits of family peace and economic propriety which Valcárcel's clerk still tried to retain. It was not in vain that he had spent his childhood and the greater part of his youth at the side of his honorable, if humble and resigned, parents. And though the ideal for Bonis was to indulge in dreams and great passions, he wanted to do this without endangering good domestic customs. He loved a well-ordered home. Looking over prints in books, he was always moved by pictures like the one of a clean, serious, old woman knitting by the firelight while at her feet a cat plays noiselessly with a ball of strong, thick wool, symbol of the bourgeois' defense against the winter. Although he envied the courage and nonchalance of artists who have no home, who forage about the four corners of the world, this admiration was born of the contrast with his own tasks, with his invincible fondness for an ordered, tranquil, sedentary life. His fondness reached such a point that to enjoy imaginative, romantic freedom, it seemed indispensable to him to have his physical necessities, so many and so complicated, carefully arranged. For Bonifacio, his slippers embodied all of these sentiments. In his dreams as a youth, when he had imagined a castle built atop rocks, a beautiful Nazarene peering out of an ogival window, a silken ladder, a lute played by a gallant (his own dream self) who steals the virgin from the castle, he had always balked at the unlikelihood of running away to distant lands without his Turkish slippers; yet it was quite clear that the slippers were incompatible with the lute.

There was more, however, to his longing for a serene home than simple physical comfort. In his ruminations, he returned constantly to the idea of the family, an honorable family without adultery, without mixed blood; the subject furnished him with delight. Would a family be incompatible with "passion," like the Turkish slippers with the lute? Perhaps not, but he had not once found the ideal conjunction of these two beautiful ideals. His own family was not a true family in his eyes; God had not decreed it. His wife was a tyrant, and lately a concubine as well; but worst of all, there was no son. And in Serafina's house, where he had found real feeling, there was neither the beatitude of the home nor even the hope for a long-enduring union of kindred souls. The singers would depart one day soon. They were Wandering Jews. It was already miraculous that with the combined subscriptions, company scandals, weeks of strikes, extensions, delays, loans, unpaid debts and abuses of credit, Mochi and La Gorgheggi had been able to stay in town for as many months as they had. Any day now Bonis expected to find Serafina's suitcases packed. "Time to go," Mochi would say, and Bonis would have no right to oppose him. He himself had not a groat; he could hardly offer them money enough to remain in town. Art and Necessity blew like the wind and carried away into the wide world his "passion," the sole refuge of his grieving soul, which needed the affection, the chaste caresses (as Serafina's had indeed become), the personal dignity which it lacked at the side of Emma, who would submit herself only like a female animal, likely to change without warning, in the middle of lovemaking, into the same old despot, who seasoned her caresses with grotesque surprises to punish her confused husband. Completely abandoned on that day, he would be forced to return to the dominion of Emma, of the cold, incisive state of Nepomuceno with his accounts, the dominion of Sebastian, the cousin, and of all the other Valcárcels who wanted to make mincemeat of him with their contempt.

La Gorgheggi finally woke up, smiling and out of pain. She thanked Bonis for watching over her sleep like a father, and her new feeling of well-being made her tender, sentimental and finally led her to embraces. They were gentle, broken for long, reasonable dialogues, so unlike the ardent clutches she had once resorted to. My wife should make love like this, thought Reyes. Serafina had grown accustomed to her innocent lover as well as to the provincial life of the sedentary bourgeoisie which he himself represented and which she had also observed during her protracted stay in that poor city. Her last hopes of becoming a "star" had begun to fade, and Serafina was thinking of another kind of happiness. The prolonged strike helped, for to have no rehearsals and performances, no theater at all, this smacked of a kind of emancipation, almost—almost—moral regeneration. Just as courtesans who have reached a certain age and have become rich aspire to respectability as the final luxury, so too Serafina dreamed of independence, of fleeing from the public, forgetting the *solfeggio* and establishing herself in a small town where she could live peaceably as an influential lady, respectable and prominent. Further, she was becoming well acquainted with the life of that city which she had once bitterly scorned. She was interested now in the local gossip and anxious to know about the "life and miracles" of this or the other lady; she grew very annoyed one day simply because Bonis had not managed to secure her an invitation from one of the parish churches to sit at the Petitioners Table on Holy Thursday. She did sing in the cathedral with Mochi and Minghetti one night, an occasion which filled her with a strong sense of satisfaction. Her head was whirling with the notion of giving a great concert in benefit of the hospital or the poorhouse. When she broached her plan to Mochi, he pushed it in a new direction: a great concert, but not in benefit of the poor, rather in benefit of the singers, survivors of the shipwrecked company. Mochi mentioned the project to Minghetti, the baritone, and he thought it a magnificent idea. He suggested to the tenor that they take advantage of that concert to reanimate the philharmonic instinct in the town, which had grown tired of the opera—the theater had been closed for some time now—then let La Gorgheggi appear in an evening gown at one of the society salons and sing in recital. She would select good pieces of music in order to arouse her fans' musical interest. This move would facilitate the plan for opening a conditional subscription on the basis of a trio. They had a tenor, a soprano and a baritone; if they could find a contralto, a bass and a chorus, they could form another company which would pay the debts, and then with less hurry and anxiety, they could wait to scrape up another contract somewhere else. It was necessary that some citizen take the initiative to put the project in motion. Who but Bonifacio Reyes? Serafina took it upon herself to beg him to undertake it. It was, of course, no sooner said than done. That afternoon, between caresses of blissful serenity, La Gorgheggi entreated her lover to adopt the idea with energy and enthusiasm, to take it upon himself to prepare for the concert, overcoming any obstacles that might crop up. How could Bonifacio do less for that woman to whom he could no longer give money, to whom he could only give that sense of acceptance which she needed so desperately? He proposed the players' project to the directing committee of the Casino, a social club established on the main floor of the Café de la Oliva. In the club, there were a ballroom, reading rooms and a gaming room, the last often the scene of great stakes and losses. Conscientious of its duties, the board of directors promised to study the question. There were repeated deliberations, a vote, and, by a small majority, the project was approved. The concert would be followed by a dance, but with no buffet supper.

Bonifacio tried to hide from his wife the fact that he had had anything at all to do with these transactions, that he was, in fact, the mainstay of the projected festival, but she nonetheless found out that the concert was in preparation and that her Bonis was organizing what was to be a very lavish affair. If she had not talked to him (except indirectly and without insisting) about other things of which she was aware and had been for some time, she now found it convenient to reveal herself clearly as in the know. Consequently, she remarked to him one day over dessert and in Nepomuceno's presence, "My dear Bonifacio, why are you being so quiet about what you are preparing for me? Do you actually want to surprise me?"

"What I am preparing for you?" he gasped.

"Why, the concert. I already know that you and a few others want to quietly give a hand to those poor actors who have stayed in town and must be having a wretched time. That's very well done. It is a great idea and a great work of charity. We will give out alms, and we'll enjoy ourselves. Magnificent. True, Uncle, that it is an excellent idea?"

"Excellent," assented Nepomuceno, cleaning his lips with a napkin and lowering his head.

"Count on me and, as well, on Señorita Marta, Marta Körner, the engineer's daughter, you know, my little friend, who will go with me. My uncle will accompany us, isn't that so?" Emma went on, looking at Nepomuceno. "And perhaps Cousin Sebastian, who will be coming to the fair about then, will help. You will have to be the one to arrange matters on that score. All right, we already know, dear fellow; don't be modest. We already know that you are the director of the festival. What of it? All the better! Thank God you are finally doing something beneficial. What upsets me is only that you never told me that you were a *friend* of the players, such a close friend. Could you imagine that it would displease me? Why? I am not proud; I don't believe that my name would be tarnished because my spouse is on friendly terms with some artists. On the contrary, if I were a man, I should do the very same thing. Didn't the famous Sweet Soprano marry a local gentleman? Isn't it so, Uncle, that we're not ashamed to know that Bonis sees a great deal of the players, a very great deal, and is well acquainted with them all? We found out through Señorita Körner, isn't that so, Uncle? And *I* even put on airs about it. So you see."

Bonifacio, feeling mixed emotions, stared at his wife with wistful eyes. A blind instinct told him, "Be on guard! Don't trust her! Don't give yourself away! There is a trap!" Another, perhaps more powerful inclination revealed to him an open sky and moved him to compassion. Perhaps his wife was capable of understanding him, of actually sympathizing with his love of art and artists. He did not reach the point, however, of hoping that she would overlook his affair with Serafina; it was, on the contrary, absolutely imperative that she not learn anything about that, but as to the rest, why not? That is to say, except for the debts and the loan. He looked at Emma. He looked at the uncle. If honor and honesty and loyalty existed in the world, they were now to be seen here in the faces and especially the eyes of the uncle and the niece.

He confessed everything which he believed it convenient to confess. His honesty was appreciated, and uncle and niece both manifested their true and unlimited admiration for his ideal and the hours of revelry and innocent joy which Bonis placed before them with some eloquence. Although Nepomuceno and Emma each had other, less worthy motives, their enthusiasm for Reyes' project was in part sincere. As to Emma's forgiving the quixotic dreams of her husband and his acquaintance with the players, nothing was easier. Wasn't he a musician too? And what could be objectionable in the fact that when he went out, he used all his free time to cultivate the friendship of that excellent gentleman, Mochi, who knew so much about music, who had such fine manners and who was above the envious attitudes of a town so limited, narrow-minded and monotonous.

Oddly enough, Nepomuceno said more than usual at this meeting. He, too, was a painter, or rather, a musician, yes, for in the Economic Society he had himself assisted in the creation of a class of *solfeggio* and piano!

"Ah, music! Naturally, it is a wonderful thing. I have heard that at times it tames wild beasts," he philosophized.

"Certainly!" rejoined Bonis, extremely pleased.

And in his own way, he recounted the myth of Orpheus and Eurydice, which was quite new to Emma and interested her greatly.

134

"Speaking of the piano," Emma interjected, "although it is late and the barley reeds are too old to make pipes for Pan, I would like to learn to play, just a little—just enough to pick out with one finger the operas you play on the flute."

The idea struck Bonis as highly laudable. He returned to the thought, although without much hope, that "music tames wild beasts." He said, "Well, look, if you decide, Minghetti, the baritone, is an excellent teacher."

Emma, glowing, could not help rising to her feet, and without trying to restrain herself, she began to clap her hands.

"Oh, yes, yes, sublime, sublime, what an idea! The baritone! And we will pay him well. It will be a work of charity. But, what a shame; will he leave soon?"

"Oh, that. Well, according to circumstances, if the subscription is renewed, if the company is formed again, if they are helped, then . . ."

"Indeed, we *are* going to help them! Right, uncle?" Emma exclaimed.

The uncle nodded his head again. What plans had she in mind? His eyes burned, focused on the tablecloth; he speculated on the hundred ideas which his eyes did not explain, but which were all too certain.

The night of the concert arrived. The salons of the Casino, a branch of the Café de la Oliva, were opened. There was even a small buffet, in spite of the committee's agreement, and the most select persons of the town turned out to sample sweet sherbet and examine, at close quarters, the singers, so often applauded when they were outfitted in costume jewelry and gold braid, now all wearing formal dress.

A solemn night for Bonis, for Emma, for Nepomuceno.

Chapter Twelve

In the crystal chandeliers burned many dozens of spermaceti candles. At the far end of the salon, on a makeshift platform, a respectable orchestra of local musicians, teachers they were, inaugurated the festival with a symphony from its musty repertory; there sat the horn player, a living reproach not only to the Italian language, but also to the notion of tuning; there the spiritual violinist, Secades, who had dreamed of being a second Paganini, a man who had spent night after night, day after day, searching in the strings which his bow caressed for either the true lament of sublime love or for the exact imitations of natural sounds, for example, say, the braying of a burro. A touch of bad luck—he had never progressed beyond the bray and could only simulate Balaam's ass, but the ineffable plaintiveness of love, the sigh of sublime passion, were reserved for other strings, for other loving bows, not Secades'. Now, aging and disillusioned, he concentrated on his other occupation—unofficial broker; indeed, in recent years he had paid more attention to banking and to his credit columns than to the art which had stirred his childhood dreams. Half-asleep now, he played, like all his companions, just to earn a small stipend, without faith, without emulation, just barely retaining a little melancholy affection and superstitious respect for good music—old music—ignoring the "new ideas" which companies had been trying to bring to his locale for many years past. There, too, was the ancient ophicleide player, Don Romualdo, bald, dignified, with an enormous belly, who played chirimia in the cathedral, ophicleide in the profane world. About him there was an aura of provincial glory. The whole town, even the deaf, recognized that what Don Romualdo did with his strange instrument was marvelous; he made it weep, laugh and almost, almost cough. Yet, in spite of so much fame, the force of time and the wear and tear of long years of admiration had thrown a heavy cloak of public indifference over his celebrity. He knew very well that, without for a moment doubting his grandeur, his countrymen had grown tired of admiring taciturn melancholy; he continued to play with his usual care although these days it seemed in vain. In brief, he was as sad, as disillusioned as his companion, Secades. With no illusions of returning to his old glory, he sat on the same cushion of bitter resignation upon which Secades had sat, pausing in his journey toward fame. It was the same thing: never to have mounted to "the temple of Fame," or to have arrived once and then descended.

With such notables as these, the orchestra squeaked like the turning of screws in an unoiled machine. The string instruments were asthmatic; they sounded of wood as cider tastes of the barrel. The brass section was maddeningly loud, almost heartless; those serpents would have been sufficient to bring down the walls of five Jerichos. Fortunately, the public listened to the orchestra no more than it would listen to rain falling.

Emma entered the salon after the first number of the program had been performed. Again she attracted attention, this time for two reasons: her costly and ostentacious dress and the fact that she came in on the arm of the German engineer, Körner, a fat, tall, ruddy man with the eyes of a petulant child: blue, clear, very deep set. He resembled a large, very well cared for pig, but he was actually a "spiritual" man, full of Mozart and the destiny of Prussia. He spoke Spanish as though he were inventing a language, with quasi-Castilian words and quasi-German idioms. Though a dreamer, he was able to manage a factory with great ease, and as an accountant, he reminded everyone, not a soul could surpass him. He knew something about everything. He secretly despised the Spaniards, idolized his daughter Marta and had come to that poor province to make his fortune.

Father and wife were followed by Marta Körner and Bonis, arm

137

in arm, and they, in turn, were closely followed by Don Juan Nepomuceno, alone; this last appeared to have pomaded his side whiskers,
which shone like pure silver. Marta Körner was a twenty-eight-
year-old blonde, very fresh, heavily made up and soft skinned. Her
principal physical merit lay in her figure, but she valued above
everything grace in her expression and distinction in her ideas. She
spoke always of the heart, raising her lovely hands to her palpitating,
pearly breast. She attributed the treasures of her person to the subsoil, but the wily Nepomuceno, among others, placed a higher value
on the surface.

Marta differed from her father in her musical tastes. She preferred
Beethoven. What they were both agreed on, however, was the
absolute necessity of making, at best, a fortune; at worst, half a
fortune. Körner had come directly from Saxony to manage a foundry established by an industrialist at the foot of some iron mines in
the mountainous region of the province, where the poor and intrac-
table Valcárcels maintained their haunts. Cousin Sebastian, who was
somewhat more communicative than the other Valcárcels in that
area, introduced Körner to Nepomuceno. At first, the German and
his daughter had lived in the rough, roadless places never giving a
thought to the fact that a few leagues away was a city which might,
if only remotely, recall the civilization and culture they had left behind in their own country. Although surrounded by all the comforts
that could be hoisted, as Sebastian joked, with a crane to those
heights upon which they dwelled, the Germans lived in a rustic
manner with no social relationships whatsoever. They began to learn
Spanish in the obscure, corrupted dialect of the region. The disdain
with which they had at first regarded and treated the coarse people
in whose midst they had to live began to change imperceptibly into
curiosity; by stages it grew into interest, imitation, then emulation,
until finally the pair no longer took pride in ridiculing their neighbors, but rather in trying to dazzle them. Körner longed to achieve
distinction among these crude mountaineers, and since his talents as
a dilettante in the various arts and a reader of sentimental literature
were worthless there, he had to take advantage of other qualities

which would be better appreciated in that land—qualities, for example, like the enormous capacity of his stomach. He did not gain the reputation he wanted until one day when the news, quite true, ran rapidly from one mountain village to another that the German had won a bet with a foreman at the mines. The Spaniard had eaten one and a half-dozen fried eggs while he, Körner, went on to gobble two dozen very easily and finished off that heroic feat by devouring two sea bream. Now this was something! Those who had remained indifferent to the glorious wars of Frederick the Great (of whom, by the way, Körner was as vain as though he were the illustrious monarch's own grandson), those who heard him speak of Goethe and Heine and Hegel without listening, all recognized the glorious future of a race that produced such commodious stomachs. Add to this the fact that the engineer also played ninepins with singular dexterity and with the power of many horses, or at least two or three of those villagers. With capabilities of that order, Körner now managed to win the sympathy and even the admiration he craved. But this kind of glory finally tired him; at bottom, he was repulsed by the patent danger—which he came to see very late—of being transformed into a sort of bear, legendary and musical, but a bear nonetheless, an ur-troll of flesh and blood. He grew very fat and put aside his transcendental meditations; his simple tastes, easily satisfied by mountain life, cut him off from the complicated plans for progress and the comfortable life which he had brought from his country. Moreover, in the mountain factory, although he was paid well, esteemed, and satisfied in point of material conveniences (for he had a good house, emoluments and concessions), he did not really prosper: he could not become rich. He attempted to work his way into the firm as an industrial partner, but he gave way in the face of difficulties which the foxy proprietor put in his way. His disposition was becoming bitter, and he felt a strong desire to leave that troglodyte's existence, increase his value and place within reach of "demand" his daughter Marta's honest supply of increasingly evident charms, charms which the years were passing by there in the mountains. On the pretext of work, retaining his position in the foundry, Körner began to make frequent visits to the capital in search of some business opportunity which would afford a better future. It was on one of these trips that Cousin Sebastian introduced him to Nepomuceno. The German, who was sagacious and worldly-wise, was quick to understand what role this financier played in his niece's household; he saw clearly that there was money there, that this money was running out fast and that the current of that river of silver was directed straight towards Nepomuceno's pocket although with great losses and divagations in a delta of expenses—the pockets of dressmakers, traders in cloth, hatters, jewelers, grocers, proprietors of sweet shops, game and fish markets and so forth. Körner tried to turn Don Juan's head by persuading him first that he, Nepomuceno, was a talented accountant, a Necker, untapped, unrecognized, idle; if given a chance elsewhere, he would shine like a star of the first magnitude in the heaven of Administration and Finance. In conscience, according to Körner, Nepomuceno was *obliged* to give the world such gifts, to find employment worthier than the simple stewardship to which he was limited now. There was more: in the interests of the doomed Valcárcel estate, which apparently was in danger of being utterly wrecked by Emma's extravagance and her husband's secret expenses, Nepomuceno must use the capital to produce something more than the ludicrous percentages that come from mere territorial rent. So much rental, so many tiny small holdings, were ridiculous. *Sursum corda*! Clear away the rust! Put this stock into industry, and we'll talk! To this assembly of arguments, he added, by way of embellishment, apéritif and complement, others—for example, that Spain was very backward in spite of the richness of its soil and subsoil. In Körner's opinion, the Inquisition as well as the Bourbons were to blame and too, of course, the abuse of the constitutional system, which was a poor thing to begin with. While he was on this theme, he lamented general Spanish decadence and even reached the point of speaking to Nepomuceno of the possible rebirth of a national theater if everyone did what he counseled: put his capital to work and take advantage of the treasures of the earth. Körner

140

did not know that Nepomuceno was ignorant of the fact that in years past such an admirable theater had actually existed, and so, in this aspect, little would be squeezed out of him. But whereas the patriotic idea of contributing to a rebirth of the national spirit through well-directed industrial movement failed to move the uncle, Marta's eyes and, more important, her figure, which had an almost hypnotic effect over the financier, did. The first time he saw Marta, on the first visit he paid Körner—who was to show him certain plans and the budget for a factory of chemical products, a great project the German entertained—Nepomuceno remained openmouthed, transfixed. He felt an itching in his throat and in his whole body an unexpected sense of youthfulness which, accurately speaking, he had never experienced in his life. Hers was the flesh of which he had always dreamed!

They were on the stairway. Marta had opened the door for him. She was poorly dressed, somewhat disarranged, but she was even more attractive and seductive because of the few tatters that covered her. Initially, Nepomuceno took her for the maid. He mounted the stairs, greeted Körner, and after just a few minutes, feeling the absolute necessity of seeing the girl again, he said, "Could I have some water, please?"

Nepomuceno's plan was to appropriate Körner's domestic and set her up in a house, perhaps even marry her. She *had* to be his. What eyes, what a body! He smacked his lips thinking that he was going to see her again, that she was now about to enter with a glass of water. In fact, the scrubbing woman brought the water. Nepomuceno did not find out until the next day, from Sebastian, that his sweet tormentor was Marta Körner herself.

A week later, Körner's daughter sang, accompanying herself on the piano, a sentimental *lieder* entitled "Vergissmeinicht," "Forget Me Not," not Goethe's but one much, much sweeter. When she dedicated it to the silver-whiskered administrator, with an expressive look and a languid gesture, she left him forever subdued by her charms. She had forced him to participate in those sentiments of *sehnsucht*, the existence of which Nepomuceno had never so much as suspected. At that late time in his life, Don Juan learned who Faustus was and what pact he had made with the Devil; he conceived the idea that Margarete—blonde, badly dressed, her eyes cast down, carrying a water pitcher under her arm as she made her way to the fountain—that Goethe's Margarete was clearly his Marta. That plump, white, fine-skinned, spiritual señorita had, within a few hours, revealed to him a new world, the world of intense, poetic love. He desired to be Faustus so that he could become fresh and young again but preferably without selling his soul to the Devil—not that he objected to selling it, but the Devil would doubtless have turned down the contract. He did not think of dying his whiskers, but rather of "gilding" them, that is, letting the Körners realize that he had not administered the Valcárcel estate for so many years in vain. The German did not take long to deduce what effect his daughter had produced on this arbiter of Emma's rents. After one or two conferences on the proposed factory of chemical products, Körner wheedled himself into the family circle. Nepomuceno could no longer pass a day without its corresponding session of long plans and calculations. Although the Körners were only residing temporarily in the city, they had a fixed house belonging to Mountain Enterprises. On the long, rough worktable he kept in his office there, Körner heaped a pile of stupendously large books on commerce, filled with imaginary benefits and profits, a sort of bookkeeping romance he had created out of his own head. In spite of his knowledge of, and experiences with, complicated and obscure accounts, Nepomuceno did not understand a word of it. Beside those volumes, which resembled the gigantic books used by the choir in El Escorial, Körner laid out his plans neatly drawn on pieces of lined tracing paper. Nepomuceno found them easy to admire since he knew that Marta herself helped her father trace those thick, rainbow-colored lines. The young lady of the house often attended her father's conferences in the capacity of assistant; she rolled and unrolled the plans, placing her delicate fingers on the areas that needed to be studied. With this excuse, she passed close to Nepomuceno a hundred times a day, grazed him with her dresses and even on several occasions made him feel, accidentally, the sweet but distracting weight of her body; in short, she totally confused him; she maddened him, and Emma's uncle now found that he could no longer live without those economical-technical conferences about the factory of chemical products. He began to believe that he was irrevocably in love with the project. That factory could not help but produce mountains of gold; while still in the planning stages, it already had his "organic chemistry" in a state of revolution. The long hours of interminable business discussions passed in minutes for him. Both the German and the Spaniard agreed that only money was needed for the colossal project to be put into practice and to unwind as easily as a silken thread. Money was needed? It would appear.

In the meantime, Nepomuceno had showed the father and the daughter, by means of veiled hints, that it might be well to treat with kindness his weakness in the area of the heart. Instead of opposing his implicit confession of passion—far be it from her to classify it as senile—instead of rejecting the cautious gallantries of her father's new friend, Marta made him understand by means of philosophical sonatas that, in spite of appearances, she placed little importance on the physical, pooh-poohed the action of time on people and cared only for the eternal element of love, of love which is never old. In short, she needed money. Their factory and his passion would blend in perfect harmony, with complete prosperity, as soon as the capital appeared. Through half-suggestions and signs the Körners were made to see the benefit of treating Emma Valcárcel with the greatest possible amicability. The undertaking was not difficult; Nepomuceno was to arrange for this relationship to blossom during the exact time that Emma determined to launch herself into the world and to enjoy her diminishing riches without limits or remorse. Thus, the superficial relationship of mere courtesy which had existed between the Valcárcels and the Germans for some time through the intervention of Cousin Sebastian was magically transformed into an assiduously cultivated friendship, becoming more and more intimate as Emma marched farther and farther along the wide and easy path of her new life. As we have already remarked, in her plans to revenge herself on her "thief of an uncle," La Valcárcel had decided to corrupt Marta once she had gotten herself married to Nepomuceno. This notion afforded her a great deal of amusement. For this reason, then, she gladly applied herself to strengthening the relationship with the Körners. What she had not foreseen was that, with the extraordinary seductiveness of feminine intimacy—novel, piquant and "taking"—Marta might win her affection, the affection of that poor Emma, whose natural depravity had not until then made room for a sort of literary, German-romantic weakness. A virgin, Marta was nevertheless a sensualist in mind, for her random and unconnected reading, which had shown her the methods of immoral if picturesque human behavior, had also provided her a moral criterion which was capricious, oversubtle and basically cynical. No matter how close his relationship with Señorita Körner, no man could ever really know the depth of her thoughts and vices; moreover, of purity nothing remained in her but a real enough instinct for physical defense against male attack. Marta might accompany a man partially in his sensual transports, but she would always hide from him another type of moral corruption, the emotional depravity which she carried within herself and which she could confess only to another woman in whom she found a similar temperament. Emma and Marta came to a quick understanding. After no more than a few weeks of seeing each other frequently and familiarly, they could already be seen in La Valcárcel's sitting room, laughing loudly, almost hysterically. When they presented themselves before the men, before Nepomuceno, Körner and Bonis, after these gay exchanges filled with secrets and quiet malice, they would smile smiles that were only poorly disguised sneers at the worthy but dull men who were incapable of ever penetrating the mysteries of that curious friendship. Marta boasted of having a complex character which the uninitiated could not begin to understand. She spoke disdainfully of middle-class morality—with people she believed would understand. Her gaiety, her readiness to play games, to frisk about, to get up in the middle of the night in her

144

gown so as to shock the maids, to run through the house and then to return to the warmth of her bed, vibrating with "unseemly" emotion and gay voluptuousness, formed a contrast, an "antithesis," she used to say, to her exquisite sensibility, to the *claire de lune* which she let others believe she carried in her soul. All the worse for the stupid who could not understand these contradictions.

Like her father, Marta was a Catholic, and she affected the devout pose of Spanish women as though it were a formula which she had discovered, suggesting that her soul had been infused with the religion before it made its appearance in Germany. Yet she felt, nevertheless, that her religiosity struck a new note, the "artistic" note not to be found in the Spanish lady. An enthusiast of *The Essence of Christianity*, Marta adapted it to her own fashion. She joined it to the Gothic romanticism of her German poets and novelists; then, afterwards, she varnished the whole picture with the hundred showy colors which characterized her tastes in the decorative arts and her itch for painting. Although she loved music first of all, she also loved color, and she gave especial importance to the blue of the Conception and the dark chestnut of Our Lady of the Carmelites. She was already speaking of the Sistine Chapel, a topic of conversation not commonly heard in the Spain of those days, and of the marvels which she had seen in Florence and other cities in Italy where she had traveled with her father.

Marta would never admit that her greatest, most intense delight lay in being tickled, especially on the soles of her feet. Under her arms, on her back, on her throat, many people had tickled her, men included, but as to the soles of her feet . . . ? Only rarely could she manage to find someone who would cater to that preference. Some maid with whom she had grown intimate perhaps. A village girl, maybe. And now Emma, from whom after only two months of acquaintance she had obtained this wonderful boon. Emma, convulsed with laughter, granted it to her gladly. She too wished to sample the strange pleasure of which her friend was so passionately fond, but she did not really find it amusing; on the contrary, she could not tolerate it for even half a second. Emma, rather, was tickled by Marta's psychological and literary subtleties. What things that woman knew! She divided the world into two types of people: the chosen and those who were not chosen, the superior souls and the vulgar ones. The trick lay in being a chosen soul; then, one was just as free as Castile is wide. There was no longer a common morality, necessary social ties, anything. It was sufficient to maintain appearances, to avoid scandal. Love and art were sovereigns of the spiritual world, and the superior woman enjoyed the privilege of using art to further love. The beautiful and emotional dilettante was the artist's prize, and the pleasure of rewarding the genius was the greatest God had conceded to his feminine creatures. When she was still very young, in Saxony, Marta had been engaged to a great musician, a master of the organ; and once, to a painter who beautifully imitated Rembrandt, she had granted favors of an intimate and familiar nature although, of course, without losing her virginity, which had to be reserved for the "Philistine," as she referred to him, whom it would be convenient for her to marry. She would marry in order to be rich, a not unreasonable condition, necessary if she were to satisfy her "artistic interest," which, the moment the notion of comfort enters in—luxurious pieces of furniture, a box in the opera and so forth—is apt to be expensive. Marta hoped to marry a very rich but ordinary man, to use that vulgar creature's money to patronize great artists and to save her love for one or more of them, "unipersonal" constancy also being vulgar. Since Marta read many books of ancient Spanish literature, a fad among the literary men of her own country, she set up as the model of her theory the wife of the *Jealous Estremanian* who, without actually committing adultery, had slept in the arms of the gallant Loaisa, sinning only in her thoughts. The *Jealous Estremanian* had been so noble that he died leaving his wife all his fortune and the charge that she should marry her lover. However, since modern husbands and impure reality were not so generous as Carrizales, the superior woman must suck the pecuniary juices out of her husband as soon as possible.

All of this, explained in a very different way, but always with the intent of edification, soon became part of Emma's general philosophy as well. Her frustrations, facilitated by a certain moral laxity natural to her, found a marvelous outlet in such episodes where spite and deceit may even exceed the sensual gratification others seek. To deceive for the sake of deception: the idea was charming. Yet at the same time, Emma realized that it might be a heavenly treat to "have relations" with a superior man like an artist, say, with a baritone as handsome and famous as the celebrated Minghetti. Secret for secret, Marta received with pleasure and with an ample measure of confidence Emma's account of her flirtation with the baritone. She did not deny Emma, but in her heart she pitied her Spanish friend, for although she herself, in fact, had deeply admired the comely figure and well-fitted breeches—one or the other—of the "king" in this or that opera, she did not see how the shapely singer could ever be classified as a truly superior and artistic man. There was, however, no reason to be picky. Clearly, *she* was above attachments of that sort.

Apart from being tickled, Marta was also obsessed with writing very enthusiastic and very confidential letters to her favorite authors; some answered, others did not. She would send her portrait along with her epistolary confessions, and more than one writer made the effort to begin a correspondence, considering the pretty girl who incarnated that repugnant spirit. Consequently, she began more than two "artistic" and "platonic" love affairs through writing. More than that, she kept a commemorative album, filled with many unknown signatures and even a few notable ones, in which questions like these were answered: What is your favorite color? And your favorite virtue? What author do your prefer? For a woman who knew that Liszt liked truffles and who had wept in secret over the hidden sorrows of a poet of Young Germany, the baritone of Mochi's company was bound to seem insignificant, even if well formed.

Now Mochi, accompanied by Serafina and the baritone, entered the salon just as a theater buff, a watchmaker by profession, finished singing an Italian *romanzetta*. He had a "suprasensible" tenor voice, as the wags used to say, for when he had to mount the highest notes, his voice just disappeared as though it had been carried off in a balloon to the Seventh Heaven, and no matter how much he gesticulated, he was never heard; he seemed to be speaking from very far away, from where he could only be seen. The public was still muffling its laughter when the general attention swung in order to digest the beauty of Serafina, who, with her modest gaze and her sweet aroma, was wearing a black dress with a long train that revealed her white shoulders and the graceful curves of her breasts. She reached the foot of the platform, where the president of the Casino waited to give her his arm, lead her up to the two steps which separated her from the piano and leave her after a low bow. She stood beside Minghetti, who was dressed in a formal frock coat; his white hands with their pink nails flew over the yellowish keyboard, moving through the octaves with elegant ability.

Bonis had disappeared. Shortly afterwards he was seen talking with Mochi in a nearby sitting room. Nepomuceno and Körner accompanied Emma and Marta, all of them seated in one of the first rows, which on those occasions were always left for the ladies who arrived late, simply because those who, to their shame, arrived early sat in the most hidden and separate areas, sidling away from the entertainment as though it were a poison or as if sitting so close were the same as participating. Nor were there lacking ladies who confused the singers with the magicians whom they had also seen perform in that very Casino; they did not want anyone to burn their handkerchiefs, even in jest, or to guess what card they were thinking of.

Emma had never before seen La Gorgheggi at such close quarters although she had thought of her often and for quite some time. She admired her, in spite of herself. She regarded her as a "lost woman" of the major kind, and this in itself attracted her, envy becoming confused with admiration. Now that Serafina was a mere four steps away, where peering between spermacetti candles Emma could see her naked arms, her corseted waist and her breasts, now that Emma could appraise her features, her gestures and even hear something of her voice, which seemed to sing even as it spoke,

148

she examined the singer more closely; La Valcárcel measured her figure and scrutinized her soul, for she wanted to estimate by comparison how thick or well formed the invisible extremities and other parts of her body would be. Insomuch as Emma could see, Serafina was very pale; she must have been that way all over. No, it was not rice powder; it was a healthy pallor, an English complexion, a true freshness and beauty which could easily withstand gossip. It was said that her voice was failing, but her elegant figure was vigorous and firm; there were no signs of decay there. How that woman must have enjoyed herself! What does she say to her lovers? Emma ruminated, remembering the secret of those strange, matrimonial events which had taken place of late, of that lovemaking she had indulged in from time to time during the night, suspended between dreams and nightmares, with her dunce of a Bonis. It was a source of shame which she dare not even confess to Marta. Did that lovely jade tell her lovers what she herself told Bonis? Emma recalled— she thought of it for the first time—that she had not even known those absurd phrases of love before, that Bonis himself had taught them to her during those frenzied moments which the two never spoke of after dawn. Was that the very same thing La Gorgheggi told her lovers? Was Bonis one of them? Was what she had heard and guessed true? It seemed impossible. Bonis was such a dolt and had not even a *real* to call his own; how could that great lady, that songbird who seemed to be such a great lady, a queen, ever have loved him, even in jest? Nonetheless, it was possible. There were indications. Strangely enough, Emma was not jealous; she felt instead a strange but very great pride, as if the emperor of China had sent her husband a fine blue or green decoration, or as if Bonis were her brother and had just married a Russian princess. No, it was not that; it was something else—something very different. Suddenly she recalled some of the theories of her German friend: that matrimony was conventional, that jealousy and honor were conventional—all things invented by men in order to organize what they call Society and the State. If she wanted to be a superior woman (and she did want to very much indeed; the notion was entertaining), she would definitely have to renounce the vulgarities of the ladies in her town. In Madrid, in Paris, in Berlin, the fine ladies knew that their husbands kept mistresses, and they did not throw plates at their heads for that reason. They simply had lovers too. But Bonis, that dunderhead Bonis, had he dared, *without her permission* . . . and at ultimely hours . . . ? Oh, no, it was clear that he would have to *pay* for that! It was clear, whether it were true or not, for the truth of the matter was another question entirely. Bonis was certainly *not* a superior soul, and he would have to pay for that mischief with his hide. Considered carefully, there was no reason why that lost woman should not love Bonis. He was handsome, devoted, discreet and obliging. Hadn't she too loved him? Was a player worth more than she, Emma, now on the verge of becoming a superior woman? And a very superior one at that. But hadn't she really been one all her life, without realizing it? Before Marta ever appeared in her house, Emma already delighted in keeping her temper over what would have made others angry, never getting excited or breaking into a fury when everyone else expected, even wanted her to. And now she had brilliantly conceived the idea of taking revenge on her unscrupulous uncle and her idiotic husband little by little and in her own way. Oh, how she would show them that she had always been special, a truly superior woman!

At the request of Mochi, who wanted to feed the religious sentiments of the gathering, Serafina sang a hymn written by an Italian master in honor of the Virgin. As soon as the public caught on that the present concern was God, it stopped scraping chairs and whispering; people withdrew from wordly preoccupations and listened in silence as though demonstrating that they not only understood how sublime were the mysteries of the faith, but also the mysterious relationship between music and the metaphysical. Serafina, who would have given so much a few weeks ago to have been invited to beg for the poor at the church door, now took advantage of that opportunity to show her refined piety, thus in this way exploding the rumors that she was a Protestant. She was really very beautiful with that air or modesty and shy devotion, with that clean, rather broad and convex brow, bathed in an expression familial, sweet and, at that moment, religious. The waves of bright hair, serving as an ornate frame for the smooth curve of that pure white forehead, were symbolic of an ideal that had lost itself in a beautiful poetic illusion.

As soon as he heard Serafina's voice rise in the silence of the salon, without thinking, without being able or even wanting to help himself, Bonis drew near the threshold of the farthest door so that he might listen from there. Although it was not really noteworthy or very original, the Italian program supplied fairly good music for the untutored. It was sentimental, slow, soft and uncomplicated, rendered in a tolerable and rather suggestive patois. Ay, thought Bonis, this is true peace of soul. In another time, not long ago, I loved the passions which I knew only through books. But peace, this peace of the soul, also has its poetry. Who would give it to me? It would be like this music: sweet, tranquil, serious, powerful in a way, but measured, soft, a friend of the contented conscience, loving the love which falls within the natural order, as the seasons follow one another without rebelling, as night and day run behind each other, as everything in the world obeys its law without losing its own charm, its own vigor. That is the way to love, to love forever, under the aegis of an invisible God who smiles with the canopy of the heavens, with the movement of the clouds and the twinkling of the stars. My Serafina, my spiritual wife, whose voice reminds me of my mother, Bonis mused, because your song without actually saying anything of this sort speaks to me about a tranquil and ordered home that I do not have, about a cradle that I cannot rock, at the foot of which I cannot watch, about a lap that I have lost, about a childhood that has vanished. Strictly speaking, in the whole world I have no relatives except this voice. A strange thing happened to Bonifacio as his thoughts continued in that vein; he suddenly conceived the idea that Serafina's hymn was a narration of the Annunciation: "And the angel of the Lord announced to Mary . . ." How strange! Did not he, Bonis, know that that voice was announcing to him as though through an extraordinary prophecy that he was going to be a . . . a mother! Just as it sounds, "mother." Not father, no; much more than that—mother. The truth was that his heart opened; the pure tenderness in which he was enveloped made itself felt as an almost physical sensation running through his body to his stomach. This must be what is called the Great Sympathetic System, he thought. And so sympathetic! *Dios mío!*, how delightful, but how strange! It recalls the beauty of the Conception. Oh, music like this, this voice, drives me almost mad! Yes, all of these ideas are absurd, but how they fill the soul! It is more than love, or rather an absolutely new kind of love, less selfish, not selfish at all. What did he know! He had to rest his head on the cold metal of the door frame and turn towards the sitting room. His eyes grew dark, filling with tears, and he did not want anyone to see him cry. It would be fine, he said to himself as the hymn continued, if Emma asked me now, "Why are you crying, good-for-nothing?" Well, I am crying for love, new love! The voice of that woman, of my mistress, has announced to me that I am going to be a kind of virgin mother . . . or father, no, mother . . . that I am going to have a son, legitimate, of course, that although you, Emma, give birth to him physically, he is going to be *all* mine. No, he did not think that the son would be his mistress', not that, may Serafina forgive him, but not that. It would be his wife's, but in such a way that Emma's inner corruption would not leave a mark on him. His very own son, child of his family, his race . . . a son he shared with the "voice" although Emma would give birth to him "for the world," according to the correct order of things. Bonifacio was afraid of making himself sick with so much foolish, feverish thinking, and his legs began to waiver, the fatal sympton of all his fainting fits. The music ceased, the "voice" was quiet, the applause broke forth, and from out of Bonis suddenly dropped all his ideas and sensations and emotions. He returned to reality and found himself with his arm being held by Mochi, who guided him through the salon toward the piano.

Körner rose to his feet, applauding with his fat hands; they sounded like mill paddles. Marta applauded, too, eliciting great surprise on the part of the local ladies, who believed that passivity in the face of art was a privilege of their sex and who unanimously considered it unworthy of a modest lady to clap for a player, just as they believed that rising during a visit in order to greet or say good-bye to a gentleman constituted a slight on their sex. Emma began to applaud as well, and La Gorgheggi did not take long to fix her attention on those two ladies who were seated so close to her and who were the only ones to join the strong sex in applause.

To Marta and Körner, the Englishwoman was almost a compatriot because she was a foreigner; and because she was an artist, they regarded her as much more worthy of respect than the affected ladies of the town, despite their pretensions and worldly preoccupations. Körner drew close to the piano and spoke to Serafina in English. At that moment Mochi and Bonifacio, arm in arm, also reached the platform. What with Körner's linguistic abilities, Minghetti's gregarious nature and the link between Reyes and Mochi, everyone was soon speaking together enthusiastically in a patchwork of English, German, Italian and Spanish. Marta shook the singer's hand, and the latter, with a graceful audacity which amazed Bonis, forcefully and effusively squeezed Emma's thin hands. Seeing his wife and his mistress, united with clasped hands, Bonifacio once again thought of the miracles of the Devil, and the vision of the *tigribis agnis*, which he had read of in many newspapers and even a rhetoric book, appeared before him as well. The tiger was, of course, his wife, who at that minute was radiant nonetheless. Emma had been born for just such a moment, and she felt a sort of wild pride seeing herself among that particular group of people, especially greeted with so much respect and deference by such a beautiful and vivacious woman. Serafina had dazzled her. Emma had often thought that there was a select body of woman, only a few, who possessed a certain indefinable but powerful quality, a *je ne sais quois*, and she felt curiously envious of the men who fell in love with these types. These "chosen" women, whom she imagined to be so loved by men, were not at all like the majority, for Emma was totally unable to understand why men should love the ordinary run of women, beauty notwithstanding. La Gorgheggi was much taller than Emma, so much so that the wife standing beside her experienced a feeling that she had a kind of masculine protection, and this enchanted her! Furthermore, finding herself so close to the woman who had attracted the attention and admiration of the whole town from a distance, Emma enjoyed a sensation of sweet vanity and curiousity satisfied. It gave her the greatest feelings of self-importance to think that she alone now received those smiles, those looks and those words which were ordinarily reserved for the public domain. However, Emma was even more drawn, almost seduced by her notion of Serafina's irregular life; she was a "lost woman" on a grand scale. The sinful curiosity with which Emma had always regarded vulgar women of the town, a curiosity she did not trouble to hide, seemed to expand and virtually ennoble Serafina. By smelling, touching, seeing and listening closely, Emma wanted to uncover in depth the intimate history of pleasure and adventure of that gallant and artistic woman. She suddenly saw, in images almost palpable, the ideas of bourgeois order, of stale domestic morality, cracked and discolored in a sad, pale, disgusting region of the spirit—darkened, neglected, regrettable. It all seemed ridiculous, like the antiquated and poor wardrobe of a village woman, a badly made dress in faded colors. She herself had worn such a dress, and for this she felt a deep and retrospective shame. For all her love of originality, she stood for so many, many provincialisms; she had endorsed the domestic morality of those locals, frumpy ladies who never applauded singers or had lovers. The idea passed through her mind that La Gorgheggi was a great captain of Amazons, the commander of a New Morality of free, undaunted women; Emma would stay by her side as a loyal bugler, a standard-bearer faithful to her insignia. When La Valcárcel noticed that the local ladies looked surprised, even shocked, over the intimate conversation into which she and her friend Marta had entered, her pleasure doubled. How marvelous that someone so prominent should do something completely new, unheard-of, amazing, irregular and even subversive, in the midst of all the pretentious gentry of the town!

Although affecting a certain sangfroid at first, Marta, too, was enchanted and filled with pride as she talked with Serafina. She soon realized that she had been outdone, even vanquished, for she perceived true superiority in the actress, which, if it were not of the suprasensitive kind she attributed to herself, was nevertheless much more effective. Marta, parading her knowledge of English, French and Italian, finally followed La Gorgheggi in her effort to speak Spanish so that Emma could understand. The actress directed her gracious manners and the irresistible charm of her gestures, her sweet voice and her discreet aspect upon Emma. She looked at her with bright, wide-open eyes, sparkling with sympathy and newborn affection. Emma was completely swept off her feet when Serafina, raising her fan to her forehead, exclaimed:

"Ah! Yes, yes! *Eccola qui!** You know, I said to myself, this lady, this Señora de Reyes . . . I . . . have seen her, have seen her, I should say, in another way, in some other day, as it were . . . far gone. And suddenly now an expression, this expression of *le sopra-ciglie*† places her before me. Oh, yes, it's all exactly the same! More than her portrait, she, she herself . . ."

Emma opened her mouth, pleased, but without comprehending. Marta was jealous, fully suspecting that Serafina was going to say that Emma resembled some illustrious woman. But La Gorgheggi, who did not explain, only added:

"Ah! Mochi and Minghetti! Please, come here, come here. Let's see now; tell me whom this lady resembles. Who could it be? Who could it be that is exactly like her?"

Mochi smiled, looking at Emma only out of courtesy, without trying to divine any resemblance at all as though he were in the theater, feigning curiosity and interest in a dialogue. Minghetti, however, treated the event more seriously. He brought his strong, dark, Levantine face with its laughing and passionate, blue eyes, its thin moustache and pointed, rather curly beard, close to the burning, almost frightened face of Emma. He fixed these impudent and gay eyes on the lady's face and took the liberty of moving the cande-

* "This one"
† "eyebrows"

labrum on the piano a bit so as to bring the light closer to the features, which he examined with deep absorption.

Mochi said automatically that he could not guess the resemblance; he admitted to failure. Minghetti persisted. "Wait a moment, wait," he urged, as though hoping to evoke an image. Emma was now fascinated, for at the time, Minghetti, close as he was, smelled of the New Man, and his eyes, compelling her, became a drunken feast of delights which she savored fully. But when Minghetti reluctantly announced that his memory, too, fell short, Serafina exclaimed:

"Oh, what men! Don't you remember . . . La Parini? *La Parini!*"

"Yes! The Great Tragedian of *Firenze*! Exactly, exactly, like a mirror image!" cried Mochi, careful to avoid saying that he did not see the similarity. Minghetti, who had never seen La Parini, shouted:

"Of course! The expression in her gestures, the same vivacious smile, the fire . . ." And beaming at La Gorgheggi, as though telling her in secret, he added, "But the features *here* are more perfect."

"Quite, quite! Even more perfect," agreed the soprano, who then went on to explain further that La Parini was an illustrious Florentine artist, unrivaled by the tragedians of her time. Although Emma could not find in the newly discovered resemblance all the value that Marta, prompted by her envy, gave it, she indeed felt a knot of pride in her throat. She saw herself bathed in glory and immediately thought: it seems quite impossible that in this ugly town of my birth anyone could enjoy herself so much as I am doing at this moment, seeing my reflection in this man's eyes and hearing these things they are saying to me.

The conversation was soon interrupted so that Serafina could sing again. This time she sang a tercet with Mochi and Minghetti. After the ovation that followed, the delightful exchanges recommenced, becoming more and more animated, and now some of the more audacious and carefree young gentlemen of the town also participated. Near the railing of the balcony, Emma and Serafina spoke alone for a few minutes, almost caressing each other with smiles.

Bonis spotted them from a distance and came closer, but neither one of them noticed his presence. He once again drew away to contemplate his handiwork from a corner.

Together! They were together! They spoke with each other, smiled at each other, seemed to understand each other. He saw a symbol, the symbol of the absurd pact between duty and sin, between austere virtue and seductive passion. What mad things occur to me tonight! he thought to himself, and he began to imagine that those two women who were speaking like magpies, nodding, smiling and growing enthusiastic over their conversation, were saying to each other (how perverse!) something along these lines:

"Yes, señora, yes," began Emma (according to her husband's absurd hypothesis), "you can love him as much as you wish. I understand that you have fallen in love with him and he with you. So be it. In Turkey, they behave like that, and, doubtless, the Turkish women are as honorable as we are. Everything is a matter of custom; as Señorita Körner would say, 'Everything is conventional.'"

"Well, yes, señora, I love him, why deny it? And he loves me" (here, more hypothesis). "But he esteems you as well, in spite of that strong temper which people say you have. He esteems you and respects you. You will see just what close companions we will be. Why not? You don't know what artists are, what it is to live for art and to disregard the minutia of town life and everyday morality. Fine morality! Everyone *must* love everyone else: you, me; I, you; your husband, both of us; both of us, your husband! The world, this sad, finite life, should be composed of nothing but love, love and music. Everything else is a waste of time."

That imaginary dialogue, thought Bonis, was nonsense, true . . . and yet, why couldn't it turn out like that? He had read that the ancient patriarchs maintained a number of wives. Abraham himself, for instance. The idea of Abraham reminded him of barren Sarah, his wife. "Isaac!" whispered a voice in his brain. Emma was Sarah. Serafina?—Agar. Ishmael did not fit; he was a trifle out of place, given Serafina. But Isaac, Isaac! Who knew? Why did his heart

157

tell him: remember Sarah and hope? Twice on that night in which he should have been concerned with other developments, his soul had been filled with love for his Isaac. He felt a vague fever; he did not know where. Perhaps he was going mad. First, he had compared himself with the Virgin, now with Abraham. In spite of such nonsense, an intimate, superstitious hope took possession of him, dominated him.

When he looked again at the group of people, his wife and Serafina, who had been joined now by Mochi, Marta, Minghetti and Nepomuceno, Reyes felt a sort of repugnance; that moral calm which at times took hold of his spirit, of his innermost being, sounded an alarm in his breast, in his conscience. He was seized by a strong desire to separate his wife from all those people, and without being able to help himself, he approached the group. Showing a certain seriousness which contrasted with the general happiness, with the vague air of concupiscence that enveloped the group, Bonis said in an energetic tone which surprised Emma, the only one who noticed his "new voice":

"Ladies, gentlemen . . . enough chatter. The public is growing impatient, and the best thing that we can do now is to begin the second part of the program, no? Music is worth more than all this gabble, isn't it?"

The lot of them stared at him. Surely he was joking. Nonetheless, his expression and the tone of his voice seemed serious, even imposing. Minghetti, bowing comically, exclaimed, "He who commands, commands! Obedience to the tyrant, perhaps even to the future impresario."

Serafina, turning her back on the others, took advantage of the moment to look fixedly at her lover; she opened her eyes wide with an expression of affection mingled with mockery, which quickly intensified into a look of passion. Catching this look Bonis trembled within, but he pretended not to understand; he did not so much as smile.

"Go on and sing, go on and sing," he urged, pretending to follow up the joke about his role as a despot.

158

Mochi bowed, and after making a sweeping obeisance, Minghetti sat down at the piano to accompany the tenor and soprano in the duet with which the second part began. Nepomuceno sat down next to Marta, while Bonis edged in very close to his wife, who was breathing heavily, absorbing all her good fortune through her mouth and her nostrils.

And while Emma, without realizing what he was thinking, devoured the soprano and the baritone with her eyes, Bonis passed his sad and tenderly curious glance from the pale, withered face of his spouse to that stomach which had dashed his hopes and, listening to the romantic music of the duet without paying much attention, he said between his teeth: "It doesn't matter. After all, Sarah was older."

Chapter Thirteen

The concert ended at one o'clock in the morning. Instead of the gathering breaking up, the young people, as was customary in town, began to dance with the greatest eagerness, much to the pleasure of the girls, who tolerated the two or three hours of music only with the expectation of spending another two or three hours dancing. Emma had no intention of retiring as long as a single living soul remained there. As to Marta Körner, she was too occupied to think of the time, for her time was spent in the big game hunt to which she had dedicated herself in dead earnest. She neither saw nor heard what took place in front of her; there was nothing else in the whole world for her except Don Juan Nepomuceno with his great side whiskers! Before the concert ended, they had made room for themselves in an out-of-the-way corner of the hall; once there, the German girl bared her soul (to say nothing of her white breasts) to the honeyed steward, the future administrator of the chemical factory. Although engaged in deep conversation, first with Mochi, then with the military governor and finally with the chief engineer of roads, Körner watched over them from a distance, very satisfied with his daughter's conduct; with his whole heart, he approved of the cleverness and delicacy which his deserving offspring demonstrated when two or three highly distinguished young men approached her to ask for a waltz; they were courteously but coldly turned away by the robust German, who was not dancing because— and here she gave a bungled excuse, intentionally awkward. Things had to be made *very* clear to Nepomuceno, even if she risked annoying the dancers. Marta was even pleased to snub them, because that amounted to as much as a declaration; she showed the true reason for the rebuffs she felt obliged to give: it was more important for her to talk with Nepomuceno than to hop around the dance floor, arousing the devil-knew-what appetites in those gay and florid youths who were, heaven knows, a lusty lot.

With Marta's second refusal, accompanied by a look and a smile which conveyed a special meaning for him, Nepomuceno clearly understood. He was grateful with all his heart for the "sacrifice" which she made in his favor, and he would have melted with pleasure had he not already done so—all thanks to the overpowering proximity of the German and the both spiritual and not so spiritual things she was telling, and more than anything else, thanks to the fact that, now and then, quite frequently really, their knees happened to touch. What eloquence, what natural warmth that woman exuded! thought Don Juan (applying the same verb to both nouns).

Marta was speaking of the Ideal, but she arranged the whole matter in such a way that her ideals were mixed as though by chance with autobiographical descriptions which caught her in solemn moments: changing her clothes, lying in bed half-asleep . . . Nepomuceno found out, for example, that she had read something entitled *Dramaturgy in Hamburg* by Lessing, and he also learned that, like the author of *Laocoön*, she loved very tight stockings, fastened above the knees and colored pearl grey. The tenderest item, perhaps, was the story of Goethe's mistresses, a theme which had fascinated the little Körner for many years. Marta told Nepomuceno, with a warmth comparable only to that which her own knees transmitted, of the noble pride of Frederika Brion, who never wanted to marry because no man was worthy of one who had once been loved by Wolfgang. Confused in everything, especially in his own state of mind, Nepomuceno began to imagine that the German geniuses were a group of satraps who spent their lives despising vulgar creatures and handling the finest morsels of the Eternal Feminine. When they reached the part about the "little mothers" of the famous Goethe, Nepo could not help but picture those "mothers" as very delicious and buxom wet nurses. In any event, no matter what the cases of Heine and Young Germany were, he himself was on fire; moreover, with so much science and poetry and touching of legs, he could only make the reply, without his knowing it, of that character in the comedy *De fuera vendrá*. That is, nothing came to his lips except a solemn promise of something that would take place in the near future: matrimony.

Meanwhile, following the example of a few other married women who were dancing, Emma accepted the invitation of the president of the Casino and danced a set of *lanceros*; then, shortly afterwards, she joined Minghetti in an intimate polka, an accepted brand of impudence which was becoming the rage in those days and which precipitated not a little moral damage in the town.

Minghetti's polka was a total relevation for her. The baritone, who had not ignored the burning looks which that señora had left behind her on promenades, at mass and in the street, understood everything that night, and he formed a plan of seduction which was convenient for him from many points of view; so during the concert itself he began to make her dizzy with looks and flattery while he was still at the piano. Later he risked inviting her to dance nothing less than the polka. It took some nerve, but he played for the highest stakes. Once she accepted the polka, he already knew what he had to do next; while his knees spoke the same language as Marta Körner's (although without the collaboration of the German classics), he concentrated his thoughts on projects and calculations of the mathematical variety. Half-serious, half-joking, he declared his love for Emma as they whirled around the salon, and she, convulsed with laughter, very pleased, certainly not in the least scandalized, called him mad and allowed him to hold her tight as if she did not feel it, as though her honor were above every suspicion and those accidental squeezes should be disregarded. She called him a madman, a humbug, but when they sat down together after the polka, instead of growing annoyed at the singer's insistence, she became rather serious, sighed two or three times like a misunderstood working girl and finally offered Minghetti her disinterested friendship, pure friendship, loyal and firm. Without dropping the theme of his incandescent passion, the baritone, who never missed an opportunity, answered with an extremely discreet narration about his and his companions' tight economic straits. Minghetti, a "bohemian," (although he did not understand that term) was not ashamed to speak of his poverty or of the picaresque schemes and artifices to which he had resorted many times in order to extricate himself from his difficulties. He well knew that part of the charm of his person, irresistible to so many women, consisted in playing up the disorganized life of the congenial, generous, happy, almost childish adventurer, a man not particularly scrupulous, except in matters of gallantry and valor. He was quick to observe that this element of seduction consistently produced the greatest responses in Emma. She herself confessed that she had begun to take notice of him and to see in him that personal appeal which the Andalusians call the "angel," on that famous night when he had sung the *Barber* . . . against his will.

"Oh, yes," he exclaimed, smiling. "When the Civil Guard hunted me down!"

So Minghetti, right there and then, used this incident, which had provoked so much talk in the town a few months ago, as a good starting point for relating in his own fashion the history of his sorrows and grievances as though making fun of his misfortunes. He hushed up many things which he judged unlikely to make him appear interesting, but he did not hesitate to confess certain not overly honest maneuvers; he ventured to refer to them, not out of love of truth, but because his moral sense did not tell him that these were unsuitable, even distasteful. Fortunately, Emma was equally unaware of a delicacy of this order, and in every victorious tale she admired the art and forgot the victim—or, rather, the fool. Bonis' wife listened, enchanted, to these picaresque tales in which the various deceptions were explained by and forgiven for the liveliness of the passions and the repeated reverses brought about by adverse fortune.

In sum, the baritone's true history, distorted in his narration for convenience, could be recounted as follows:

Cayetano Dominguez ("Minghetti") was a native of Valencia. In his infancy, he had experienced the drudgery of poverty, which instead of converting laziness into industry, usually leads to perpetual battles with the penal code and its agents, interspersed with intervals in prison. Jail, the frequent residence of his respected father, had taught Minghetti the repeated lesson of the orphan's sad life. At last, the author of his days left the house never to return, dying, after regaining his liberty, in a mysterious adventure in La Huerta. Poor Minguillo, as he was now called by the other delinquents of his neighborhood, finding himself alone in the world (his mother had died giving him birth), was subjected to an apprenticeship which had no small effect on him, mostly bad. He suffered misfortune, hardship, dereliction; at twelve years old, he was a complete man and almost a total rogue thanks to the resources of his invention, the eagerness of his work (when he did honest work), the wiles of his industry, the force of his cynicism, the vigor of his muscles and his utter contempt for every law, moral or juridical. These, he felt, were created solely for the rich; faced with the more important necessities of finding food and shelter, the poor could not fulfill them: hunger and homelessness were the greatest crimes.

From the hands of a distant relative, who beat him and called him vile names, he passed into the service of the Church as a choirboy; he even began to sing in the cathedral choir, as a soprano. This period of his life, according to him, was the most pious, without being exactly perfect. So, he averred, he did not commit misdeeds for their own sake, but for money. His voice, meanwhile, served the choir, and he sang like an angel in that cathedral without ever being scolded for laziness or lack of skill; he was an assiduous worker, and his dexterity in every occupation he undertook was remarkable. His voice finally broke, so he went back to the street. The year he lost his voice was also the year when his passions began to exert themselves; both coincided with the period of greatest poverty in his life. It was hardly inconceivable, or at least it did not appear so to him, that in those days the expedients to which he resorted for sustenance and whatever else a single and unscrupulous young man needed were absolutely incompatible with the civil and criminal laws. This is not to say that he reached the point of robbing, at least not with violence, but rather that, remembering family traditions, he invented happy and flashy industries like games at the fairs, fitted with harmless gimmicks and innocent shams, all a just castigation of avaricious dolts and overconfident simpletons. For all this, the only profit which stuck between Mingo's fingernails scarcely amounted to the necessary time and effort of his work—a small recompense, considering the risk, not to mention the talent and the wit employed in the schemes he invented. His voice. Oh! his voice was the traitor! He had not thought of that for a long time, except for singing occasionally in taverns and on nocturnal strolls for the edification of his fellow vagabonds in the underworld or the seduction of some girl who would ask for other pay as well.

His relations, interrupted but not broken, with the "men of the soutane," the clerics, offered him the chance of entering the seminary as a servant (having covered up, of course, a large part of his history). He had periods, it seems, if not of repentance (since he did not believe there was anything to repent), then of weariness, a sort of "mysticism" which demanded the solitude of a retired life—long hours of hieratic severity, candle in hand in the dark recesses of the choir—and the absence of bad company, but also, more important, assured bread, gained without the need for illegal exertions. For all these reasons, then, he took shelter in the solitude of the cloister, and he was the most lively, compliant and alert servant in the seminary; he did not then realize the magnitude of the horrors in which he was forced to collaborate. Many years later, when, free and an artist, he looked upon himself, by reason of his accomplishments and his standing, as very advanced, a free thinker and the like, he took advantage of his memories of the seminary to use them as an argument against religious institutions. "Don't tell me what those little curates are!" he would exclaim, and when no ladies were present, his narration, probably exaggerated, was truly shocking in that it touched on certain violations of the natural instincts.

It is clear that he did not speak of adventures of this nature to Emma on the night in question. It was not until later, when they became more intimate, that she learned of these particular storms which her friend had endured in his picaresque youth.

He left the seminary through a window, carrying a shotgun; nothing less was demanded by the hurry and the danger with which he rushed to defend the cause of the people and the town in a rash revolutionary attempt to which he was pledged, thanks to some irregular friendships he had made during the frequent night excursions he undertook with his other companions, in particular one seminarian who was fond of going to the theater and more immediate places of corruption as well. After that he walked around the countryside in a state of rebellion, day after day, until his shoes wore out, and then he emigrated with another group of "the deceived," as the captain general of Valencia once called them in a long harangue. He ran so far that he did not stop until he reached Italy. He lived in Turin, in Rome, in Naples—God knows where and how! It turned out, however, that he returned to Spain as a chorus singer in an opera company, speaking Italian and become worldly-wise, and he persuaded everyone that his vocation was music, that his forte was the seduction of easy women and the temptation of all women.

In Barcelona his voice attracted the attention of a maestro, who put it to advantage by teaching him music, real music. He applied himself in earnest to studying. He left the theater for a few years. He lived by heaven knows what expedients, odd recourses; perhaps he was a gigolo. At inn after inn, rooming house after rooming house, he awakened guests with baritone "gargles" which exercise the voice and keep the muscles of a powerful throat from falling asleep. Those little gargles, reminding one of an agitated turkey, were forgiven because of his grace, amiability and wit. He was a babyish Tenorio, childlike even in love; he permitted himself to be spoiled at every opportunity, and in loving him, women could not help but expend many of those maternal caresses which all of them have buried within themselves.

He sang entire operas into the ears of his mistresses as though kissing them with the breath which seemed to issue forth perfumed by the melody. One of his sweethearts once said that this well-formed man with his extraordinarly beautiful, fresh complexion exuded an irresistible aroma of Italian music. From the time of his first recital in Barcelona, he called himself sometimes Minghetti, other times Gaetano, and when he returned from his second trip to Italy, which lasted two years, he almost regarded himself as a foreigner. As to his instinct for swindling, which had no immediate application in his new position, it found room for natural expansion in his relations and contracts with other singers, their wives, the impresarios and the guests at various inns. The incident which Emma had mentioned involved a mischievous trick of which the good Mochi had been the victim. Julio and Gaetano had quarreled over a question of money, over whether or not the Valencian, Gaetano, had been paid, for he denied giving a receipt. That night Minghetti disappeared on foot. Julio complained to the authorities that the baritone had absconded with his advance pay, leaving the company in the lurch. The Civil Guard undertook the charge of bringing the quartet back together and did so; as a result, Minghetti, resigned, smiling as though it had been a joke, performed before the public once again, singing the *Barber* with a great show of malice that won him an even greater ovation as a sympathetic tribute to his amusing trick and to his happy nonchalance. On that night, Emma came to know of him in the gallery, where she overheard the story of his flight, bruited about enthusiastically by the public, which is always disposed to forgive handsome and witty swindlers.

Only a few days after this solemn night of the dance when she had first learned of the baritone's adventures, Emma and Minghetti had become very close. He sang in her ear, but only in the capacity of an initmate friend. The ploy about the piano lessons was carried out. Minghetti became La Valcárcel's music master, but it was quite clear that after a short time the lessons had become purely a matter of form, a pretext for the professor to sing his ballads, accompanying himself while his disciple, seated alongside admiring him, turned the pages whenever he signaled to her with a nod of the head. Emma managed, nonetheless, to murder the polkas and bang out a waltz she liked. Bonis could in no way object to all this because the lessons were given with his blessing, and, furthermore, he could see that his wife actually did spend a few hours every day studying melody and pounding the keys.

Other things were under way now as well: the progress of the factory for chemical products and the reconstruction of the opera company built around the trio, La Gorgheggi, Mochi and Minghetti. Both enterprises became confused in Reyes' head because those who were involved in either one or the other often ate together in Emma's house. They gathered every night in her "salons" (she wished them to be called this, after the rearrangement of the furniture, that is, and the demolition of the partitions, all of which changes mounted up to quite a respectable sum that, however, was not respected by Nepomuceno, who performed marvels of prestidigitation with it). The most important link between the theatrical enterprise and the factory was, of course, the "capitalist" who supported them: Emma. A few local fans invested in the theater, but their stock was insignificant in comparison with Emma's; in consequence, she became the one great patron, represented by Nepomuceno in everything that referred to the economic part of the business and by Bonis in that aspect touching on relations with the musicians and singers. Bonifacio, in turn, relegated to Mochi the position of technical director, handling whatever matters fell within his field of competence. The impresario became director of the new company, but with the single change that he no longer ran the risk of losing a *cuarto* and was, even better, the only one who stood to gain if there were any profit, no matter how small.

From the days of the Sweet Soprano, the players had never remained (for weal or woe) so long in the town. They were almost taken for neighbors now, and Julio and Gaetano were already discussing, though with a certain discretion and measure, all the burning questions of local interest in the Casino. As for Serafina, she became the glory of the promenades, and the citizens pointed her out to visitors as one of the local marvels, a phenomenon.

The Körner family also managed to establish itself, but with an even firmer foundation, joining their name to the cause of industry which the papers, dealing with local moral and material interests as they did, defended with so much concern. Körner made a trip to Germany on behalf of the new society for chemical products in order to bring over all the pertinent news and to order all the material necessary for the factory, the construction and operation of which he himself must direct. As to the payment of these expenses, we have already seen that the diminishing inheritance of lawyer Valcárcel's daughter covered all the expenditures, or nearly all, since to conceal their actual holdings, they had offered some stock to friends and relatives. The result was that most of Emma's capital was compromised so seriously in what Körner called the "chemical-industrial adventure" that Nepomuceno, responsible for that fraud, believed himself obliged in conscience—in the small, bad conscience that was left to him—to explain with absolute, or almost absolute, clarity the whole situation to his niece and, further, the risks she might run. Nepomuceno asserted, "According to all probability, we'll come out of this rich, but there is no reason to hide the fact, dearest niece, that our money, rather your money, is exposed to heavy losses, not to be expected, of course, but possible."

Though her uncle spoke of these matters, Emma was only conscious of her passions, her joys, the disordered, turbulent and happy life in which she had wildly immersed herself. She was so happy with this sense of abundance that she was convinced that she had triumphed over the capricious wheel of fortune; moreover, Körner, who had become a close friend, had convinced her, by telling her of things which she could not understand, that the "small advance" of only a few thousand *duros* would inevitably result in a real fortune, worthy of the great lords of other countries who did not count millions, as did people here, in *reales*, but in solid silver coins. She too wanted to be a millionairess, and her heart, as well as Körner and Minghetti, told her that she would be; that status, they said, represented a kind of miracle of science and ability. If the Germans could not perform miracles of knowledge, who could? It was simply a question of extracting from the seaweed, which the waters cast up in such abundance on the coasts of the province, a tremendous amount of material which was indispenable in an infinite number of industries. It seemed hard to believe that as much money as she had been promised could come from something so repugnant and evil smelling: seaweed! Why, it even disgusted the mules! But the sages—and Minghetti—said so. It must be true. Onward, risk everything! If she were ruined, so what? It would be amusing. Anyway, she was not at all sure that she would not elope with the baritone one fine day. It, too, seemed hard to believe, just like the business of the seaweed, that Minghetti was as much in love with her as he swore he was; although persuaded that she had improved greatly and that her "autumn" was very interesting, her middle-age succulent and sweet, Emma knew that in the end he was much younger. And she? She was, well, somewhat "fatigued."

Between Germans and Italians, real ones and false ones, a kind of pact, tacit at first, afterwards very explicit, had been established for their mutual protection. The factory people, Körner and his daughter, helped the theater people; the theater people, Mochi and Minghetti and La Gorgheggi, helped the factory people. Nepomuceno, whose interests favored the Germans, encouraged Emma to spend money on the operatic enterprise because Marta and her father asked him to do so; La Gorgheggi and Mochi worked on Bonis' spirit so that he would not puncture his wife's fantastic visions of opulence, the source of which was the "industrial-chemical" idea which both the Germans and her uncle had put in her head.

Most of them were seduced by, corrupted by, as well as joined together in, the sort of solidarity of vice fostered by the lives they led. They were gay, always united by concerts, in country picnics and private banquets, sure that the world was their oyster, as Emma loved to say. La Valcárcel's house where, wearing capes and slouch hats, the silent relatives from the mountain had once been parasites, these foreigners camped, an irregular society which, to the amazement and envy of the townfolk, lived in a way that was not customary in that dull place, with an arrogant and alluring contentment which others observed from a distance, critical but envious. Many young men from the "best families" who at first had censored Emma, Bonis and Marta behind their backs, now remained quiet or even defended the Reyeses and their friends simply because a few of La Gorgheggi's smiles, Marta's provocative, albeit "spiritual," insinuations and, most important, Emma's invitations to informal dances and banquets had converted them. There was more. Because of the vile gossip and, too, at the insistence of Bonifacio, who had become intolerable both in his moral quibbles and in his complaints about appearances, Emma contrived to entice to some of her parties, even if they were not on very intimate terms, two or three of the most distinguished families in the capital. One of these was the family of an Andalusian magistrate, who had two daughters, both as beautiful as figures painted in watercolors on a tambourine. The father was a gay fellow in the civil government, and his two motherless young innocents spent their lives fulfilling and furthering their father's joy. Yet they were very bored in that dirty, humid town, and they seemed to see the sky open up at the possibility of a friendship with Emma and company. The magistrate, who was a great braggart and spoke often of the riches he had out there, somewhere in the country, threw himself with vigor into the factory project and, although cautious, became involved to the extent of some ten thousand *reales* which he multiplied, adding a number of zeros to the right, whenever he spoke to his colleagues and friends about his part in the business enterprise. But Ferraz and his daughters were not Emma's greatest acquisition. Through the mediation of the Andalusians, La Valcárcel had the opportunity to offer a real service to the Silvas, three girls rich in titles, debts and fashion plates. The titles and debts were their father's, but the fashion plates were their very own. There were no girls more elegant in town. They were three, and when they promenaded together, aloof with upright postures, a sort of moving sculptured group, they brought to mind the large prints in the fashion magazines. They could make seven dresses out of one; it was a marvel to see them reverse the top and the bottom and to take up or let out everything, even hats, using the bouquets of flowers and the gherkins and other fake vegetables from five or six harvests of fashion for decoration. However it happened, they set the fashion in town, and because of their nobility and arrogant manner, they found that they had sweetheart after sweetheart, in troops. While the father could think of nothing but his own efforts to seize the wheel of fortune in the gaming room of La Oliva, the daughters were very busy little "peddlers," shouldering their only merchandise—their beauty—through plazas, churches, promenades, dances and the theater. But one day a relative died, and the enforced mourning brought a real cause of grief: the coliseum was going to open with the reformed opera company, and now the Silva girls could not go on Thursdays or Sundays to show off their graces and sit erect in their big-cushioned chairs on the very edge of the railing of their box, like rigid and melancholy cranes on the margin of the sea. The defunct relative was a second uncle, but he was a marquis. If he had been an ordinary man, the Silva girls would have continued to wear their colored dresses and to be as ubiquitous as ever, but mourning for a marquis cannot be left undone without sacrilege. The opera box was out, definitely. It was then that Emma was able to gain the friendship of these elegant aristocrats by doing them a favor and thus killing two birds with one stone. Since she had become the "impresaria," and the singers were now her initmate friends and, as she said, very decent people, there was no reason why the Silvas could not attend the performance behind the scenes. The Ferraz girls proposed the expedient to the Silvas who, without consulting their father (whom they never consulted about any measure), accepted, mad with joy. They could not shine so brightly behind the curtain, but at any rate, they were certain to enjoy themselves; they would see things very pleasant and very new and could even flirt with the singers, a few of whom, like Minghetti, were very handsome and congenial. Emma thought it was her duty not to let those señoritas go alone behind the stage and into the obscure areas around it; and from the first night, also without consulting anyone, she accompanied them and introduced them to La Gorgheggi, who offered them her dressing room so that they could spend the intermissions in pleasant company. Marta and the Ferraz girls once attended the spectacle in secret as well, running and playing in those narrow and dirty passageways and corridors between curtains and trapdoors; but in general, of course, they preferred to show themselves in the management's box, Emma's which was next to the president's.

Naturally, when it was learned that the Silvas went with Reyes' wife to see the opera backstage, there was a great deal of gossip; at the same time, they were pitied because they had become absolute orphans, having such a father as they had. Poor girls! They had not had a mother when they needed one most. After Emma's act of charity, they were much maligned, but they paid no attention. They were proud to be seen in La Gorgheggi's company, as was Emma, and the respect with which everyone treated them offstage and in the singer's room also flattered them greatly. That alone sufficed. Serafina was in her glory, finding herself admired by those aristocratic young women whose fine manners and even the mourning they wore lent a certain dignity and nobility to her gatherings during the intermissions.

"I am happy, Bonis, very happy, and I owe it all to you!" she exclaimed one day, catching her lover by the wrists, drawing him to her breast and kissing him with a burst of gratitude which Bonifacio valued at its worth.

Yes, she *was* happy, he thought; it was better that way. Emma was also very well contented and actually treated him better than before; occasionally she even let him understand that she was grateful to him for her initiation into that new life of "art," as they referred to their trotting out. Everyone was happy, except Bonis . . . at times. He was not satisfied with either the others, with himself, or with anyone at all. One should be good, and no one was. There were no longer any completely honorable people in the world, and it was a shame. There was no one whom he could trust, not even himself. In fact, he fled from himself and from those scrupulous soliloquies of which he had once been proud and which had delighted him so much that he had almost swooned from the sheer pleasure of examining his own conscience. In brief, he saw clearly now that he was a rather wicked person. But what good was all this severity with which he regarded himself when he awoke, his gorge rising, if after getting up, washing himself and splashing a great deal of water over his neck, an eagerness for pleasure, a certain concupiscence, the laziness of sin converted into habit, were rekindled in him along with that vigor of life, that force of his healthy and virile maturity? Things were going badly. His house, his wife's house, had been boring, intolerable, a jail, a place of tyranny before, but now it was worse than all that, it was a . . . a brothel! Yes, a brothel. Bonifacio ruminated, here everyone comes to amuse himself and to ruin us. We all seem to be foolish actors, piddling adventures, heretics . . . a promiscuous crowd. This word *promiscuous* had a terrible significance in Bonis' soliloquies. *Promiscuous* was . . . a mixture of grasping love affairs, of scandalous complacency, of abominable confusions. Sometimes he imagined that the exaggerated familiarity of the Germans, the players and his wife resembled the roomy bed of misery. Possibly there was no actual instance of dishonor, but the danger existed, and appearances condemned them all. Marta, for example, who was going to marry Uncle Nepomuceno, accepted the surreptitious gallantries of Cousin Sebastian, a lecherous and well-preserved fifty year old, who had changed from a romantic into a cynic because he believed that change spelled progress. Once idealistic and poetic, now Sebastian could not catch sight of a cook without giving her a pinch, and he attributed this inclination to the fact that we now live in a "positive" century. He, Bonifacio, had been forced to let his mistress enter his wife's house and allow them to be friends and eat together. Emma, although doubtlessly honorable, let Minghetti draw too close to her and speak to her in a low voice. He was not really suspicious

. . . but, why? Perhaps the consciousness of his own guilt closed his eyes, he did not dare accuse anyone because he had lost the spiritual touch, because in the midst of so much falsehood, impurity and disorder, he no longer knew what was good or bad. Decorum? Honor? Delicacy? In another time, when he fleeced the Valcárcel estate in competition with Don Nepo, when he soiled the honor of his house with adultery, masculine adultery but wrong nonetheless, he found excuses in the middle of all that remorse for his conduct; love, art and sincere passion explained it all. But now? For a long time he had been "unfaithful" to his own passion, Serafina, surrendering night after night to an absurd and extravagant lust for Emma, lewd and all the more repugnant to him because the nuptial bed formed a theater for his strange adventures. All this had opened his eyes and made him understand the spiritual misery that he bore within himself, that maybe his passion was not so great as he had believed and that, consequently, it was illegitimate. Furthermore—and, oh, this was painful—Art too had bad as well as good points, and everything in that company that glistened was not necessarily Art. No, there was no need to deceive himself any longer. This *was* a brothel, and he was one of its many corrupted souls. There was nothing good except that fleeting peace, quiet and tender, which awakened within him from time to time and which made everything around him, in contrast, seem totally abhorrent. He felt, as the result of such thought, an ardent desire, not to die, since the pain of dying and the uncertainity of the afterlife frightened him, but to be transformed! To be regenerated! He dreamed of something like a new man grafted on the now decrepit torso which he had dragged about the world for such a long time. He was not yet old, but he felt as though he had lived for centuries. From the memories of his childhood, those dream days of unconscious life to the present—what a distance! How much he had undergone! How many turns he had given to the same ideas!

Poor Bonifacio rubbed his forehead and his whole head with his hands, pitying that brain which boiled, which crackled, which begged for rest and peace, but even more, for the aid of newer forces.

One day Bonis came across the word *avatar* and looked up its meaning in a dictionary. Something like this would be perfect for me, he thought. Another soul that would enter my body, a new life without the compromises of the other. He did not hope for miracles. He did not even like them. Miracles were absurd, irrational, and he longed for order, for law directing everything, a constant law without exception. Miracles were romantic, revolutionary, violent, and he no longer favored romanticism, nor violence, nor the extraordinary, nor the passionate. However, there was a kind of love superior to passion, a sublime love which was not sensual. No matter how refined and platonic the sensual might be, to love a woman was always . . . to love a woman. No, there must be something else! The love of man for man, of father for son. A son, yes, a son of my soul! That is the "avatar" I need. A being which is I myself, but created anew, outside of me, the blood of my blood!

And Bonis, weeping at this thought, said to himself, leaning his head against a wall, yes, yes, this has been the greatest desire of my life ever since I could formulate it: a son!

Something like the caress of a hand of light which with its contact alone could cure the wounds in his heart passed over him. He felt an emotion of tranquil satisfaction in the face of the clear, evident consciousness that at the bottom of all his errors, almost always dominating them, there had been a latent but real and vigorous longing for a son, for a love which was not commingled with concupiscence. In him the most serious, the most profound emotion, even more important than his love of art or the desire of passion for the sake of passion, had always been his frustrated sense of paternal love. His desire had taken a palpable form, constant, fixed, rooted in intense memory. It was always for the son: a boy, a single one. His only son.

A girl? No, she could not extend him, carry him on, perpetuate him. He could not conceive of the being who would inherit his blood, his spirit, as feminine. It had to be a man. And only one, because the love that would consecrate the son had to be absolute, unrivaled. To love a number of children seemed in Bonis' mind to constitute an infidelity to the first. Without realizing it, he compared the affection for many offspring to polytheism. Many sons were many gods. No, only one! That one, that one of whom his heart spoke, that one who almost—almost—appeared before his eyes in the air, the sole hallucination of his now sleepless nights.

And from whence would his only son come? There was no room for sophisms about sin. He must be born of Emma.

But, oh! he did not deserve a son. No, surely he could not come.

After the night of the dance, the sources of that social promiscuity in which the players, the Germans and the people of the household, his Emma, the uncle and he himself lived—after that night in which, if he were not so opposed to admitting the direct intervention of the supernatural in his affairs, he would have seen the hand of Providence, the revelation of destiny, had he not then been at the very peak, the total realization of the great things of which he had so often dreamed? No, not in the least. He had bungled again; he had allowed himself to be dragged along with all the others into a lazy and vicious saturnalia, and he had even reached the point of viewing his mistress with fascination in his own home, at his wife's table! He had begun to imagine such an abomination as legitimate behavior, according to the comfortable philosophy of those who finish dinner half-drunk—behavior which at an earlier time had seemed to him the wellspring of poetic inspirations and artistic morality, exceptional and therefore privileged. And he, Bonifacio, was the same person who, hearing Serafina sing a hymn dedicated to the Virgin, felt that an actual divine love was being formed in his own body! With a bizarre, hysterical and false mysticism he had compared himself, absurdly but sincerely, to the Virgin Mother. How often afterwards had he seen things in a very different light? How often had he begun to think: this is all a question of geography. If I were a Turk, all this would be legitimate, so why not imagine that we are living in other latitudes? But why in those other moments when he reflected so sadly, why did he not repent? No, he could not because his conscience told him that a few hours later when his stomach was full and his fantasy excited by wine and coffee—and perhaps by Minghetti's and Emma's music—he would once again become that corrupt, complacent Reyes, well content with the species of free love that he had brought into the house. Serafina would come, and while Minghetti and Emma continued their interminable lessons, the two of them, Serafina and Bonis, in the summerhouse in the orchard—oh, misery! oh, shame!—as usual would be lovers, lovers without even the weak excuse of blind passion, lovers because of habit, convenience, the force of sin itself.

No, he would not have his son! Wretch that he was! He did not deserve him! He renounced all hope of such felicity.

But if not felicity, he could at least have true repentance. Why should he not aspire to moral perfection and go as far as he could along that road? Among all the great things he had thought of becoming in this world—a great writer, a great captain (this a very few times, only as a child), a great musician and, more than anything, a great artist—his dreams had never led him to the vocation of saintliness. If he had said to himself once, I know that I cannot invent great passions, dreams or novels, why not perform *all* of these; I'll be the hero myself, and then why not aspire to heroism of another nature? Could he not be a saint? He lacked the talent, the ability to be an artist, a writer. For sanctity, this was unnecessary.

So poor Bonifacio, who at times would wander wildly about the house, the streets, the solitary paseos, found a copy of *The Golden Legend* in his father-in-law's library and saw that, in fact, there were many saints with little talent, saints who were nonetheless visited by grace. That was it: one could be a simple saint, even a simple-minded saint.

Leave everything! Since he had no son, leave everything and follow . . . follow whom? He did not have faith enough, no, far from it! He had grave doubts, yet his ideas were so disordered that it was impossible for him to clarify those niggling questions in order to regain a firm belief. The old books which he had read avidly to prepare himself for his son's education had produced, finally, an intellectual indigestion brought on by reservations and denials. He was not a believer . . . nor had he even ceased to be one. Certain things in the Bible he could not swallow. When he heard that the six days of Genesis were not days but, rather, epochs, even according to a purely orthodox viewpoint, he felt a great sense of consolation, as if a weight had been lifted from his shoulders, as if it were he who had invented the idea of the world created in six days. But Noah's Ark, with all its species of animals remained; the Tower of Babel remained; the sin which passes from father to son remained, and Joshua stopping the sun, instead of stopping the earth, remained. No, it was impossible. He could not take up his cross because he was not a simpleton like those of the Middle Ages; rather, he was an educated simpleton, a simpleton who frequented cafés, a modern simpleton.

What Bonifacio did not lack was a sincere longing for sacrifice, for self-abnegation and charity. To make a fool of himself for the greater glory, for what lay above, seemed very reasonable, harmonious as an interior music. One night, he read a book in bed which mentioned a half-mad Italian mystic of the Middle Ages called "God's Juggler." This mystic seemed to be heaven's clown; filled with the love of Jesus, he laughed at the Church and looked upon his own condemnation as an accomplished fact, but if he were sent to hell, he would carry with him his divine passion, which no one could tear away from him. Jacopone da Todi, as he was called by the people, who laughed at him and sometimes admired him, performed ridiculous acts; consequently, his penitence was never praised but rather became the object of jokes. He would go out walking on his hands, head down, feet in the air, or he would anoint his naked body with oil all over and then roll on a mountain of feathers which stuck to his body, and in this way, he passed through the streets so that the children ran after him.

Bonis wept with sentiment reading of the heroic feats of this mystical clown, author of the *Lauds*, immortalized afterwards. He, Bonis, was no poet, yet with his flute he believed that he too could say many things, even convert infidels! But the real trial remained: detachment from everything. To go out in the world, begin wandering, leave everything, and now that he had no son, to become a village saint, a mad saint, all this was very reasonable, but, ay! his conscience told him that he would never dare to leave everything, especially his slippers, to take up the cross. Perhaps he could not even bear to leave his wife, or his mistress.

Chapter Fourteen

Great events eventually arrived and pulled Reyes away from the fleeting, if mystical, whims which he himself in his hours of rational and moderate reflection termed sickly. The unhappy man could not help remembering the very well known passage from *La somnambula*, "Ah, del tutto ancor non sei cancellata dal mio cuor"* (according to the way *he* sang these lines), when the time came to take leave of Serafina Gorgheggi, who, the company again having disbanded, was leaving with Mochi to fulfill a contract at the theater in La Coruña. That separation had hovered over him like a constant threat, the bitter drop in the otherwise felicitous days and months of great passion, and after that, like a necessary and even deserved and healthy sorrow, at least in the eyes of Bonifacio, who was full of old remorse and new moral plans.

But when the moment arrived, Bonis felt it like a critical operation performed on quick flesh.

Explaining everything to himself with complete frankness, in an intricate skein of sophisms, Bonis recognized that one's basic, natural affections, purely *human*, were the strongest and the truest and that he was a sham mystic and an incurable romantic. Ay! In spite of the lukewarm feelings he had had for her for some time, separation from Serafina was an acute pain, one which horrified him and made him almost sick with suffering. It was exhausting, when his mind was tense, to gather his weak forces in order to support those very real pains, but there was no remedy. The very thought of trying to

* "Ah, you are still in my heart."

181

maintain an opera company any longer became absurd. All the expedients invented to retain Mochi and his disciple were no longer valid; they had nothing more to offer. Never before, even when the Sweet Soprano actually sang, had the players of a company stayed in town so long as a year—over a year—in succession, whether working or on strike. Perhaps before this time an occasional chorus singer had remained, but married to someone from the town or working in another capacity. One orchestral director had, in fact, become a citizen, directing the municipal band, but sopranos and tenors had never stayed for so many months. Once the harvest was reaped, they left the fields. The phenomenon of Serafina, Julio, and Gaetano's stay was as amazing as if the swallows had decided to pass a winter in the snow. Only, in the case of the swallows there could have been no gossip, suggesting, among other things, that they were fed by the sparrows. Now horrible charges were uttered concerning the prolonged residence of the players, who had not even had contracts every season. The departure became necessary, not really in order to silence the rumors which they all ignored (except, perhaps, Bonis), but rather because they had no decorous, or even semidecorous way to continue keeping up appearances. There were not resources enough to continue paying the great expenses run up by the remaining players of the dissolved company. The necessity to terminate that state of affairs, as Reyes called it, became clear. The theater company in general had lost heavily in its enterprises, but the principal players, Mochi, Minghetti and Serafina, continued to rely more or less directly on lawyer Valcárcel's greatly diminished fortune. An opportunity to earn their living out of town arose, and no matter how painful the leave-taking, they were forced to take advantage of it. The only intransigent one was Emma. She held a conference with her uncle, who had been named vice-president of the Academy of Fine Arts, an organization now united with the Economic Society of Friends of the Country, and as a result of that conference an agreement resulted: Minghetti would stay on in town as the director of the Academy's musical section. The salary which the members offered the baritone was hardly spectacular, but he was

182

well enough satisfied, for in addition he planned to give piano and singing lessons. Between one thing and another (and *another* the local gossips whispered parenthetically) he could get along until he grew tired of that sedentary life and decided to accept one of those contracts which, according to him, had been offered in various foreign countries.

Serafina was sorry to leave the town; she had almost begun to forget that she was an actress and adventuress, seeing herself instead as an honorable lady on good terms with the best society in a provincial capital and with a faithful, gentle and handsome lover. She had begun truly to love Bonis, with an affection essentially fraternal, though it flared up into lust from time to time and changed into a jealous passion when she suspected that the silly Reyes could tire of her and love someone else. For quite a while, in fact, she had noticed in her dearest "ninny" a dissimulated coolness and distraction, a certain tendency to flee from her little intimacies. At first she suspected something of those strange "Walpurgis" nights at home with Emma, which seemed to preoccupy Reyes so much for a time. Afterwards, following up her lover's aversions and distractions, she came to understand that it was not a question of any other love affair but of certain "ideas" he entertained. Perhaps he would turn into an absolute imbecile, and at this thought she felt a sense of remorse: "This one's brain is getting addled because of me." More than once, after one of those slight quarrels engaged in by old lovers—pacific and faithful, but tired—she heard Bonis speak of "morality" as an obstacle to their mutual felicity. What Serafina could never divine, however, was Bonis' principal "idea," that idea of having a son; and of course it was this, and this alone, which actually separated him from his mistress, from sin.

But on the night when the coach set out for Galicia, Bonifacio, mounting with a leap to the footboard of the front compartment, secretly managed to give La Gorgheggi a last kiss; he felt that his passion had not been an "artistic" lie because, with that kiss, he bade good-bye to a life of intense, ineffable delight which could never return; with that kiss he took leave of the last vestige of his youth.

In the midst of the crowd that had gathered to see the singers off, after the coach had disappeared, Bonis, in the shadows, felt very lonesome, abandoned, sunk once again into insignificance, into his old self-contempt.

As he returned home, through the streets which lay dark before him, he distinguished two figures walking close together among the crowd of his male and female friends. Their arms were linked, as was permitted in that age to señoritas and gallants. It was Marta Körner and Juan Nepomuceno who had pressed ahead, trying to avoid the watchful eye of the German father, who did not approve of such familiarity. After the departure, which had moved and excited them, the mysterious streets, only dimly lighted with oil lamps, encouraged them, and as they whispered to each other, the breath of passion was clearly evident—Nepo's passion for the marriage bed and Marta's passion for a husband. They were absorbed in their conversation, oblivious of those who followed them, believing themselves a thousand leagues from anyone else. At times they raised their voices, especially Marta. Unintentionally at first, but afterwards with great interest, Bonifacio heard them say strange things.

It was essential to speak to Emma as soon as possible! thought Bonis. It was absolutely necessary to tell her of that couple's carefully guarded secret: that they were going to get married within a month's time. And it was particularly important to settle the accounts, to tally their respective capitals, although the uncle would continue to administer his niece's money—as long as there was anything worthy of mention to administer. Emma was lost; she had done nothing except spend and squander, without ever understanding that she was on her way to complete ruin. To speak to her of mortgage was to speak in Greek. "Fine, mortgage yourself," she would say, without ever having any more idea of what a mortgage was other than its being a means for her to procure the money necessary for her follies.

"Now, look, Marta," the uncle was saying to his German sweetheart, "she is a woman who hasn't any clear idea what percentage means, and when she is told, for instance, about a very high interest rate, it sounds the same to her as if it were only a token charge. Nothing matters but the money she is given from moment to moment. It is as though she imagines, gullible as she is, that *she* is the one who robs her usurers, those people who steal money from God knows how many souls. In order to do away with these evils, I myself have had to become my niece's only Jew! I! I am the one who supplies her with that money, at moderate interest, and she does not even realize it because she never, never asks."

Marta listened to Nepo with more pleasure than if he had been reciting Goethe's "Early Spring."

"You mean . . . they are going to ruin themselves?"

"Positively. There's no help for it now."

"It's their fault."

"Theirs. He started; she followed. Then both of them . . . afterwards everyone. You have seen it yourself; that house is an almshouse, the players have eaten up her fortune, and since the factory is not going well, I'm afraid . . ."

"Oh! but there's no need to mention that."

"No, of course not . . ."

"Papa is hoping to build up the business; his agents have offered him new markets, dependable outlets . . ."

"Yes, yes, of course, but it will be too late for the Reyeses. Our effort, what we do with our *own* capital, Marta . . . with ours, do you understand . . . well, this will salvage the factory, yes. But it will be too late for them. Our future lies in gunpowder."

At that point Marta squeezed Nepo's arm, and Bonis could no longer hear what they were saying. He dropped behind. He was the last to enter his house, where the group that had set off from there to say goodbye to La Gorgheggi and Mochi had returned. Serafina, it should be pointed out, left for the coach from Emma's house, because the latter was forced to stay in that night. She was feeling indisposed, so they had to say their farewells in La Valcárcel's bedroom.

Bonis paused in the doorway when everyone else was already

upstairs. What a din! What clamor! It was always the same. No one, it was sad to realize, now even thought of their two friends who were driving along into the distance up the highway, nothing of the sort. Chairs were being dragged about; there was the sound of the piano and afterwards the clicking of heels. They were dancing.

I have brought all this about! Bonis groaned. And they are dancing on the ruins. The Reyes family has ruined itself. The Valcárcel house has failed—and the last *ochavo* is being joyfully spent by all these thieves and vicious parasites that I have brought to the house. "He began it!" the greedy uncle said, and he is right. I did begin it, and I still owe what . . . I've robbed. And everything that followed—the theatrical enterprise, the factory, the banquets, the picnics, the informal dances—we threw them all away to those greedy toads, all because of my weaknesses, my passions; and even when that passion had begun to fade, I was afraid to settle the accounts, afraid my adultery would be discovered, yes, adultery, that's what it is called! I tolerated it all; I brought it all about. It is my fault, and the worst is what her uncle just said: "He began it!"

Bonis buried his head in his hands and hesitated at the doorway, dimly lighted by an oil lamp. He could not make up his mind to go upstairs. With that mob inside, his house disgusted him. If I were to sweep them all away! And myself along with them . . . everyone . . . everyone! he thought. How could he endure that life, especially now that neither pleasure nor sin attracted him?

Egoist! he accused himself. Since your bed mate has gone, you moralize about the others. But, the impending ruin? When Nepomuceno informs Emma about all of this, it will be certain. We will be poor. For my sake, Bonifacio thought, I am almost glad . . . and yet, the horror of it all is that it is my own doing.

The noise of the dancing, which had been resounding muffled and continuous within his head, suddenly ceased. Then he heard many footsteps rushing in the direction of Emma's bedroom.

"What is happening?" Bonis muttered, startled. He assumed as he had in former days that Emma had become sick and would lay the blame on him. As he turned toward the stairway, the door suddenly burst open. A pair of figures appeared: Cousin Sebastian and Minghetti. Rushing down two steps at a time, they ran smack into Bonifacio.

"What's the matter? What has happened?" he shouted, picking up his hat from the floor, he who should have been the master of this household.

"Upstairs, man, upstairs! Always gazing at the stars, eh? Emma in that condition . . . and you outside!"

Cousin Sebastian's phrase reminded Bonifacio of a whole treatise on archeology; it was part of the classical repertory of his earlier domestic days.

"But . . . what has happened? What's wrong with Emma?"

"She's ill—a fainting fit, a bad headache," said Minghetti. "We have to find Don Basilio quickly. She's screaming for him."

"Go on up, man, run. She's calling for you, too. I never saw her like this. This is *very* serious. Go on up, go on up . . ." His voice trailed off. Quickly, the two emissaries hurled themselves into the street, competing with each other in speed and zeal.

"You go to the Casino; I'll go to his house," said Sebastian, and each broke into a run, one up the street, the other down the street.

Bonis entered trembling, as he had so often in past times. What would it be? Would the horrendous times of the sick shrew return? In comparison, these recent days of "moral laxity" smelled of flowers! And in the future, what weapons would he use in the battle? He no longer believed in passion although the last traces of it had pained him that night. And now he scarcely believed in his Ideal, in Art. It was all deception, a trick, the temptation of sin. Yes, his slavery, his disgrace, that life of a dog tied to the leg of a mad woman's bed—all was returning! He no longer had force to resist; for the Ideal, for passion, he could suffer all, but without that? Nothing. He would die. Sickness again . . . and now, now, with poverty almost assured . . . how horrible! Oh, no, he would run away.

He entered, heading down the passageway. All was confusion in the house. The Ferraz girls and one of the Silvas were running from side to side, giving contradictory orders to the servants. In Emma's room, Marta and Körner sat beside the bed; they looked like statues in a mausoleum.

"She's asleep," the father said solemnly.

"Silence!" exclaimed the daughter, with a finger to her lips.

"But, what has happened?"

"Shhh! Silence."

"But . . ." Bonifacio began in a lower tone, drawing near. "But, I want to know . . . and her uncle? Where is her uncle?"

"He's changing his clothes," Marta answered in one of those hisses which are more disturbing than a shout.

Reyes smelled the odor of antispasmodic drugs, an odor which tormented him with memories. There was also a certain stench, a nauseous stench. He drew closer to the bed, at the foot of which sat a pile of undergarments that Emma had stripped off, according to habit, after she had gotten between the sheets. Remembered sensations spoke to Bonifacio of other griefs, and quickly reflecting on all of this, he felt alarmed.

"But, what has *happened?*" he asked without lowering his voice sufficiently, forgetting his wife's sleep, thinking of very strange things.

"Don't shout, sir!" The German girl's reprimand was severe.

Bonis brought his face very close to his wife's.

"She's asleep," repeated Körner.

God knows whether she is or not, thought Bonis. Pale, looking very ill, disheveled and with the ten years which she had managed to throw off once again hanging upon her features, Emma opened her eyes, and the first thing she did with them was cast a glare of hatred and another of fright at her afflicted spouse.

"What has happened, dear, what has happened?"

The sick woman tried to say a few words. In fact, she apparently even had in mind to make a speech for she sat up in bed and stretched out her arms, but the strain made her nauseous, and Bonis, without time to withdraw, was covered with the same spew from which the uncle was drying himself. Körner discreetly fell back a step, and Marta caught hold of the bell with the intention of calling for help—she was not a female to descend to certain strong particulars at the sickbed. The stomach, she used to say, is not our slave; it enslaves us first. The Ferraz girls came running, and later Eufemia with water, sand, a towel and whatever else was necessary. It was made clear to Bonis that he stank, and he hurried away to change his clothes.

When he returned to his wife's room, he saw the uncle, Körner, Marta, the Ferraz girls, the Silva girl, Minghetti and Sebastian in the drawing room.

"Is she better? Is she alone?" he asked.

Sebastian responded as though from charity alone, "No, she is with Don Basilio."

Before making up his mind to enter the bedroom, Bonis scanned the whole gathering. He saw in them something strange: they did not seem to be alarmed but rather filled with malicious curiosity. There was only surprise and uncertainty, not shock or fear of danger.

"Is something wrong? What is wrong?" he pleaded, as his unhappy face turned in vain to those near him, imploring them for tenderness, for charity, for something.

"Dear sir, you may go in," said Körner. "In the final analysis, you are the husband, no?"

So Bonis entered. Beautifully dressed as always in an off-white, well-cut overcoat, a curious smile on his face, Don Basilio was waiting out a storm of shock and rebellion against the designs of nature, to which Emma had wholly abandoned herself, clutching her disheveled head with her trembling hands and calling upon God in an insulting tone of voice using the familiar form.

"*Dios mío!* What is this?" asked Bonis, shocked himself, his hands forming a cross in front of the doctor.

"Why, nothing . . . your wife is extremely nervous and has taken rather badly a piece of news that I thought would fill her with satisfaction and legitimate pride."

"Be quiet, Aguado!" she howled. "Don't make fun of me. I'm not

189

in a mood for jokes. *Dios mío*! What will become of me? How awful! How terrible! Yes, what will become of me? *Dios de Dios*! And at this time. . . . I am going to die for certain, for certain; my heart tells me so. I *won't* have it, I *won't* have it, I *won't* have it!"

"Is she delirious?" cried Bonis, horrified.

"Why?"

"Well, she is saying . . . that she won't have it. Have what?"

Don Basilio laughed heartily. "What she means is that she won't have a child. But you'll see that when her time comes—although it's still far off—we'll give birth to a robust baby."

"Soul of mine!" shouted Reyes, suddenly aware of everything, less because of the proof before him than because of a voice somewhere in his conscience which spoke to his brain: "Serafina has gone, and *he* is coming. He did not want to come until he found your heart empty, to have it for himself alone. Passion has gone. Your son is coming."

He flung himself to hold his wife's head in his arms, but she met him with her fists, punching him so forcefully that he lost his equilibrium and almost fell on top of Don Basilio.

"Nervous, extremely nervous," the doctor remarked, concealing the agony of a bunion which that jellyfish had stepped on.

The explanation began.

Emma clung with true panic, like a castaway to a plank, to the notion that all this was absolutely impossible. Aguado, with statistics supplied by his own clientele, demonstrated that impossibilities of that nature had forced him to spend many sleepless nights. And without going any further, he cited so-and-so's wife and such-a-one's wife, who had produced unexpected babies after years and years of apparently permanent barrenness.

"Oh, the mysteries of nature!" Don Basilio gloated.

But had they not assured her so many years ago, when she had the miscarriage, when she was half-dead, her insides in a pitiful condition, that she could never again become pregnant, that all that had ended, that something or other had gone wrong with her womb? Emma demanded.

"Yes, they may have said that, señora, but *in illo tempore* I did not have the honor of numbering you," he smiled proudly, "among my clients. I've heard rumors of someone who may be a great midwife, but who is enormously ignorant of obstetrics and gynecology and every other kind of 'ology' divine or human."

While Emma poured forth her laments, screams and protests, swearing and forswearing that she was determined not to give birth, that the pregnancy was a disguised sentence of death, that it had come too late and other things along those lines, Aguado turned to Bonis in order to explain what had taken place there.

As soon as he, Basilio, had approached his patient, he had noticed some strange symptoms which had nothing to do with her habitual nervous crises. He had informed himself as to certain intimate details, although this with great difficulty because of Emma's horror of all calculations, arithmetical previsions and recollections, not only in respect to her uncle's accounts. As a consequence of this information, what he could see before him, and an examination, he had discovered that this lady, like so many others, had returned to the long-abandoned jurisdiction of maternity. He spoke a great deal of the womb and the placenta but much more of the "mysterious march of Nature through, permit me the Gallicism," said Aguado, who was a purist within his limits, "through physiological phenomena of every order." Indubitably (and he did not say so just to flatter himself) he had expected no less from the homeopathic and hygienic regimen which he had wisely prescribed for his client; for without those pills and more particularly without the physio-moral influence of nourishing food, of walks and especially of amusements, that organism would have continued its valetudinarian life without even a remote hope of having sufficient residual strength from which to draw a new life, an alter ego. There was no doubt that Aguado was determined to impress Bonis, since normally the famous ladies' doctor was not so tiresomely pedantic.

In any case, Bonis had to restrain himself from embracing the doctor. He had accepted the absurd idea that his wife's pregnancy depended on that very argument between her and Aguado. If Emma won the dispute, good-bye son! If the medic had the last word, birth was assured!

Since there was no reason to hide the matter, it was not hidden. Those in the drawing room immediately heard of Don Basilio's diagnosis. There were shouts of joy, of surprise and even a few of malice, and, as well, jokes, revelry and the pretext to continue enjoying themselves and making a happy disturbance. Emma continued to protest. She felt better, it was true, after giving full vent to her feelings, but the shock of the night had had a bad effect on her. She was not sick as she had feared, but she *was* in an "interesting condition," and this was horrendous. Now, they paid no attention to her, but laughed at her and even left her alone while they wandered around the house and took refreshments and played the piano and sang. All the time that she herself confessed that nothing actually hurt, she nonetheless tore her hair, insulted her male and female friends—half in jest, half in earnest—calling them "executioners" and proposing that they give birth in her place, for then they would see.

She kept on denying her condition as if it were a question of honor, just as Marta might deny it if she found herself in a similar situation; but Emma, of course, denied it half-heartedly, only trying to deceive herself. As to the rest, she understood well enough now after hearing Don Basilio and answering his wise questions that she had been blind, that she herself should have understood what was underway a long time ago when she had noticed strange things take place in her intimate life.

Bonis had attempted to remain with his wife while the others, once Don Basilio had departed, rushed to the dining room where the refreshments awaited them, but he had to leave her too—he was summarily dismissed. So Reyes disappeared, and, as Don Juan Nepomuceno had gone out with the doctor, the guests were left in full possession of the house.

In the dining room, the burlesque character of the jokes with which the unexpected event had been received became more marked. Calculations were made regarding the greater or lesser proximity of the birth, presuming that all things followed their natural course to their happy conclusion. Hypotheses respecting the probable causes of an event of that size abounded and were mixed, reaching the point of absurdity and ending in a variety of documentation, examples of one similar case or another, far stranger. Körner demonstrated great erudition on the subject, but local, more recent incidents were preferred as better, more credible testimonies. Emma would not have been amused to hear herself compared with sixty-year-old pregnant ladies or to know that, as an example of miraculously preserved beauty, someone cited Ninon de Lenclos (of whom Señorita de Silva had never so much as heard!). Oh, Marta was quick witted! It was she who changed the conversation from tocology to aesthetics so that she could display her knowledge without loss of decorum, the prerogative of a modest virgin ignorant of obstetrics! That clever girl was so coy in the matter of feigning innocence that she reached ridiculous exaggerations. In order to rival the ingenuousness of the Ferraz girls during the first news of the happy event, Marta was inclined to let it be understood that in her judgment newborn infants came from Paris! But, with true innocence, the younger Silva girl revealed all that she knew about the whole matter, and this was quite a bit. Marta quickly furled her sails and did not engage further in these ludicrous philogenetic and ontogenetic "legends," as she herself would have called them had it not been thought ill mannered.

Everyone agreed as to one point, one on which the doctor had insisted: the principal cause underlying the restoration of Emma's feminine health and of her motherly faculties was the new life which she had been leading for some time, the amusements, the room for expansion. Consulted on that particular, Minghetti nodded his head in assent and continued eating pastries. His table companions looked at him with sly half-glances, and the more perceptive noticed an air about him which Körner, speaking in a low voice to Sebastian, referred to as *gené*, leaving Sebastian, who spoke no French, in the dark. Nepomuceno returned as they were getting up from the table. They all took leave of Emma, repeating the jokes.

Körner and Sebastian, who displayed an amount of experience which the Ferraz girls could not understand in a bachelor, recommended such and such precautions, and all the virgins, including Marta, offered to serve their friend in every way compatible with the state to which they still belonged.

Emma raged, flailing the air, and her anger increased because she could not explain, in any decorous way to the girls, the arguments with which she continued to dispute the physician's sentence. Descending the stairs, some insisted that La Valcárcel's fury was contrived, that, in fact, she was well satisfied with the discovery; others thought, more correctly, that if this new potential flattered Emma to some degree, the terror of childbirth and the loathsomeness and repugnance of maternal duties after the birth left no room for satisfaction.

"And, furthermore," said one of the Ferraz girls to the Silva girl, "did you see her face after just these first signs and the shock?"

"Oh, yes. She looked like a cadaver."

"What she looked like was a fifty-year-old woman."

"She's not far short of it, is she?"

"Now, woman, don't exaggerate. It's just that her makeup had flaked off."

"Well, she has aged ten years, then."

"That, yes."

On the street, they suddenly became quiet, thinking unanimously about Minghetti and that friendless expression he seemed to wear in Emma's room. Sebastian accompanied the Körners home. Nepomuceno had been forced to remain behind because the German father had become very particular, now that the wedding was near, about gossip; he did not want his daughter to be seen in the dark streets at such hours with her betrothed, even though he himself accompanied them. Körner insisted that in Germany it was quite customary to let fiancées walk about alone with each other whenever they wanted, that it was held in good repute, but that in meridian countries every precaution was insufficient. In point of fact, he feared the good Nepomuceno's ardor.

"But Reyes?" asked several of the family's friends as they separated. What had he done with himself? He had not stayed in Emma's room.

Actually, Bonis had locked himself in his bedroom, seeing that his wife had so pointedly rejected his open-hearted joy; the future father, who had only desired to share the delight of this unexpected and welcome news in the sanctified love and company of his wife, now was alone. In the absence of his wife, Bonis had to content himself with the humble bachelor's bed in his room, the single witness to his many thoughts, his many dreams, his many feelings of remorse and the many pains and humiliations he had swallowed with his sobs. This bed was his sole confidant, his best friend, not the large bed in his wife's room, no—only the poor walnut boards and those sheets without lace (because lace and petit point made him nervous), that blue-flowered coverlet which told him so many sad, sweet, gentle and poetical things all consonant with his essential self. It seemed to him that by dint of his looking year after year upon those flowers, as his thoughts wandered through the enchanted worlds of his illusions, of his sorrows, a sort of blue moss of dreams had clung to the coverlet, the threads of his own idealism. In short, that coverlet and a rose-colored one in the same pattern were like intimate friends, confidants that he had never found in the world of the living.

He often thought of this: strictly speaking he had no human friends capable of understanding and of sacrifice, neither true childhood friends nor friends of maturity. *Il suo caro Mochi?** Bah! Mochi had deceived him for only a little while. He was a leech, God forgive him. No, his only friends were objects: the mountain on the horizon, the moon, the parish belfry, certain pieces of furniture, the shabby clothes which he used at home, the worn-out slippers, the bachelor's bed more than anything. These inanimate beings, created by industry, which Plato felt corresponded to no idea whatsoever, were, for Bonis, like paralyzed souls who heard, felt, but could never respond, even with signs.

* His dear Mochi

Nevertheless, that solemn night as he took off his boots to put on his slippers and sat contemplating the blue-flowered coverlet, the neat folds of the clean, humble sheets, the narrow, soft pillows, everything seemed to smile at him with its freshness and its aspect of intimate familiarity. Total felicity was impossible unless his feet were relaxing in the softness of his loose wool slippers.

"Ah, ha, ha!" he exclaimed, feeling very comfortable and resting both hands on the bed. A knowing smile passed over his face, reflecting the joy in his heart. Now, for meditation. For dreaming. Solemn night! There were no miracles; he was certain of it. And it was better that there were none. Miracles and the true God were somehow incompatible. There was, however, Providence, a plan for the world in preestablished harmony with the natural laws (he did not use these words; he did not think this in words). There were providential coincidences which served the pious man as propitious signs emanating from God and brought about by Nature. It was no miracle that the doctors who had long ago condemned him with his wife's barrenness were mistaken. It was no miracle that Emma should bear a child at the age of almost forty. Nor was it miraculous, although admittedly surprising, that the son's arrival was announced on the same night that his passion ended. Serafina had gone, and "Isaac" was coming. He *should* be named Isaac, according to Bonis' reasoning, but instead he would be called God-knew-what—Diego, Antonio or Sebastian—at the pleasure of his mother, the tyrant of them all. Isaac! The strangest, the most surprising coincidence was that his visions had begun on the memorable night of the concert, that concert which had spawned a great part of the misfortunes relating to his home and the wholesale corruptions which entered it all at once. During that concert, too, was born his growing desire for peace, for pure, tranquil love and, as well, that vague hope, rejected and revivified from moment to moment, of finally having a son, a legitimate, only son. Most marvelous, although not miraculous, no, was the fulfillment of what he ridiculously called in his own mind "The Annunciation."

He felt so excited within himself, so filled with tenderness that

196

he was a little afraid. "Oh, if this is what it is like to be mad, then I welcome madness!" he said aloud. He was so happy, so proud. There could be no doubt. Providence and he understood one another. It had been a sort of contract: "Let her leave, and he will come."

But, had she really gone away—completely?

"Yes," said Bonis emphatically, standing up and kicking the floor. No one is left here but the father of the family. Here, in this heart, there is no longer room for anything but fatherly love, my love for my son.

A secret voice told him that his new love was a trifle abstract, somewhat metaphysical, but that would change. When his boy was actually there, it would be something else, different. Not knowing what his name would be, thought Bonis, contributed somewhat to the failure of actual human love for the baby of his heart. Isaac! No, he would not be Isaac. . . . Moreover, Isaac had not been his father's only son. Although it seemed irreverent, the most appropriate name, to be precise, would be Manolín . . . or Jesús. No, comparing himself with God the Father or even Saint Joseph was too much!

The idea of Saint Joseph made him sit up in the bed where he had stretched out without undressing. Although Bonis was not a believer in the strict sense of the word, and although his doubts had carried him many times to exegetic questions, he thought that history had done Saint Joseph small service, maybe with the best of intentions, but still small service. He felt a personal compassion for Saint Joseph. Let's suppose, he reflected, that he and no one else was the father of his "putative" son, that he was the actual father, without becoming heretical or compromising the so-called miraculous—sublime, extranatural, but not necessarily miraculous—bond between the Divinity and the Son of Man; let's suppose this for a moment. How terrible, then, to tear away this glory from Saint Joseph . . . the love of *his own* son! It was given to the mother. And the father? And the father? Thinking these rare thoughts, his eyes filled with tears. Was he mad? How could he now weep, even though filled with infinite compassion for the patriarch, Saint

Joseph, when he should have been so happy! But, truthfully, that was history. History did not know what it was to be a father. "Nor I myself, really," Bonis said. "When I have the boy at my side in a crib, I won't be thinking of Saint Joseph or any of this theology . . ."

In that instant a thought flashed across his mind: the child must be named Pedro, like Bonifacio's father. "Dear father! Mother of mine!" he sobbed, hiding his face in the pillow, which became soaked with his tears.

That was the source; there was the origin of true tenderness: the bond between fathers and sons. Bonis envisaged that bond as a chain linking past, present and future, unifying mankind, as a symbol of disinterested love and self-effacement, but Bonis further realized that every link was broken by death; the chain also represented forgetfulness, indifference. He seemed to be alone in the world without the links of unselfish love or anything that would help him, but he understood, nonetheless, that he was the product of another's denials, in a limitless series of loving sacrifices. Infinite consolation! He must have been born of an act of love as well; there was no rational motive to suppose for one moment that his ancestors loved their son less than he would love his. Bonifacio had turned slightly toward the wall. The lamp, placed on the night table, cast the profile of his face across the white stucco. His shadow, as he had already noticed with a melancholy sense of satisfaction, resembled his father's just as he saw it in distant memories, but that night the similarity was much clearer and more accentuated. "Strange!" he exclaimed aloud. "I scarcely resembled my father, but our shadows . . . yes, very much: this moustache, this movement of the mouth, this curve of the forehead, this way of raising the chest while giving a sigh—all this is as I saw it a thousand times, at night, too, while my father read or meditated. Curled up close to him in his bed, I daydreamed, happy with infantile security because of that protection I had at my side which covered me with wings of love, a refuge in which I believed I was absolutely safe." Bonifacio paused. Father of my soul! How much you must have loved me! he shouted within himself.

Bonis forgot that he still had not had supper and felt a faintness take hold of him. He began to feel ill, without really realizing it. His legs trembled as the memories of his childhood piled up in his head and acquired a solid force, a firmness of outline which bordered on hallucination. He felt himself fainting, and as if he had cut into layers of geological strata, he contemplated simultaneously a number of periods of his early life. He saw himself in his father's arms, in his mother's arms. He tasted on his pallate flavors that he had liked as a child. He once again smelled odors that had impressed him like poetry in his remotest age.

He began to be afraid and jumped out of bed, tiptoeing in the direction of Emma's bedroom. La Varcárcel was sleeping; now she was really asleep, with her mouth slightly open in the unconsciousness of deep fatigue. The old wrinkles in her forehead were once again menacingly prominent. Bonis felt a twinge of grief on the behalf of all his ancestors. He heard, with familial pride, the voice of battle, of resistance, of name against name—a thing which had never happened to him during his long years of resigned domestic captivity. The Reyeses seemed to rebel in him against the Valcárcels. Oh! What he would give in that moment to have seen, to have read, that book about family crests of which his mother, more than his father, had spoken so often, proud as she was of her husband's lineage. The Reyeses were of a good family, natives of a coastal village called Raíces. Bonis had passed through it once in a coach, but he had never thought of his ancestors. Now who might have taken the book? A relative, an uncle? His father, Don Pedro Reyes, a court attorney who had very bad luck and very little talent, scarcely ever spoke of the ancient grandeur, more or less exaggerated by his wife, of the Reyes family.

His father was a simple, sad man, hardworking but without ambition. His unstained honor had been put to the test a hundred times, but he received no recognition for his honesty, for Don Pedro was so modest that he was almost heroically incorruptible. He was so broad-minded when it came to forgiving another's misconduct that his moral standards would always be suspected. He loved silence, he loved peace, and he loved him, Bonis, and his brothers, all dead

199

now. Yes, now, with an extraordinary clarity, with a talent for observation which he had not realized he had, he saw the recondite merits of his father's character. His romanticism and his misapplied reading had always prevented him from admiring that noble figure, now evoked by his own shadow on the wall of his room. Close to the sleeping Emma's bed, Bonis adored like a Chinaman the sanctity of the paternal shades. Oh, how clearly he saw it now; deed after deed in his father's life which had seemed insignificant to him before took on new meaning. One time, he recalled, he had even caught himself thinking: I am an ordinary sort of person. I'm not a man of genius. I'll be like my father—a simpleton, a common man. And now his soul screamed, a common being! Why not? Imbecile, imitate your father's commonness! Remember, remember: what did that man long for? To escape from sordid business, from the commerce and the lies of the world, to shut himself up with his children, not in order to remember his grandparents' nobility, but in order to love his family in peace. He was an anchorite, the self-effacing anchorite of the family. His desert was in his home. He went out into the world only because he was forced to do so. His house spoke to him in silence, with the placidity of domestic peace, of all the "idealism" his loving and humble spirit could imbibe. His smile, when he spoke to strangers about matters of the street, was of a profound yet hidden sadness. He expected nothing from outside the doors of the house. He did not really believe in friends. He feared evil, which he felt was widespread, and often spoke to his older sons about the necessity for preparing to defend themselves against the intrigues of the world, without doubt a great enemy. Yes, his father used to speak to his children about what awaited them outside in the same way that prehistoric man, sheltered in a cave, might teach the rest of his family to fight with the beasts of prey they would be sure to encounter as soon as they departed. Bonis remembered more: although he tried to hide it, his father let it be seen, in spite of himself, that he was basically ineffectual, that he was afraid of that terrible fight with existence; he showed himself pusillanimous and resigned to his poverty, to the impotence of his honesty, assaulted as it was by the treason, sin, cruelty and tyranny of the world. He considered his home a refuge, an island of self-sufficient love separated from the rest of the universe with which he could have no connection. For these conjectures as to what his father had been and thought, Bonis drew upon a multitude of accumulated memories filled with meaning, but in his historical hypotheses, in his recomposition of the family sociology, they did not help him to perceive the struggles his father must have endured between disenchantment, fear of the world, horror of outside conflicts and the necessity of protecting his children and of arming them for the battle to which life, once he was dead, condemned them. Don Pedro had died without providing a single son with a position. He had died when his family, because of its penury, had been forced to renounce the last vestiges of good bourgeois form in its social and domestic life-style. Then, poverty had given a plebian aspect to the decayed lineage of Reyes. His mother, her soul riven by this comedown, had died only two years later.

Another Reyes was now coming, a morsel of the spirit and the blood of his father. Bonis had once conceived the idea that sons resemble their grandfathers more than their fathers. The word *metempsychosis* resounded in his ears. He had greately valued that word long ago for its exotic quality, and now its significance pleased him. "It will not be *exactly* metempsychosis," he said, "but there may be a bit of that—in another way. Who knows whether the immortality of the soul isn't something like this and explained by this sort of renaissance? Yes, my heart tells me so, and my intuition tells me so: my son will have something of my father about him. Now the Reyeses are born rich; they return to their ancient splendor!"

As he thought this, a cold sweat ascended along his spine. He remembered, synthesized in two or three phrases, the dialogue which he had overheard that same night, the one between Nepomuceno and Marta. Ah! Was that the destiny of the Reyeses? If one more was born, was he to be born into ruin? They *were* ruined— or soon would be. That is what the uncle had said, and his information must be sound.

Bonis sat down in a chair, not daring to do so on his wife's bed.

He again reviewed his situation. *Dios mío*, simple joy is impossible in this world! This night that I thought would be filled with nothing but joyful fancies, interior happiness, torments me instead. My son ruined! And ruined because of my fault, he thought. Yes, yes, I myself began this work. And worse, my ineptitude, my ignorance of the most important things in life—numbers, money, accounts—poor prose I called it all. Art, passion? No, instead *that* was poetry! And now my son is to be born ruined.

Emma moved a little and sighed as though in complaint.

For a moment, Bonis was determined to wake her up. There was little time to lose. He wanted to disclose the terrible secret to her as soon as possible, that very night. Not even one minute could be wasted. From the next morning on the two of them would have to change their way of life totally. They would have to put new supports under this house, and that meant no delay, none whatsoever!

My son's welfare is in question. From now on, less analysis and more action, he assured himself. *I* shall be the head of the house. *I* shall be the administrator of our goods. And this factory, this factory which produces I don't even know exactly what . . . we will see. Oh, Señor Don Juan, my dear Nepomuceno, there will be a *scene*! I already know, and I am resolved. Bring on the scene! But all of that tomorrow. Now, the immediate, the manly act worthy of fatherhood must be performed tonight; I must wake up Emma to inform her about everything.

Emma suddenly, however, woke up without anyone's pleading. Bonis had no time to broach the question of his secret discovery, for she began to insult him as she had so often done in the past because he "stood there, gaping." She drove him out of the room with shrieks, screaming that he call Eufemia, and through the agency of the maid, finished by slamming the door in his face.

That too had to end, he thought, but—after the day of birth. It was of prime importance to avoid a miscarriage, so nothing should be done to displease her. In giving birth and in nursing—if nurse she did (and he, of course, hoped that she would)—they would talk about everything. They would then see if a Reyes could or should be the slave of a Valcárcel.

202

"Nevertheless," he said, "I should go in once again, with the greatest courtesy, in order to announce the danger."

He raised the catch of the door which had just been closed on him, but he let it fall again. He felt very weak. He had had no supper. He saw red sparks in the air. He wanted to eat something and leave it all for tomorrow. It was already very late anyway. The problem was that he had no appetite, a thing which he seldom lost.

He took two soft-boiled eggs and then went to bed. He did not fall asleep for a long time, and when he did, he softly dreamed, almost weeping, of Serafina, that she had died and called him to her arms from the bosom of the earth. She was holding a flask. The flask contained a human fetus immersed in preserving fluid.

Chapter Fifteen

Emma defended her hope that the doctor had been mistaken for as long as she could and with a multitude of ingenious recourses. Against all proof deduced from the intimacies to which she had had to confess—intimacies which as a general rule were proof enough—she maintained that her nature was exceptional, an enemy of even the most ordinary physiological rhythms. But her great argument consisted in presenting herself in profile. "You see? Nothing!" and she drew her corset tighter and tighter each day, without fear, deprecating counsels of prudence and health. She acted like a poor maiden for whom losing that status represents a great source of shame and who, therefore, attempts to hide the proof of her ignominy.

Her gossiping friends were mistaken in seeing any dissemblance in La Valcárcel's obstinate opposition to the fate of things. No, she was not flattered by the thought of being a mother at such a time. Furthermore, her terror of the dangers involved, which seemed supreme, left her little room for vanity of any kind. Sickness, death—*that* was what she saw. "I cannot give birth to a child. My heart tells me so. I will not give birth," she said with a shiver when by herself she began to give way to the evidence. "At my age! Bearing a first child at my age! How horrible! How horrible! With my brittle bones!" she moaned. Emma shut herself up in her bedroom. She looked at herself in her full-length mirror, in undergarments, even without undergarments; she examined herself carefully. She measured herself. She compared herself with other women. She took the dimensions of the width and length of her torso and whatever parts of her body she believed, in her instinctive but vague notions of tocology, were essential to the arduous passage. And throwing herself naked into an armchair, without thinking of chill, she began to cry furiously, to cry without tears like a spoiled child, screaming "I don't want to! I cannot! I'm no use!"

Death was probable, sickness certain, those terrible, insupportable, insistent pains! However easily she might give birth, those pains would definitely come. No! No! Never! What for? Once again the bed, once again the feeble body, the pallid complexion, the *skull* standing out under the yellowish skin, the weakness, the nerves, the biliousness . . . and the dreadful abandonment by the rest, by Bonis, her uncle, Minghetti! Oh, yes, Minghetti, like everyone else, would let her die, would let her suffer without dying or even suffering with her. Labor! Useless cruelty, immense danger, for nothing: what stupidity! Happy women, women dedicated to gaiety, to art, to . . . baritones—these superior women did not bear children, or they bore children only when it was convenient. To give birth, what idiocy! Why had she not foreseen the possibility? She had let herself be surprised. But who would have suspected it? And her anger, as usual, exploded against Bonis, who was forced to desist in his efforts to perform a duet of mutual endearment based on the approaching "joyful event." One thing Emma would not tolerate was anyone's speaking, even in jest, of the danger she was in as a stroke of good fortune.

Finally her denial of the coming "catastrophe," as she called it, became a patently useless and ridiculous affectation. Emma gave up tightening her corset, stopped defending herself. If, in the first months, her pregnancy had not been very conspicuous, it soon became quite obvious. It was not "exaggerated," according to Marta, but it could not be ignored. He was there all right, the *parvenu*, as she called him in French while laughing maliciously, knowing that no one but Minghetti could understand her. In *his* snide conversations with Marta, Sebastian, laughing as well, referred to the baby as "the little surprise."

The first day of her "defeat," La Valcárcel was transported with grief; she could no longer deny, but she could protest. Then, that situation actually began to seem tolerable. She grew accustomed to the idea as a necessary evil. She wore out her fear, and for a while she only complained out of habit, still with a vague uneasiness, but as if the day of crisis were drawing away into the distance instead of approaching. Her first expression of vanity lay not in being a mother, but in her size. Since she was pregnant, then she would be good and pregnant! And finally, boasting, she actually exhibited without support or binding that which she had tried to hide at first. Furthermore, it was noticeable that her face had not grown worse. Those ten years which the day of shock had registered were no longer there. Her flesh even looked better. The tenseness of her features and the tint they had taken on was not unbecoming. One saw what it indicated, but it was really attractive. Actually, as a state of being her condition was indeed interesting.

But all these consolations were still insufficient. From anyone's point of view, hers was a burden bulging with dangers, inconvenience, evils future as well as present. She never spoke to Minghetti of what was about to happen to her. It was a theme which the two avoided in conversation. Yet, without any doubt whatsoever, the baritone was upset. He felt a sense of exasperation which tingled his smiles with cynical bitterness. He felt as though he were thrust into an atmosphere of ridicule. If it were not for the lack of contracts, the world of art having forgotten him, he might have preferred to leave that pleasant life, his emoluments as the director of the Academy of Fine Arts (office expenses Mochi called them), everything. The friends of the family, including Marta and the Ferrez girls, each in her own way, spoke to Minghetti about Emma's condition with malicious phrases and half-sketched smiles. Minghetti could hardly disguise just how much the conversations annoyed him.

"How discreet!" everyone said. "The real Tenorios always act in that way—the truly gifted ones." No one had been able to catch in Minghetti the slightest gesture of arrogance. It was even pointed out that he looked upon Bonifacio with greater respect than before.

In fact, he had been discovered many times regarding Emma's husband with a singular expression in which no one could divine so much as a trace of mockery. In short, as everyone said, he was discretion itself.

The only time that Minghetti and Emma spoke of her pregnancy was to torment Bonis and Señor Aguado. Emma insisted that she must bathe in the sea. The season was right, and the event would still wait a little longer; there was time to go and return. In those days, bathing in the sea was not yet so common as it is now. Although Emma's town was only a few leagues from the coast, the number of families there who made the trip in summer was scant. For the very reason that the whole business was out of the ordinary, Emma insisted upon it.

The doctor did not deny that a bath in the waves might be quite harmless. It depended, of course. The event might be closer than expected, and in that case it would be rash. But this was not the worst danger. The worst, the most truly dangerous and foolhardy action was, of course, the ride in the coach. The round trip over that rough terrain, those roads with ruts and holes, was madness.

"But Minghetti said . . ." Emma began.

"Señora, let Minghetti sing his arias and his romanzas, but he shouldn't meddle in other people's business."

"Minghetti has traveled . . ." she tried to say.

"Oh, yes, but not in *your* condition!"

"That's not the point. I say that he has traveled, that he has seen a great deal, and he assures me that . . ."

"That ladies *comme il faut* should not have children? Yes, I already know his theory."

But against Aguado's advice, the Reyeses went to the sea and bathed. Bonis was tempted to object, to inaugurate, in fact, the new energy which he had decided to put into practice in the future, since the continuation of his line was now assured or almost assured; but Emma's temper grew so furious the moment her spouse suggested that they weigh carefully the doctor's arguments that the unfortunate Reyes continued to postpone his resolutions of taking control of the household and being his wife's husband until after the birth.

No, we will not destroy the greater good, Bonifacio thought, for the sake of a lesser one. We will not irritate her. A miscarriage would be a horrible catastrophe, the very destruction of my hopes, of my entire life! After the delivery then we will talk.

But Nepomuceno, Körner, Cousin Sebastian, Marta, the Ferraz girls, even Minghetti—they were not going to give birth; why didn't he take a stand with them? Why didn't he throw those parasites out of the house? Why didn't he impose some order on the expenditures and the customs of his own house, desecrated by those perpetual sprees? And, most important, why didn't he take Nepomuceno into another room and confront him, saying: "So, so, my little friend, we have reached this point! Let us see, the very least you can do is explain all this about our imminent ruin, no?" Why did he not venture to take a stand with the uncle and the family friends? The trip to the coast provided him with a respite. In fact, it was merely an excuse. "We are going soon, and I can't take all that in hand now," he reasoned. "But on the return, oh! What will take place on the return! Then I'll have it out with Emma's uncle, for sure."

The only thing Bonis had dared to do before going to the baths, however, was poke about the family business a bit. Timidly, he ventured to propose that Körner and her uncle take him along to see the factory, which was a league away from town, a league along a rutted road. No one suspected that the trip was full of malicious and intentional espionage. Bonis' ineptitude in every type of serious business, both industrial and economic, was such that everything the uncle and the German said was literally Greek to him. They spoke of the bad state of the "old business" in his presence, but he understood not a word. The "new business" was something else again, but, here the Valcárcel funds—as the engineer referred to them now with absolute contempt—had no bearing. The chemical products factory languished. The project for extracting useful substances from seaweed had been almost entirely abandoned. In theory, the business was infallible; in practice, it was a calamity. It was not abandoned entirely, however, because of their stubbornness. All the material gathered at the cost of the large but unrewarded sacrifice of the Valcárcel funds had been put aside for other adventurous, economically insane speculations which made it possible for Körner to try out innovations he read about in the technical journals, experiments which in commerce, in Spain's sad commerce—especially in that corner of Spain, cut off as it was from the rest of the country by an almost complete lack of communications, without even a railroad—resulted in disaster. They were mad. Little money, to be sure, was invested in these adventures of chemical romanticism simply because there was little left. There was nothing at all left of the capital which up until then had provided for everything.

But the new industry was something else again. There was no uncertainty, no conglomeration of trials and errors where probable results were ignored. It was altogether different: a gunpowder factory, the first and only one in the province. Körner took charge of the technical side of the business while Nepomuceno remained the head of the joint-stock company. The Valcárcels, nearly exhausted economically, were only left with a little something, almost a pittance, and they scarcely realized it. The gunpowder factory was built on the land of the "old one," as the original factory had come to be called. No one knew why so many hectares had been purchased for the old factory, but the purchase was "fortunate." The new investors had been able to acquire all that was necessary for this gunpowder factory, and since it was useless to the Valcárcels, it was bought from them at a very low price. That administrative plot, which Körner and Nepomuceno had orchestrated, had cost them not a few disputes and not a few compromises and not a few *reales* to overcome the scruples of the law and the public administration in matters relative to personal tax. But today a big meal here, tomorrow another one there, little gifts, slaps on the shoulder, recommendations and other expedients had sufficiently smoothed the way.

In his visit to the factories, Bonis picked up nothing except an invincible fear which preoccupied him the whole time they were close to the gunpowder. The idea of flying, much more likely there than a league away, did not leave him for a moment. As for the old factory, the one for "chemical products" (always this vague term!), it did not seem to be in such a bad way as he had believed. He expected to see an absolute physical ruin, the walls cracked and split, the machinery rusted, the chimneys smokeless. But there was nothing of the kind. Everything was in sound condition, almost new, alive; there was noise, there was heat, there were even a few laborers. Where was the ruin? He did not dare ask about it, because he did not want the others to suspect that he might know something about the state of business. When we come back from the baths, and I ask her uncle for his accounts, I shall find out whether this is bringing us anything or whether it is in fact ruining us, he procrastinated.

He returned, bouncing about like a quail inside the coach, and as he entered the city, he determined never to establish on his own an industry as dangerous as gunpowder.

Körner and Cousin Sebastian (for Uncle Nepomuceno was very fond of Sebastian just then and had brought him, with pleasure, into the business, interesting him with the inducement of big profits) noticed at the same time and communicated to each other the observation that for some weeks past Bonis had been listening very attentively to their conversations about the factories, hovering over the table in the study and looking out of the corner of his eye at the papers they brought in and carried away.

"It looks as though that imbecile wants to find out what is happening," Körner remarked.

"Yes, I've noticed that, but haven't you also noticed that stupid expression he wears? He doesn't understand a word."

"Oh, yes, but still, I don't trust him. He has a way of looking . . . like a spy. So, we'll have to spy on him as well."

One day, after hearing them comment persistently on Reyes' idle curiosity, the uncle became worried. He said nothing, but he, too, dedicated himself to the task of observing his nephew-in-law. On the night table in Bonifacio's bedroom, Nepomuceno noticed several books which gave him something to think about. They were not the verses, the novels, or the books of "logical and ethical psychology" which Bonis usually read. There sat a volume of *The Hundred Treatises*, a popular economic encyclopedia, which along with an abridged course on the raising and breeding of chickens and other poultry included a compendium on Civil Law. On top of this volume, he saw another book, the title of which read: Laspra, *Forensic Practice*. Then, there was another with the title *The Annotated Commercial Code*. What did all *that* signify?

The next day, Ferraz, the happy magistrate, met Nepomuceno in the street and said to him, "Are you people going to have some kind of lawsuit?"

"What lawsuit? With whom?"

"Well, I only mention it because every afternoon I see Bonifacio in La Oliva talking with the Papinian of the Marketplace, young Cernuda."

Hello! Is this what we're up to? thought Don Nepo, but he was careful not to say anything aloud. Instead, treating as a jest the news which had really alarmed him, he said aloud, "Bah! He's probably thinking of becoming a lawyer and taking lessons from Cernuda. Listen, friend, now that he is going to be a father, he wants to become a wise man. So, he studies a great deal. eh?"

The two laughed over the joke and especially the cute bit of malice, but Don Nepo had something else to think about. This business with Cernuda was serious. He would have to keep constant watch.

Körner, Marta, Sebastian and the uncle advised Emma to take the waters as soon as possible. Minghetti's plan won out. They looked for a coach with good springs. Warning the driver to proceed at a walk, the married couple, along with Eufemia went to the seashore.

Emma thought that she would feel something strange with the movement of the coach. She expected a kind of curious but natural miracle from that imprudent trip: that through no fault of her own the child within her would be destroyed. Gaetano had said that the trip might bring about a failure of birth. Frankly, La Valcárcel wanted to abort the baby and had not the least compunction about it. It would not be her fault, but rather the fault of the vibration, the swaying, the natural laws of which Bonifacio spoke so much. The latter was boring the driver with his precautions, with his continuous warnings.

"Careful! Eh? What is that? A hole? You've jerked us! Slow down to a walk, to a walk! There's no hurry." He looked at his wife. "How do you feel, dear? These highway engineers! What roads! What a country!"

And Emma, oblivious of, or rather encouraged by, the danger, thought: Oh, yes, the country, the engineers. Laugh away, you fool. The laws, the laws of nature which you think are unalterable and so very interesting, these are going to give you a shock.

She dozed, half-dreaming, half-voluntarily imagining; she envisaged a deformed ridiculous creature, a wrinkled old man who resembled the baby Jesus, his skin loose, covered with the fuzz of a winter peach, issue forth from her womb, then fall little by little into an abyss of humid, thick fog. He took his leave, making faces and waving good-bye with his hand, the only pretty thing about him— a mother-of-pearl hand, beautifully shaped, a sweet little thing. And she caught that hand and kissed it, and she said to the hand which she grasped between her own two, "*Adiós, adiós* . . . it cannot be, it cannot be. I am no good for motherhood! *Adiós, adiós* . . . look, the laws of nature have made you fall, taken you from my breast. *Adiós*, my child, my little hand. *Adiós* . . . *adiós* . . . until eternity!" Then, the little finger, which seemed to be made of wax, decomposed and melted into the dark mist which enveloped it and Emma as well, suffocating her, asphyxiating her. . . . She opened her eyelids with a start and saw Bonis who, moved to tenderness—with the gaze of Agnus Dei, as she said—fixed his clear eyes on her stomach which carried there his only hope, his only dream.

They reached the coast without any incidents, and Emma bathed the next day, taking the precautions which the local doctor, consulted by Bonis, advised. It was from this doctor that La Valcárcel learned, horrified, that in the matter of her return to the city, what

212

she believed could have been an abortion would instead be something much more dangerous than the normal delivery: an actual delivery much too early—not an abortion at all! A seven-month-old baby with a precarious hold on life and great losses on the part of the mother, *that* is what the trip to the city could produce if great precautions were not taken. Emma screamed! She invoked the heavens! She insulted Bonis and the absent Minghetti and Don Basilio. She, who had wanted to deceive nature! She had fled from one danger only to court another, greater one!

"But, why didn't they tell me at home?" she screamed.

"Dear woman, didn't Aguado and I warn you?"

"Aguado spoke about losing the little creature, not about losing me myself. My god! I won't move. I'll give birth here, in this village. I'll die here. I'll not go a step farther!"

It cost a great effort to get her into the coach. The local doctor had to assure her, on his word of honor, that he would be responsible for there occurring no change—if they took the precautionary measures that he indicated. His instructions were followed to the letter. The best coach was borrowed from a countess who lived nearby. Her coachman had to swear that the horses would not take one step longer than another, and the carriage was filled with pillows; Emma traveled almost suspended in air. She had to confess, finally, that she hardly felt the movement. During the trip, which lasted three hours longer than the previous one, she slept with her hands locked over her stomach. When she awakened, she saw Bonis' face fixed with an intensely expressive look on the same sacred bundle that her fingers pressed. Actually grateful, she smiled at the husband who had helped to preserve her from laying down her burden before its time. Ashamed of the caress as she always was of these weaknesses, she showed him her gratitude by giving him a gentle tap with her foot. And Bonifacio, who felt tears well up in his eyes, thought: best of all would be to love the son and love the mother.

When she descended from the coach by the door of her house, Emma demanded that two men, who *had* to be Bonis and Minghetti, assist her. She let her whole body fall on them, assured of not being abandoned to her own weight. Afterwards, while Bonis and Don Nepo and the others who had gathered in order to meet her gave orders for the baggage to be carried into the house, she embarked on the long trek upstairs supported by Gaetano's arm. On the first landing, she stopped. She breathed heavily, looked fixedly at the baritone, then finally inquired, "And if I had died on the road . . . through your mistake?"

"Bah!"

"Yes, bah! I could have bled to death. That was perfectly clear."

"No, little one, no. You'll give birth without any pain, and you'll have a strong child."

Emma suddenly turned livid, for following his speech, feigning distraction, Minghetti freed his arm and went on upstairs ahead of her without any more courtesy, his hands in the pockets of his pants and whistling a cavatina in a snakelike hiss, one of his many accomplishments. La Valcárcel went up by herself, clutching both the banister and her stomach as though she were afraid of giving birth on the staircase. She went to bed immediately and called for Don Basilio. She demanded an examination which, done, revealed that there had been no change and that her "moment of peril" would come on the appointed (or, in this case, the *assumed*) day.

"The ones who are away," as all the happy company called Mochi and La Gorgheggi, wrote and asked about Emma's health with a great show of interest. Minghetti was charged with carrying on the correspondence on the part of everyone at home. Few letters were sent to La Coruña, but an abundance came from there. The absent singers felt a sense of nostalgia for the *vita bona* they had left. Serafina wrote the most. In a beautiful English hand, she filled sheets and sheets with her polyglot idiom, using English for the most difficult things she wanted to say—things which went undeciphered if Körner or Marta was not present to translate them—Italian frequently, and Spanish most of all. Even in Castilian, there were paragraphs the "home correspondents" could not understand, not because of the words but rather because of the ideas, a flow of veiled allusions, deployed with great artifice, which went straight to Bonifacio's heart and awakened his memories. Yet in spite of his feelings of remorse, Bonifacio wrote less and less often to Serafina, despite her urging. The singer had a veritable passion for epistolary expression, and she was capable of sustaining the flame of a more or less moribund romance by heaping up reams of perfumed sheets filled with minute lettering crossed like a delicate fabric. But if Bonis had consented to "continue their relationship" by writing, he had absolutely refused to let the actress write to him directly. Although he felt certain that Emma had discovered her husband was, or had been, La Gorgheggi's lover, there was really no reason to tighten the screws. She was evidently turning a blind eye. If he challenged the dignity of his deceived wife, Bonis explained to his "accomplice," perhaps then *she* would tighten the screws and there would be a real mess. Serafina had answered this with a strange humor: "But if your wife lives like a great lady, unconventionally, and she knows what the world is? . . ."

This notion of his wife's perverse tolerance aroused Bonis' moral sentiments; he would not admit the hypothesis. No, his wife could not despise him or herself up to that point. In short, he was intransigent. Serafina could not write him love letters, which were certain to fall into the hands of Nepomuceno or Emma because they would surely not respect his correspondence, any more than they respected his other individual rights. La Gorgheggi, then, was forced to resign herself to writing, not only to Minghetti in her name and Mochi's, but also to Emma, her dear, dear friend; and even in those letters to Emma there were veiled replies of the most artful kind to the few letters Bonis sent her. Too, the future father saw that those sheets, which alluded to his wife's approaching delivery, were filled with obscure references and remarks, not answers to anything at all that he had written, but more like shows of utter malice; he felt, as a result, a great moral repugnance, and he finally broke off completely with Serafina. He put an end to his letters. In any event, that correspondence would have had to end quickly, he reasoned, as soon as the son was born.

But there was a bit more: Reyes became superstitious in his own way. Although he rejected as absurd (if attractive and pretty) the idea of making a promise to the Virgin of Cueto—a miraculous statue to that neighborhood—he decided to "sacrifice" all of his vices, all of his sins, to the success of the delivery. Strict morality, he thought, will be for me, so to speak, Our Lady of the Good Birth! He examined his conscience, and he found no other serious sin, except of course that of his "adulterous letters." So, he suppressed them. After a few weeks, Serafina complained with her customary belletristic secrecy, but Bonifacio pretended not to understand. Eventually, he did not even bother to read those letters which came first from La Coruña and later from Santander. He finally learned, because Emma herself relayed the information, confirmed by Minghetti, that Serafina was now in an unpromising situation, with misfortune following misfortune. Mochi, bored, had run off to Italy with no money, but many debts, leaving his friend and disciple in Santander, where she remained without a contract, without money and with well-founded fears that her maestro and spiritual *babbo* would not come back for her, in spite of his promises.

Minghetti and Emma, who with her fear of dying at a given date felt very charitable and at odd moments sympathized with others' misfortunes, conferred as to how Serafina could be protected in a way in keeping with her dignity. The uncle was consulted as well, and he did not hide the coldness with which he received the news of that interest his niece took in Mochi's protégée. He said drily that nothing could be done for her, either with or without dignity, seeing that it would have to be done without money. Bonis was told nothing about these projects for succor, first, because of their inveterate habit of not counting on him for anything and also because, without communicating it to each other, Minghetti realized as fully as did Emma that it would be too impudent and indelicate to bring Bonifacio into such an undertaking.

One day, when according to the most probable calculations the "catastrophe" which horrified La Valcárcel was now drawing near (and in Don Basilio's opinion one should be ready from one moment to the next), Reyes ran into the mailman in the doorway of the house just as he was going out. The mailman brought only one letter.

"It is for you, sir," said the man in a solemn voice, as though stressing the importance of the incident.

"For me!" Bonis seized the paper as though it were some kind of booty, as though he and the postman were fighting over the ownership of it. He looked uneasily at the staircase and then toward the street, afraid that some witness might appear, and when the mailman was almost out of the door, Bonifacio spoke to him, trembling in the face of his fears. He called him back:

"Listen, mailman, take the money, please."

"No, sir, it's not urgent. I'll collect another day."

"No, no, I have it. Take it. Clear the accounts. Take it!" and he handed him a coin worth two *cuartos*.

"There is one too many, sir. It will stay on the accounts until tomorrow, eh? Seeing that you are so punctual, I too will be . . ."

"No, no, on no account. Keep the other, or give it to a beggar," Bonifacio returned.

And the mailman went away, laughing.

"He goes away laughing at me," said Bonis. "He must believe that I wanted to buy his silence with two *maravedis*!"

He did not read the envelope of the letter, and he kept it uneasily in his pocket. But it was not necessary to read anything. He knew. The letter was from Serafina. Of course, he was correct. In the Café de la Oliva, he read those pages in which La Gorgheggi complained like a Dido well versed in the epistolary style. How eloquent her reproaches were! All of that prose touched his soul! She complained about his long silences. She knew, through Emma's letters, that he no longer read hers, those of his beloved Serafina. It was without doubt for this reason that he had not offered her any consolation whatsoever in the terrible situation into which she had fallen. Perhaps he disbelieved her poverty. Perhaps, like a wretch, he thought that she could seek out the type of adventure which would provide her with sufficient means to live in comfort. Well,

217

no, not at all! Believe it or not, she could not keep from reflecting on, pining for, the sweet and serene mode of life that he had once shown her and which she preferred. Her true taste was for such a life.

She then proceeded to tell him, in her fashion with many romantic phrases, but with all sincerity in regard to her present feeling, that the period which she had spent in Bonis' town had transformed her, that she could no longer engage in that gay life in which her beauty had once promised her both triumphs and profit. As always she hid her old adventures, but she did not dissemble in regard to her present situation. In La Coruña, in Santander, she had resisted all the temptations of money; that was the only temptation, in fact, which lay before her. She could have had rich lovers, but she did not want them. She was faithful to Bonis after the manner of the good married woman who may not actually love her husband but does respect him and esteem him, and respect and esteem even more her good name. For Serafina, the life of the small-town gentlewoman which she had enjoyed with Reyes—of the lady who has engaged in a forbidden relationship, yes, but only one—was glorious. "The maestro," she went on to say in the letter, "has promised to come back for me as soon as he is offered an acceptable contract, but time flies and I despair. Mochi does not come, and I am delicate, nervous, worried, very sad . . . and poor. I am losing my voice, furthermore. The theater begins to frighten me. I have been neglected by my public, and this can only hint of great hunger in the near future, a poorhouse in the distant future. I don't beg you for refuge; I don't beg you for alms. But I am coming to be near you. I want to be a bourgeoise! In your house, at your side, I learned to be one in my own way. I too need that peace of the soul of which you spoke to me so many times. That and a little bread, a bit of native land—even though it be borrowed. I have grown fond of this dear corner of yours, just as in the past I grew fond of that green corner in Lombardy I told you about when you adored me like the 'madonna.' I know that love is not eternal. I don't beg for your love, either; I ask only for your friendship, for a certain affection that even the least faithful of spouses cannot deny their wives. Nor do they ever deny them refuge, Bonis. I cannot live in your house, but I can live in your town, at least for a little while. I need rest now. I am sick inside, deep inside. Disturbed. Please, let me come. I need to see the faces of friends. You don't know how painful it is not to have a true home when the body is tired and wants to rest, when the soul begs only for peace and a life of memories. I never spoke like this before, but you, your convictions about morality, even your big, dusty house with its traditional, genteel airs—all of that has found a place in my soul. I sometimes heard you say that we poor actors had left a mark on you with our happy, heedless ways. *Everything* leaves a mark. You people, too, have left a mark on me. You, you, Bonis, more than anything—especially your worries and your fear of an uncertain, nomadic life. Being blown by the wind from one side to another is terrible. I am going to see you, Bonis. I *am* going to see you. Perhaps it doesn't matter to you now. But to me, yes, it still does. I am not your wife, but you are my husband. I have no other. If I had been lawyer Valcárcel's spoiled daughter, the benediction which sanctifies your love for her would have fallen on me. Don't give Chance more importance than it deserves. You already know what I am like. Some fine day I shall come to you. Will you shut the door on me? Does the virtue for which you now stand demand that? You are still greatly loved, Bonifacio Reyes—loved by SERAFINA."

Bonifacio did not doubt the sincerity of that prose for a moment. He felt a wave of infinite regret, retrospective love; his old passions, evoked by memories, seemed purified. But he himself was disoriented; the compass needle of duty spun wildly in his head. He owed Serafina something. If she had corrupted his heart, his marital bed, he had marked her with a new instinct for an ordered, tranquil and honorable life. Furthermore, she who had once made him so happy was—begging for bread!

"Sophisms, sophisms!" suddenly shouted the "new man," as he called himself. I am going to be a father, and his father's mistresses cannot enter this house in which my son is born. The mistresses are finished . . . but, more than anything, the money is finished. I won't spend a *cuarto* now on anything which doesn't concern my son. Everything is for him, everything for him! That's final. There is no reason to think about it. This is being cruel? This is being selfish! Fine. Selfish for my son. That's not repugnant to me. For him, anything whatsoever. A father's duty, a father's love is for me the absolute. I'll cling to that absolute.

These phrases, and others in the same vein, did not always hold sway in Reyes' soul. From the time Serafina's letter arrived, Bonis' existence was a continuous fight with himself, a perpetual battle, like so many others he fought with himself—and always lost.

Serafina finally arrived. She presented herself at the Valcárcel house and was well received by Emma, by Nepo, by Sebastian, by Marta, by everyone; and Bonis himself did not have the courage to treat her coldly. What he did not do, however, was act as a lover, nor did Serafina reveal desires to renew their relations for the time. Nevertheless, he remembered what the letter had said regarding that particular. La Gorgheggi's eyes seemed to be always reciting the message at the end of that epistle, but her lips said absolutely nothing of those affections. Nor did she touch on the delicate question of the stipend which this past mistress seemed to have expected. The singer pointed out that she had come to wait for Mochi, that he had offered to come to her aid and to take her by contract to America. She asked nothing of anyone. She lived modestly in her old room at La Oliva, and Minghetti, Körner, Sebastian and other old friends visited her. Bonis only saw her in his own house, that is to say, in his wife's house, but she did not complain about this manner of conduct. When there was an occasion for them to be alone, she did nothing other than look at him with loving eyes.

Reyes was satisfied with his firmness. He had felt very, very strongly, seeing the soprano in his presence again; however, he had restrained himself by thinking of his future "priesthood" as a father. That battle which he was winning over himself for once, seemed to him like an initiation into the life of total virtue, of sacrifice, to which he felt called. With his energy employed in the fight against his one-time passion, spending all the strength of his poor will-power, he forgave himself with few scruples the postponements and extensions in the affair of the uncle's accounts. Granted, he planned to make himself clear in the matter; he planned to put that question to Nepomuceno, but the days passed and he did nothing—nothing whatsoever. He read civil law. He read a commercial code that was the appendix of a treatise on bookkeeping. He consulted young Cernuda, an eloquent lawyer, but . . . nothing else. The uncle, of course, would be preparing himself; he was only waiting for the assault. Oh, Bonis knew very well that Nepo would have the arms with which to defend himself. For that reason, he dodged the issue; for that reason, he postponed the meeting; and for that reason, to tell the truth, his legs would tremble every time he thought: this very day I'll call the uncle aside, and I'll tell him! But he was not even sure what he had to tell him.

One afternoon the mailman arrived with two letters mailed within the city. One was from Serafina, who had not appeared in Emma's house for three or four days. She wrote to Bonis, forgetting their agreement that she would not do so, and told him that she felt ill and suffered bitter apprehensions caused by her having received no letter from Mochi. She begged Bonifacio for consolation, a visit and—a few *duros* in advance. She was "infinitely sorry," but the innkeeper at the Oliva had cruelly wounded her self-esteem, had offended her, and she wanted to pay him in order to be able then, justifiably, to leave the inn and, as well, to tell that churl that he did not know in the least how to treat a lady, especially a lady left alone without a man to defend her.

In the face of this news, Bonifacio's first impulses were worthy of a Bayard and a Croesus all in one. For a moment, he forgot his "priesthood," and he pictured himself on the grid, running the host of the Oliva through with a single thrust and then throwing at his body a mesh purse like those that Mochi used in the operas. But, at that moment, the distorted handwriting on the other letter attracted his attention. He tore open the envelope and read it in a flash! The contents of the anonymous letter (such it was) said no more than this: "Thief! Sacreligious man! Where are the seven thousand reales returned in the confessional by a repentant sinner?"

Bonis, by then in his bedroom, dropped to his seat on the blue flowered quilt of his simple bed. He felt a cold sweat, and his throat constricted.

"I am becoming sick!" he murmured. But suddenly he forgot this sickness, the anonymous letter, everything, because Eufemia ran into the room, screaming. Her momentum was so great that she bumped into her master's knees.

"Sir, sir!" she screeched. "The mistress is in labor."

Bonis leaped up like a tiger, ran through the rooms and passage-ways wearing one boot and one slipper (as he was when the cursed letters surprised him) and reached his wife's room in a few bounds. Terrified, with the look of one condemned to hell, Emma was writhing, clinging with the iron grip of her fingernails to the shoulders and neck of Minghetti, who had not even had time to get up from the piano bench. He had been singing and accompanying himself as usual when his pupil let loose with a scream of shock and fear, surprised and horrified by the first pain of the now imminent delivery. She seized this maestro, this friend, not only with the instinct that any woman would show at such a pass, but also as though she were resolved not to die alone, if she indeed would die. She seemed determined not to let her captive go this time, but rather to carry the first person who fell into her hands, whoever it was, along with her into the other world.

When Bonis appeared, there was a sudden movement among all three which seemed to arise from the same impulse, the same mandate of conscience. Emma released Gaetano's neck and shoulder; the latter jumped away, separating himself from Emma, and Reyes advanced with a look of possessive authority, resolved to take Minghetti's place. Emma clung more eagerly, more confidently to the thick neck and chest of her husband, who felt a strange new delight in the contact of her fingernails and that strong, nervous pressure, indirectly indicative of the little being he had been awaiting with such longing. That was *he*, yes, he, the son who was there, making himself known through the pain of his mother and through that mysterious solemnity, sublime in its incertitude, which marks all the great moments of natural life.

In Emma's desperate squeezes with each new pain, Bonis clearly recognized, apart from the natural effect of feminine weakness in such straits, apart from mere "physiological phenomena," the real character of his wife. He saw the same egoism, the same tyranny, the same cruelty as always. Bonis attributed a certain percentage of the injury that Emma inflicted on him, as she clutched him, apparently trying to transmit part of her pain through that contact, to her desire to hurt him, to make him suffer, which she so enjoyed.

"I am dying, Bonis, I am dying!" she wailed, grasping her husband.

In Bonifacio's present state, however, that pressure seemed sweet and the voice even loving. He looked for Emma's face, which was resting on his chest, and he was met with an expression like Melpomene's in the portraits of the Gallery of Drama. The shocked eyes of the parturient, opened affectedly wide, expressed no tenderness whatsoever. She certainly was not thinking of the child. She was only thinking that she suffered, nothing more, that she would die, that it was atrocious for her to die when others would be allowed to remain here. She was in pain. She was furious. She took up her cause at the final hour, like someone condemned to death, innocent but not resigned, wildly snatching at life. There was even a moment when Bonis thought he felt his wife's sharp teeth on the flesh of his neck.

Minghetti had slipped from the room on the pretext of going to acquaint the others with the news. Said and done. Shortly after, Cousin Sebastian appeared, quite pale, and within five minutes, Marta, very vexed because this birth might possibly delay her imminent marriage and the baptism might overshadow the wedding. One would think from the way she judged it all that Emma had guaranteed not to give birth until after she herself had been wed. At last Nepomuceno appeared, accompanied by the old doctor, the famous *accoucheur*. Emma, in all deference, had saved that little surprise for Don Basilio. Until the "day of peril," Aguado; but, in the critical moment, unless the birth was too torturous, she wanted instead only the help of that popular and miraculous male midwife who had never had a client die on him. Ladies in the town had more faith in that man than in Saint Raymond. Those who did die, died always at the hands of the tocologists, who had no divine skill, no supernatural "sleight of hand." The celebrated midwife knew at what point to call for his colleagues; short on science, he had a conscience and, with this consideration, was able to boost the legend which made him infallible.

Bonis, who had always defended the city tocologists and persistently attacked the great *accoucheur's* reputation for miracles, felt himself also touched by the general faith when he saw the midwife enter. May science and Señor Aguado forgive him, but he too felt confidence in that practical quack—in spite of the fact that one day, long ago, he had mistakenly condemned Bonis to a barren wife. That false prophecy had torn from him his hopes of ever being a father, of reaching the dignity which seemed to him greatest. However it was, Don Venancio entered as he usually did, shouting, scolding, reproaching and declaring that he was responsible for nothing because he had been called too late. He greeted no one. He pushed Reyes from his wife's side with one sweep. He made Emma stretch out on her bed, and right under the stupefied Bonis' very nose, he demanded utensils of such a kind that it seemed the illustrious *accoucheur* planned to build a gallows with which to hang his son.

Sebastian, a skeptic about everything since he had given up his romantic ideas and grown fat, smiled to himself, assuring everyone in a low voice that nothing could be expected soon. Don Venanico hurried here and there, going about his business with the gestures of a fireman fighting a fire. He always did the same thing. Sebastian had seen him on many occasions, not all necessarily to be mentioned.

Marta believed that in the role of total innocent she was playing in that comedy there was only this stage direction: "Go away." So she withdrew to the dining room where she found Minghetti, who was dunking biscuits in Malaga. He was not his usual happy self.

From the dining room were heard, now and again, the muffled and muted shouts of Emma. Marta looked at the Italian with malicious curiosity. What things happen in this world! thought the German girl to herself. Fundamentally and secretly, she was more skeptical than Sebastian. Here is this one acting as though nothing mattered to him, and the other unhappy soul! . . . Minghetti continued dunking his biscuits and drinking Malaga. Finally he noticed Marta's insistent and expressive look. Taking the so-called radish by the leaves, he drew close to the haughty German, and just when she thought that he was going to reveal to her some secret or pass along an intimate confidence, he caught her by the waist and sealed her mouth with a noisy kiss. Marta's shout mingled with another in the distance, that of the woman in labor.

Chapter Sixteen

He was going to be a father! With that knowledge, all the clichés of fatherhood exploded in his brain like powder bursting in fireworks. Reyes noticed, however, with great regret, that his heart took a smaller part in that solemn event than his head and his rhetoric. Why did that new dignity—strictly speaking, the first in his life— to which he was "called" leave him a little cold? Perhaps more important, why did he still love this son of his loins, not as a son, but as a *concept*? Son or daughter? Mysterious, thought Bonis, that in this instant I doubt the sanction which reality lends to presentiment. Perhaps a daughter—although pray God it would not be! Mysterious! And he turned back the bed and slid between the sheets.

Going to bed, even for a few hours, seemed to him something like an abdication. The role of the husband, he thought, once the critical moment of birth has arrived, is too passive, too insignificant. Bonis longed to do something, to intervene directly and efficaciously in that business which was of such grave importance to him.

There was more. Although reason told him that in such situations all the fathers in the world had very little to do and that everything then was up to the mother and the doctor, he fancied that he was far more useless than other fathers in the same situation. He was too easily pushed aside; they managed too well without him.

Nonetheless, there was no alternative to what Don Venancio had told him: "You, friend Bonifacio, to bed, to bed for a few hours because this could take a long time, and we will need everyone's strength. If you don't rest now, you won't be able to give her renewed support when you are needed."

Fine, he thought; this is rational. For that reason he was going to bed, for he always submitted to reason and logic. He planned to submit even more if he could, now that he was going to be a father. He had to give example. But what seemed unreasonable to him was everyone else's indifference, Emma's included, and the looks and surprised expressions with which everyone who was close to his wife received his show of paternal and marital solicitude: Doña Celestina, the knowledgeable assistant who had come at Don Venancio's suggestion; her husband, Don Alberto, who was also there; and Nepomuceno, Marta, Sebastian and even the high-spirited Minghetti— although that last one, indeed, sometimes looked at him with eyes that somehow revealed a certain . . . respect, and something of incredulity.

Running things over in his mind and reaching certain conclusions, Bonis remembered that some time ago Serafina had tried to make him understand that the birth of his son was an event which should not be greeted too zealously. And Julio Mochi, too, in a letter written months before from La Coruña, referred to the matter and Bonifacio's paternal enthusiasm in a singularly lukewarm tone, with words behind which he fancied he could see pitying, even mocking smiles. But Serafina's and Mochi's attitudes could easily be prompted by jealousy and the fear of losing his friendship and protection. Without a doubt, Serafina saw that a rival was coming who would finally rob her of all his heart, of her ex-lover, her present friend. "Poor Serafina!" he said aloud. No, there was nothing to fear. He had heart enough for everyone. Charity, fraternity were compatible with the strictest morality. Apart from the fact that . . . no, frankly, paternal love was not so intense, so strong as he had believed, imagining it from a distance. Bah! It did not come within even a hundred leagues of the great passions. Where was that intimate, self-fulfilling satisfaction which accompanies the pleasure of love and flattered vanity? Where was that smile of life which was like a frame enclosing happiness in the sublime moment of passion? This was something else—an austere, somewhat cold sentiment, poetic, yes, because of the accompanying mystery, but more solemn than anything else. It was somewhat like an investiture, like being con-

227

secrated by a bishop. In short, it was not a source of happiness—or a passion.

Impatient, restraining himself only for the sake of fulfilling Don Venancio's rational precept, Bonis thrashed about in his bed as though he were on the rack. Of course, I must sleep, he began to think. She could give birth tonight or not give birth until tomorrow . . . or the day after. All of those screams might only be a false alarm. She's a fine one! If Don Venancio hadn't felt the child, I would still be suspicious. But, in any event, Emma is capable of complaining of labor pains a month before it's necessary. Yes, we'll sleep. This could continue for some time, and we might have to stay up and watch over her for long, long periods. If these intruders would only leave us. The strange thing is that Emma, who has always used me as a nurse and almost, almost as a night table, hasn't called me to her side now. Odd woman! And now that I would be so glad to help her!

The warmth of the sheets began to induce sleep and to incline him toward vague visions; his sleepy contemplation of flattering images and memories made him think, sighing, "If only Serafina had been my wife, and this son hers, and I somewhat younger!"

As though these thoughts and desires had been a knife thrust into his very being, though precisely where he could not say, Bonifacio felt a spiritual pain, a sort of protest, and he fancied he heard something like bubbles of noise, far away, from the direction of his wife's room, something like a baby's first cry.

Dios mío, if it is? Without wanting to admit it, he felt a sense of remorse for what he had just thought, and superstition made him think his son had been born in the same instant so that, in a way, his father had denied him and his mother.

"Soul of my soul!" shouted Bonis, bounding to the floor. "This is like being born without a father. My son! Emma, Emma, my little wife!"

Bonifacio opened the door of the bedroom and immediately heard, distinct and clear, the sibilant cry of a newborn child. His own flesh and blood was born all over again, crying.

"A boy! You have a boy, señor!" cried Eufemia, who flew in

like a tornado, close enough to touch the astounded Bonifacio, without realizing that the new father was in his nightgown. But neither he nor she took notice of this detail. The maid was very excited and deeply affected. Bonis thanked her in his soul, putting on his pants backwards and then correcting the mistake, trembling, gasping for breath, wondering all the while if he should not break with convention for good and run through the house in his drawers. But no, he dressed halfway, and bumping into walls, doors, furniture and people, he reached the foot of his wife's bed.

In Doña Celestina's lap he saw a purple-colored object, which made frog-like movements, a bit like a troglodyte who is surprised in his den and forced out into the light and the dangers of life. In a fraction of a second, Bonis recalled having read that some poor sea animals, fleeing from their more powerful enemies, resign themselves to living hidden under the sand, renouncing all light in order to save their lives, enclosed in eternal prisons for fear of the world. His son reminded him of this. He had taken so long! Bonifacio imagined that birth was forced upon him, that opening the doors of life was truly an act of violence.

"Crowning, Bonis, crowning!" said a weak and affectionate voice from the bed.

Without understanding, Bonis drew near to Emma and embraced her, weeping. Emma wept as well, nervous, very weak, wasted, suddenly transformed into a crone. She squeezed her husband's neck with the force with which she clung to life, and as though complaining, but without her usual bitter force, she continued, "Crowning, Bonis, crowning! Do you understand? Crowning!"

"Naturally! He was born headfirst!" shouted Don Venancio, who was on the other side of the bed with his sleeves rolled up and with a few spots of blood on his shirt and frock coat, very like a worker in a slaughterhouse.

"But he was crowning for a very long time, Bonis!"

"Yes, centuries," said the doctor drily.

"We didn't tell you. We made you go away, but I was in danger, wasn't I, Don Venancio?"

"But, my little one, I just went to bed . . ."

"Yes, but it was all about to happen for a long time. He was crowning, but we didn't tell you in order not to frighten you. Oh, I was in danger!"

Emma wept with a touch of rancor, even now, for the past danger, but was more affected by the pleasure of seeing herself alive, of being saved. Her soul was filled with a sentiment that should have been gratitude to God; Emma, however, was not thinking of God. Emma, of course, was thinking of herself.

"Come, come, less chatter!" commanded Don Venancio, and he covered Emma's shoulders with the fold of the sheet. "And now be careful not to fall asleep."

"No, my sweet dear, no sleep. That would be dangerous," exclaimed Bonifacio with a shiver. The idea of his wife's death passed through his mind like a wave of shock. For her to die! For *him* to be left alone without a mother! And he turned to his son who was bawling like a prophet.

A portent. In that instant, he saw in the wrinkled, indecorous and lamentable face of the newborn baby the living image of his own face as he had seen it sometimes at night in a mirror when he wept alone for his humiliations and misfortunes. He remembered the night his mother had died. When he had gone to bed desolate, he had looked automatically into his shaving mirror to see if he had circles under his eyes or a coated tongue, and he had then noticed that tragicomic expression, not pure and poetic as he had imagined, but more nearly the face of a suffocating monkey. Although he had even features, when he cried he became very ugly, ridiculous really, just as when he played sentimental music on the Valcárcel flute. His son, his poor son, cried like that: ugly, laughable, woeful as well. *He* was his exact counterpart! Yes, he was his very portrait, especially with that asphyxiated expression. Afterwards, as the baby grew a little more serene, thanks to a swallow of sugared water which must have seemed agreeable to him, he made a grimace with his mouth and nose that reminded Bonis of the child's grandfather. Oh, just like my father! Just like me in the dark!

At the same time that he felt something like spiritual relief as well as virile and even animal pride, however, he was stung by a feeling of remorse for having engendered the son, the first sorrows of paternity which, shock after shock, create an ache that hurts as if it is one's own pain, the holy charity of love for one's child. Bonis' conscience told him: "I will never again be happy and without cares, but I will never be absolutely unhappy if my son lives . . ." In his eyes, the world then suddenly acquired a solid, positive quality. He felt more part of the earth, less of the ideal, of his dreams, of his undefined nostalgia, but life seemed more serious as well, serious in a new way.

The boy continued crying, in spite of the fact that he now had protection—some embroidered, very clean swaddling clothes that struck Bonis as inappropriate to the solemnity of the moment and very uncomfortable. Oh, yes, he resembled him in his expression and his way of complaining about life! The others might not see that resemblance, but he was as sure of it as of a password. This was the son of his loins, perhaps also of his hesitations and his extreme sentimentality which was unsuspected by the world and even, strictly speaking, by Serafina.

A few hours later, when Don Venancio and the remnants of the "slaughter" (at least the dirtiness of all those critical moments seen from close by) had vanished, Bonis allowed Emma to speak again at length, and the relatives and friends even entered into the conversation.

What memories La Valcárcel dredged up! All, of course, were of the maternal lineage, and her old patronymic and hereditary mania revived. "Uncle, uncle! Sebastian, Sebastian! Let's see, who does Antonio look like?" Emma blurted out.

"Who is Antonio?" asked Marta passively.

"Why, my dear girl, the head of the house, my son! I called him Antonio to myself from the moment my head was clear enough to think of something besides the danger and the pain."

"Why, he looks," said Sebastian, "like the hero of Alpujarras, his namesake, Don Antonio Diego Valcárcel y Meras, founder of the noble house of Valcárcel."

231

"Don't say that in jest. Bring forth the portrait and we will see!" Emma demanded. There was no alternative. Between two servants and Sebastian, the illustrious grandfather (restored) was fetched and compared with Bonis' son, whom the mother drew from the warmth of the bed. Some found only a remote resemblance; others denied it amid gales of laughter. Antonio continued to bellow, and Bonis continued to see in him his own likeness, as he had seen himself in the mirror the night his mother died. What in his opinion did seem to be developing, almost hourly, however, was the infant's resemblance to Don Pedro, Grandfather Reyes, especially in the wrinkle in his forehead, in the lines of his nose and in the characteristic grimace of the lips.

For no legitimate reason, Marta was exasperated. She wore the "vinegary" expression which sometimes appeared without her realizing it and which made her look old and ugly, the sort of expression which was especially in evidence when she was jealous of something, when she felt that she had been upstaged. She now definitely saw in the baptism her wedding day completely overshadowed.

"To me," she said, "Antonio doesn't bring to mind either the Valcárcel type or the Reyes type. He looks like a foreigner. You have dreamed about some Russian prince."

The Ferraz girls, who were now assembled, laughed at the joke, pretending it was not meant as malicious. The rest were silent, surprised at her audacity. Emma did not understand, nor did Bonis. Bonifacio saw that they kept talking about the Valcárcels: whether the boy resembled his maternal grandfather, whether he would be a lawyer, whether he would be a gambler like so many others in the family and so forth. Memories of Emma's family lineage, good and bad, were evoked, but no one gave so much as a thought to the Reyes family or their past—no one at all!

Antonio went on crying, and Bonifacio was not far from doing so himself. His father! His mother! If they were alive! If they were there!

As soon as he could, Bonifacio escaped from the noise. He left to the rest of those people, now that they were enjoying themselves, all the rituals and duties appropriate to the occasion. The boy had fallen asleep, and he was not allowed to see him. Emma, now less nervous, but more fatigued and with a slight temperature, had returned to her old callousness and had ordered him away from her presence, since she did not need him. So Bonifacio retired to the solitude of his room and thought about his son.

"Yes, a son, yes!" he said to himself with his face buried in his pillow. "He had to be a son. The voice of God told me. A son. My only son . . ."

During all of that first day, Emma was sentimental and excited. Her husband believed that maternity was going to transform her, but the next morning she woke up with a fairly high fever and with no accompanying signs of tenderness. In spite of the exhaustion, she raged on as much as her strength would allow. They had told her about the time just after childbirth, which was also dangerous, and she experienced new terror. Emma even reached the point of forgetting the little one she held between the sheets, and she refused to show him to anyone, not even his father, because she did not want to have to turn over and become chilled. Bonis could not even glimpse his son, except during those serious moments when Doña Celestina changed his clothes. He developed from hour to hour. He began to look like any other newborn baby, losing that filial resemblance which Bonifacio had seen at the first moment. Reyes became somewhat confused. Then, he had to give up the idea of calling him Bonifacio or Pedro because Emma, of course, firmly demanded that he be named Antonio and called him that even before the baptism. He would be Antonio Diego Sebastian. Sebastian was going to be the godfather. Bonifacio acquiesced in everything. He did not want any disturbances yet. Any annoyance could hurt Emma. No, not now; he would postpone everything. Was he not determined to be strong? Was he not also determined to watch out for his son's interests—if it were not too late—and to provide him with the example of his own dignity? Well, there was no reason to precipitate the matter. Nor at the present time did he want to have it all out with Nepomuceno. There would be time for that. However, certain circumstances, not anticipated, forced him to marshal his strength and energy touching on this matter.

As it happened, bad news arrived from Cabruñana, the district near the sea-coast where the Valcárcels had some small holdings, part of some church lands confiscated and then sold by the state. It seems that a minor bailiff was having his own way with Emma's rents, overlooking late annuities or at least indefinitely postponing the collections and then using the sums collected to sweeten his own income. In short, he was exploiting his masters' property for his own profit. Nepomuceno paid no attention to the denunciation. The business came up during supper, but Don Juan and the cousin agreed to turn a blind eye to it all. Then, much to the great surprise of everyone present, Bonifacio began to speak. Giving nervously energetic yet restrained blows with the handle of a knife on the table, he said in a voice which trembled yet held a note of decision, sharp and shrill: "Well, I see things in another light, and, first thing tomorrow, now that the baptism has been postponed since Emma does not want the boy to catch cold in all this bad weather—I am sorry about this, of course—I'll take the Cabruñana coach, make my way to Pozas and to Sariego, and *I'll* settle Señor Lobato's accounts. I don't want him to rob us any longer."

There was a solemn silence. Bonis did not hesitate to compare it, poetically, to the calm which precedes a storm. For the present, it was the calm which brings the surprising, the unheard-of, to the fore. Indeed, Reyes understood that he was there alone, that the Valcárcels and his future in-laws, the Körners, would eat him up with great relish if they could. Not that he was not frightened or even shocked by his audacity; he was. But everybody knew that the diligent father of a family *must* be a hero. The sacrifices were now beginning; they hurt more than a little, yes, but one had to get on with it. The seriousness of a fight is only really known by its pain.

Everyone looked at Bonis and, afterwards, toward Don Nepo, who was the one called upon to answer. Don Juan, slow and tranquil, had changed greatly with the exciting lessons of Marta. Now, he relied heavily on the weakness and ignorance of the enemy. He

234

did not beat about the bush. He went straight to the point. Away with euphemisms! *Only* in the serene and relaxed tone of his voice could any leniency be imagined.

"On that matter about robbing you," he said, "I assume that you didn't say it with me in mind?"

If Bonis' words were a gauntlet, it had been picked up in arrogant fashion. Before Reyes answered, Don Nepo cast a look of triumph in the direction of his fiancée, who approved of his valor with a glance. At that moment, Bonifacio, who was ill prepared for such a snap confrontation, such a dual to the death as that, suddenly remembered with terror the anonymous letter of two days before, which, because of the gravity of events, he had completely forgotten. This is purgatory, he thought. I have sinned. I have squandered. I have robbed my son's inheritance, and now I am in purgatory: a state which is no doubt just like this, built on logic and ethics and nothing more than logic and ethics.

"For heaven's sake, uncle," he responded slowly and deliberately, trying to temper his voice with moderation and firmness. "*Por Dios*, why should I say it with you in mind? I am speaking only of Lobato, who is a great thief."

"A thief I *encouraged* year after year if, of course, we are to believe what Pepe de Pepa José, the busy little accuser, says. It would seem that Lobato and I have agreed to ruin you, then to finish off the Cabruñana property; is *that* what you are saying?"

"No one says that, uncle, no one says . . ."

"What *I* say, Señor Reyes"—and Señor Don Juan Nepomuceno delivered a not overly powerful blow to the table—"is that you are not a practical man and that this role you want to play out of making your debut as father of a family does not suit you."

From Marta a strident chortle of laughter, as violent as a series of slaps, resounded in the dining room, startling even her allies. Everyone looked at each other in surprise. Marta, her face swelling up like a serpent's, repeated that laughter and looked at Bonis cynically. Bonifacio looked back at his good friend without the least understanding of what that untimely laugh signified.

Don Juan continued. "A practical man, experienced in business, does not overstep himself in either zeal or suspicion, nor does he believe gossip. It would be a fine thing if I, *verbi gratia*, believed an anonymous letter I received a few days ago, a letter which assures me that you pocketed the sum of two thousand *duros* from a debt repaid to your father-in-law's inheritance through the secrecy of the confessional."

"Anything I took would be mine!" exclaimed the head of the house in a clear, loud, positively energetic voice, standing up but not rapping on the table.

Everyone stood up.

"Yours would be *nothing!*" retorted the cousin, Sebastian, who advanced a pace toward Bonis, presenting to everyone present his robust muscles, a body which seemed like an enormous fort. Marta, without thinking of what she was doing, placed a hand on Sebastian's shoulder as though urging him on to combat. She relied more, of course, on the cousin's strength than the uncle's, her intended's. Bonis found himself thrust prematurely and stupidly into the scene which he had wanted to postpone.

"Gentlemen, come, why make all this noise? There is no need for it. What I won't allow anyone to do—I swear to God I won't allow it—is to create a huge disturbance now. The first thing to consider is my wife, and if she finds out about . . . this, well there could be a misfortune, and God help the one who provokes her!"

The entire company sat down, taken aback. Bonis, overtaken with surprise himself, seemed like another man. Sebastian, who was certainly brave, strong and more than capable of throwing his uncle's "clerk" over the balcony, shrank a bit at what he called the "moral" force of those words and the expression of that tone. Everyone quite understood that poor Bonis was prepared to bite and scratch in order to prevent Emma's health from being endangered.

"Without noise, without noise, everything can be discussed," said Don Nepo, who wanted to make the "imbecile" talk in order to see just how much he would disclose and what laws the shining new lawyer had crammed into his head.

"Without noise, yes, disspassionately," the respectable and fat-cheeked Körner ventured to suggest, for he thought it was his duty to intervene as peacemaker.

"It is true," answered Bonifacio. "Passion never, never leads to anything."

"Exactly," continued the German, "and it should be easy for you people to understand that strictly speaking there is nothing here to worry about. Bonifacio doesn't distrust his uncle, nor his uncle Bonifacio, nor has anyone thrown doubt on anyone else's legitimate rights."

"Each one has his own interest," objected Nepo.

"Certainly, but there is no reason to speak of that now, for in the long run, there will be somebody to tell everyone which role he must play."

Bonis again felt himself swell up with new authority. That allusion to justice was so transparent. Don Juan felt a wave of anger rise to his face; however, he determined to resort to the supreme form of revenge. He restrained himself and swore that the miserable wretch would pay for it. Bearing this plan in mind, he managed to recompose himself, his fury assuaged by the sweet contemplation of future cruelties, delayed revenge. Smiling serenely, he said:

"Well, Bonis, you are right. We will settle these accounts when Emma gets well, and we shall see with figures and documents what you will have to try to understand, all right? What you both have spent, what I have saved . . . and who owes what to whom. What I must inform you of, however, is that if you two keep on spending as you have until now, bankruptcy is sure. You are, we might say, ruined. Emma has spent money like a mad woman, and you—don't deny it!—you set her the example; you dragged her into that impossible life. And every one of us knows why."

"Everyone!" solemnly echoed Sebastian, who had pursued La Gorgheggi in vain and still had designs on her.

Bonifacio, who had enough energy that night to fight with any man, did not have so much that he was able to resist proven facts, and the facts were terrible: ruined! And he had started it all! He was even to blame for what the uncle had stolen, for hadn't he allowed it? And his theft, his *thefts*—to pay a mistress's debts! He had to sit down. He was pale, unable to trust his legs. The uncle suddenly recognized the typical Bonis, the real Bonis, and he in turn swelled with recovered authority; however, he concealed his arrogance and, falsely conciliatory, said, "Do you want to see what is happening in Cabruñana? Leave tomorrow at eight o'clock, the hour the coach departs. Come to my room first, and you will see the books and the contracts from there. You can see everything, everything. So take what you need, and try to enlighten yourself. You realize, of course, that you mustn't present yourself to Lobato calling him a thief without knowing why you call him one."

Bonifacio, now having lost his strength for everything, meekly and mechanically followed Nepomuceno. Körner went out after them. Marta and Sebastian were left alone in the dining room. Körner, always faithful to his role of peacemaker, went along as counsel. Much good he did Bonis! In the uncle's room, Bonifacio suffered the humiliation he was expecting. With sly astuteness and almost feline viciousness, Nepo explained to him all the affairs touching on the Cabruñana property, and he did so in the most rigorously technical terms of consuetudinary law imaginable.

Bonis had no clear notion of the lease at all. The word *leasehold* sounded like Greek to him. *Partnership, laudemio, retraction* and the hundred other words used in civil law, added to the words which formed part of the judicial dialect of that area, passed through his ears like wind. He learned nothing. He apprehended vaguely that he was being deceived and that the uncle only wanted to stupefy and humiliate him. He fell into a thousand confusions and countless mistakes as he tried to explain to himself what they were trying to explain to him. Whenever he attempted to give an opinion of his own, Körner gleefully corrected him in order to throw his dullness and ignorance into relief.

"But, my dearest fellow," he would exclaim, "I am a foreigner! I already know more than you about all the customs of the country, the laws of Spain . . ."

When they reached the numbers, Körner was sincerely shocked. Bonis did not know how to divide and scarcely knew how to multiply.

In order to escape from that slough, Bonifacio—abashed, filled with shame and remorse—tried to take up more important questions, which had nothing to do with that horrible and obscure, but basically rather trivial, affair, so inaccessible to him, a poor flutist; he dragged the matter of the factories into the discussion, feet first.

He was very excited, his self-esteem offended, and with a lapse of prudence and at a bad time he broached the delicate question of the two factories without being fully prepared. It was three o'clock in the morning when Körner and Nepo, "deeply offended," urged Bonifacio to listen to the "complete history" of that disastrous speculation. They needed to vindicate themselves, and seeing that he had raised the question, they were determined to answer.

Whether he wanted to or not, Bonis had to hear and see and feel. They put before him minute books, estimates, pay bills, plans, files— a "dark wood" that made him lose all notions of time and space. He thought he was suspended in air, caught in a witches' Sabbath. His ears roared. While the others explained and gesticulated in what sounded like pure gibberish to him, sleepiness, anger and remorse all buzzed through his brain like a swarm of wasps. He would gladly have kicked, bitten, cried, as his eyes closed, his ears burned and his legs folded. He had fallen into a trap for his weakness and stupidity, he knew. He had gone in alone, when he should have entered with a judge, a clerk, a lawyer, auditors and a pair of Civil Guards.

After two hours of these abominations, of true agony, he only had courage enough to move quietly towards the door, followed by the two monsters who continued explaining to him, point by point, the ruin of the Valcárcels in the factory, the ruin of Antonio Reyes, of his only son. In the dining room (and now the time was almost five) Marta and Sebastian, half-asleep and yawning, were still waiting up for them. They both joined their arguments to Körner's and Nepo's as though trying to attract their attention, but hounded by that dreadful nightmare and dead with sleep, dizzy with rage, with fever and fatigue, Bonifacio arose and left the room in open and accelerated flight. He locked himself in his room, determined to leave for Cabruñana accompanied by the papers which the uncle had foisted off on him, as soon as it was day. He would leave without saying good-bye to Emma, without seeing his son, for two reasons: so that his courage would not fail him and his wife would not have time to dissuade him from this irrevocable resolution. I don't know a word about leases, he thought to himself, or partnerships or mixed contracts or numbers or factories, but I must have willpower from here on out. I said I would go tomorrow, and the sun itself will fail before I do. I shall go. Emma's temperature is not terribly off; it's falling now. Antonio is the same. I'm going to Cabruñana. I'll even come back the day after tomorrow with two or three wet nurses for her to choose from, since people say the ones there are very good. Emma won't want to nurse the baby herself, and in point of fact, she really can't. We will care for him ourselves, the nurse and I. Anyway, the less Valcárcel in him, the better.

Bonis could not sleep. Fully awake, in a thousand nightmare visions, he commingled his past remorse, his present anger and shame, his propositions for future energy and his hopes as a father. To act, he thought, is a terrible thing. It was much more agreeable to think, to imagine; but a father must be diligent, practical, positive, and he would be all those things for Antonio, for *his* Antonio. Yet at any rate, for the present, anger, irritation and embarrassment over his ignorance of so many things which everyone in the house except him knew—all that scramble of low, vulgar, pedestrian passions—deprived him of the enjoyment of his good fortune, of the joy of being a father.

In the morning while everyone was sleeping and the sun had run part of its course, Reyes stepped out of the house with only his papers in a small valise. He took the coach to Cabruñana forthwith, and before noon he was already arguing with Lobato in the middle of a field, in front of some oaks which the steward had allowed a tenant to fell because, as gossip had it, both of them would stand to gain considerable sums. Lobato, an ex-Carlist leader, was a wolf with a taint of fox about him. He spoke with difficulty, spelled out each letter when he read, and wrote in such a way that, if necessary, he could easily deny that those were letters. The point was this: Lobato was master of the territory because of his political power, because of his usury and because of the deceit to which his personal influence compelled justices of the peace and minor officials. Nepomuceno had dealt with him because with only half a word they fully understood each other, and too because only a man like Lobato who was the terror of the council board could collect the rent from those tenants who were otherwise accustomed to receive the bailiffs and the constables with stones and bullets. When traveling at night, Lobato crossed at full speed certain dark thickets where he was sure to encounter ambushes set up by those peasants who trembled in his presence during the daylight hours. On one occasion, after taking to court a tenant who owed three years' rent, he received such a blow with a stone as he traversed the wood at night that he reached his house in a state of semiconsciousness, clutching his horse's mane. And this idiot, this doltish little gentleman of whom Señor Don Juan Nepomuceno has spoken only with contempt, comes to demand money from me? Lobato, with feigned humility, mocked his master. Playing the fool, the ignoramus, he made Bonis see that *he* was the one who did not know what he was about. The tenants too laughed at the master with irony so dissimulated that it could not be taxed as disrespectful. They scratched their heads, smiled and made up their minds not to pay better than they had in the past.

Despairing, Bonis decided to leave those beautiful valleys of eternal green, of fresh shade and infinite hue, the beautiful variety of the hills and plains through which clear blue rivers wound. *Divine! Divine!* Bonifacio mused. But what a rascal Lobato is, and what thieves are all those shepherds! In another situation, without these cares and preoccupations, what happy days I'd have spent in these thickets where the whisper of the pine branches mingles with that of the sea resounding like its echo. Cabruñana was a riparian region, and its narrow, multiform valleys, rich dark green on the slopes and in the marshy savannas, appeared to be the sources of ancient rivers, now dried of their waters. The violent forms of the landscape, the velvety hillsides cut sheer in their fall as coastal cliffs, all those rocky spots and roadless places, those high meadows and plains, recalled the mysterious bottom of the sea.

His useless task done, without more benefit than scattered warnings which no one heeded, Reyes decided at mid-afternoon to ride to the capital of the council and the district, two leagues away by road, in order to spend the night there. Before nightfall, he proposed to reach Raíces, which was on the way, and stop for half an hour. Why? He did not know. To dream, to feel, to imagine those remote times in his own fashion, to reminisce at his leisure, in solitude, free from Lobato and Nepo and Sebastian, to think of the Reyeses to come.

Raíces was the site of about twenty or thirty houses scattered throughout the luxuriant foliage of a peninsula abandoned by water, in the morasses. Close by were dunes, whose yellow ridges of sand recalled in shape the rough spots which surrounded Raíces, but for centuries and centuries Raíces had displayed the dark green velvet of its mosses and sod and its meadow flowers, just like those found inland, far from the sea breezes. Raíces was a mysterious green retreat which inspired melancholy, austerity and a poetic, resigned kind of forgetfulness of the world. On the south side, the village was hidden, dwarfed by a very high hill, cut vertically, whose almost perpendicular incline exposed, like the ivy on a gigantic wall, pines, chestnuts and oaks, trees which climbed uphill as if scaling a fort. The sea and the dunes left it open to northerly and northwesterly winds, and the remains of a forest bordered it on the east and west. The dwellings, few and scattered through the dense foliage, were for the most part humble cabins, but there were several big, ancient houses of dark stone with coats of arms over the doorways.

Bonis arrived an hour before sunset at a little plaza which served as a courtyard for some of the oldest but also most noble-looking houses. Carts resting on their shafts as though asleep blocked the passageway. Half-naked children, dirty, ragged and without a spot on their bodies where one could plant a kiss (except on the eyes of a few and the blonde locks of a very few), jumped and ran through that common corral which doubtless incorporated the entire world for them. More serious and far more businesslike, some pigs rooted in a pile of manure in which, too, roosters and hens scratched and pecked; two dogs slept fitfully, bitten by thousands of mosquitoes.

The Reyes family came from this very place, thought Bonifacio, watching from a neighboring street. From out of that squalor he summoned up an ideal picture of gentle and melancholy peace, isolated, as it were, from the foolish vanities of the world. A group of chestnut trees and the wall of an orchard kept him hidden from the sight of the children and the dogs, who would have become alarmed if they had noticed his presence. He dismounted, tied his horse to the trunk of the tree and sat down on the grass to meditate at ease.

He thought of Ulysses returning to Ithaca, but he was not Ulysses, rather a poor offshoot of a dead generation. The Ulysses of Raíces! The Reyeses who had emigrated had never returned. They would not recognize him in his own native home. Since he had read the *Odyssey* many times and remembered clearly the various episodes and the names of the characters, Bonis thought: the pigs and the dogs which Ulysses found in Eumaeous' dwelling when he returned to Ithaca are here, but Eumaeous, who stood watch over Ulysses' pigs, is not; he does not exist. Those dogs would attack him just as they had Ulysses if they saw him, but Eumaeous, the faithful servant, would not rush to his aid. What had become of that Ulysses, Reyes? Why had he left there? Who could ever know! Perhaps those little ones who seem like the very children of manure, almost earthworms, are relations of mine. They are of my tribe maybe.

Suddenly he slapped himself on the forehead. His recollections of the classics brought him to think of the passage in which Ulysses is immediately recognized by Eurycleia, his wet nurse. Bonis had had no other wet nurse than his mother who had died, but Antonio, his son, needed a wet nurse, and he had forgotten that he had come to

Cabruñana to look for one. *Best here*, he thought. Yes. I will not leave Raíces without finding a nurse for my son. It is an inspiration! Who knows, perhaps he will feed on the milk of his own true people, the blood of his blood.

Since he had decided, moreover, to become every day more active and less of a dreamer, rather a practical man like the rest, like those who earn their money, since he had also decided to earn money for love of his Antonio, he left his arguments behind, got up, mounted his horse and pressed along through those streets and plazas, from door to door, searching for what he needed, a wet nurse, a native of Raíces to come to the Reyes house. Fortunately, that was a famous region for wet nurses, one of the most celebrated in the province, and without having to inquire beyond that tiny neighborhood, Bonis found two good milk cows with human features. In that region the service he solicited had become a type of industry aimed for exportation. It was agreed that the next morning, very early, Rosa and Pepa (as those candidates for the honor of nursing Antonio Reyes were named) would be in the district capital ready to take the coach in which Bonifacio would transport them to the city where they would be examined by the doctor after which the one in the best condition would receive the medical *imprimatur* and the official appointment by Emma herself.

Satisfied with his diligence and the good fortune which concluded his business, Bonis stopped, just before he left the village, at a bend in that solitary road beside the wooden bridge which crossed the Raíces, the poetic, sinuous rivulet which under the shadows of countless trees flowed to the nearby ocean without hurrying, eternally certain of reaching it before nightfall, even though the sun had already hidden behind the waves that roared in the distance. Turning the horse to look back, aware of the solitude, immobile in the middle of the road, Reyes stood still, contemplating the melancholy corner from which he was withdrawing, as if he had truly left something of himself there. Nothing concrete, nothing tangible spoke to him or could speak to him of the connection between his race and that pacific and humble spot, but nevertheless he felt himself bound to it by undefinable, spiritual chains, those that become impalpable to the soul at the very moment that one tries to test their strength.

I'll never know, Bonis mused, in what century the Reyeses left here or what they were here or how or where they lived. I don't even know anything about my great-great-grandfather except for some vague notions. I only know that we were noble a long time ago and that we left Raíces. Oh! If I had only kept that book of armorial bearings which my mother so often talked of and which my father appeared to deprecate so. Yes, I am sensitive to these things. I seem to feel a certain sympathy even for these spots. This calm, this silence, this greenness, this resigned and tolerable poverty, even the music of the sea which roars behind these mountains of sand . . . all this seems like something that belongs to me, a section of my heart, my way of thinking, resembling the character of my father. The Reyeses should never have gone from here. They were not made for the world, that's clear to see. I, the last one, who am I? A wretch, an ignoramus who has never earned a *peseta* in his life, who only knows how to spend what is not his. A dreamer who believed that some day he would become something worthwhile by feeling deeply things rare and inexplicable. And this is what the race has come to!

He paused in his soliloquy as though to hear what the silence of Raíces said to him in the twilight. A distant bell began to sound the Angelus. In spite of his religious doubts, Bonis took off his hat. He remembered the words with which his mother would begin the evening prayers: "The angel of the Lord announced to Mary . . ."

Oh! To him, too, without a doubt, the angel of the Lord had announced he would be a father. His very being, his very loins, were filled with love for that son, for that Antonio of whom he was now thinking as one thinks of an absent love, sending gazes and wishes to fly to the horizon behind which the loved one hides. A feeling of infinite tenderness flooded his soul. Even his horse, who stood peacefully immobile, seemed to understand and respect his emotion. Raíces! His son! His faith! His faith now *was* his son.

The past: death, corruption, abdication of responsibility, errors—

245

all was forgotten. What had his own existence been? A fiasco, a disaster, a thing of no use, but everything that he had not been his son could be. What in him had been aspiration, merely sentimental potential, in his son would become effective energy, accomplishment. Oh! His heart told him that Antonio would be something good, the glory of the Reyeses. And perhaps when he had made his fortune, won a great political position or, better, written dramas or—the acme of all his desires—become a great composer of symphonies or operas, a Mozart, a Meyerbeer, his father now old, doting on his son, would instill in him the idea of restoring the Reyeses' home in Raíces, and he, Bonis, would go to die there in that peace, in that sweet twilight, between the murmuring branches of century-old trees, rocked by the musical and scented breeze which moved against the violet background of the sky on the horizon, where the last breath of the lazy day dissolved into the night.

"Oh! Definitely! There is nothing of value in the world except poetry!" Bonis remarked aloud, continuing, "My Antonio will devote himself to this. He will be the poet, the musician, the great man, the genius. And I, his father, I will dedicate myself to the practical, the positive, to earning money, to avoiding the ruin of the Valcárcels and to restoring the Reyeses. So, good-bye Raíces, until I return. I am going to be with my son. Perhaps we will come back together."

Shaking his head and shortening the reins to wake the sleepy Rosinante from his lethargy, Bonifacio went on his way at a trot without turning his eyes back, afraid of his dreams, of his madness, prepared with more and more eagerness to sacrifice his temperament, the temperament of the caviling, sentimental fool, for the sake of his son's future.

He slept in the district capital, and at daybreak, accompanied by the two Eurycleias he had found in Raíces, he mounted the coach which commuted daily to the capital of the province. When he reached his home, he found the house filled with people, servants and friends, all bustling about. Dressed in black satin with a fine mantilla, Doña Celestina was standing in the middle of the salon with a bundle in her arms, a heap of embroidered white cloth, covered with lace and blue ribbons.

"What's this?" asked Reyes, who entered with his elected wet nurses on either side.

"We are going to make this Jew of your son into a Christian," the woman answered.

In fact, Emma had resolved to go ahead with the baptism. Of course, the day before she herself had demanded that no one mention a word of baptism until the cold in the little one's eyes had cleared up, but when she woke up that morning and learned that, without her permission and leaving her with a fever, Bonis had gone to the village to straighten out injustices which it had never occurred to him to straighten out before, she was annoyed. Out of revenge and considering that the weather was fairly temperate, in the time it takes to say "God bless," she had made all the arrangements from her bed, giving orders in her inimitable way for the child to be baptized that very afternoon so that the father would return to find the ceremony had taken place and would be able to do nothing but rage. Bonifacio did not rage. The sanctity of the moment did not allow for angry passions; instead, he embraced his wife, managing to do so only with great difficulty.

Emma now had very little fever. She became vivacious. Without giving a thought to the critical period after birth, even though it had not yet passed, she decided to adorn herself and adorn her bed. She delved into the bottom of her linen cabinet, which was like an old treasure chest revealing a sea of foam, of snow and cream, of fine linen shot through with the most delicate, almost spiritual, lace. In the middle of that foam, like a castaway, appeared the wasted, yellowish countenance of Emma, fallen now into the kind of ruin which admits no restoration.

She is an old woman, thought Bonifacio, resigned without bitterness, but sad for the sake of his son.

La Valcárcel approved of the competitive examination of the wet nurses planned by her husband. Bonis could not understand why Nepo, the Körners, Sebastian, the Ferraz girls, the Silva girls and their other friends laughed, some almost hysterically, at the thought of Pepa and Rosa, the robust villagers from Raíces. Every time that Sebastian and Marta recalled his triumphal entry, marching between the two villagers with their gigantic breasts, they split their sides with laughter. According to Marta, that entry was too much; one *had* to laugh, uproariously. And they did laugh.

But Bonifacio did not understand. He did not even try. What did the ridiculous giggles of the troop, those who had eaten all of his son's bread and whom he was ready to drive out of his house, matter to him?

The whole retinue began to move. Emma had decreed—and there was no point in arguing—that Sebastian be the godfather and Marta the godmother. A first-class ceremony had been ordered. The baptistry of the parochial church was covered with gold-fringed, scarlet satin drapes. The font glittered like an ember of gold, illuminated by very tall candles.

Bonis, walking alone behind Doña Celestina, who was taking care that the shawl which covered the sleeping Antonio's face did not slip to the ground, had not had time, as he passed through the streets, really to consider the grave and poetic tenderness appropriate to that occasion. He afterwards remembered having experienced, instead, something like embarrassment as he faced the cold, curious, almost insolent and somewhat mocking looks of the indifferent and easily distracted public. But when he crossed the threshold of the house of God, stopped between the doorway and the chancel and saw there within, in front of him, the lights of the baptistry, a sweet, religious emotion full of deep mystery, not lacking a bit of vague terror (due to the uncertainty of the future) had overpowered him so that it made him forget all the wretches who surrounded him. He saw now only God and his son. On previous occasions, seeing other children baptized, he had thought that it was rather absurd to try to drive out demons or whatever they were from the bodies of those innocent angels ready to receive the waters of baptism. But he now saw nothing whatsoever absurd in that act. Oh, the Church was wise. It knew the human heart, and it knew which were the great moments in one's life. Birth was indeed solemn, as was taking a name in that chancy comedy that we call life. Baptism made one consider the whole future, the mysterious and curious synthesis of longing and fear which combine in that first penetration into the future. Although he, Bonis, did not believe in every article of dogma, and even less in the "marvels" of the Bible, he recognized in these critical moments that the Church actually seemed like a mother. He placed this son of his heart and loins at the feet of the Church, without repugnance and without compromising his mental reservations.

His son, his Antonio: there he was, flesh of his flesh, fast asleep, swathed in laces, a small, colored dot lost in all the whiteness. He no longer resembled Bonifacio, but his father, Reyes the attorney. Yes, the expression of pain, the grimace of the lips, the frown— all that was his father's. Ay! How his love spilled over his soul, coursing down like tears of tenderness and filling him up inside, his love for that son, for that weak being abandoned by the angels in that world of man. It was no longer abstract, metaphysical; it was now a love without phrases, a love with no rhetoric about it, an ineffable love that pleased his conscience and gave absolute sanction to his past vow of constant and quiet sacrifice. To live through my son, for my son, I was born for this, Bonis thought, born to be a father. There, in the doorway of the church, waiting for the priest to make a Christian of Antonio, he felt the grace that God had sent him in the form of a clear vocation: the vocation of fatherhood. Yes, he agreed to himself, now I have become something.

After that he saw a round, smiling curate, covered with gold embroidery like the altars of the baptistry and surrounded by the sacred setup of acolytes, candles and crosses, which Bonis, too, felt appropriate to the occasion. He did not object to anything; everything was fine. In spite of his certainty that his Antonio, that innocent baby with a sad face, had no sort of demon at all within him, nor any personal grudge whatsoever against the Church, Bonis acknowledged her right to take certain precautions before admitting the newborn infant into the bosom of the Church. Even the stricture against his son's entering the temple before he had fulfilled the requirements of this sacrament seemed rational, although he thought that the priest might have been more careful with the catechumen, or whatever they were called, of such a young age, because the cold draft between the doors could be quite fatal and kill, right then and there, a Christian in full flower.

"Doña Celestina," said Reyes in a soft, humble, scarcely audible voice, so that the curate and the assembly would not give a heterodox interpretation to his words, "Doña Celestina, please move over to this corner; here you are in the draft."

"Let me be, Don Bonifacio," she snapped.

The presiding priest began to speak the Latin phrases Bonifacio could only half understand. He did make out that his son would definitely be named Antonio, something or other else and Sebastian. Why Sebastian? In the end, it did not really matter.

The Ferraz girls looked at the baby and the curate with their mouths open as though watching a very droll farce. They were believers like everyone else; but, for those tambourine-like young women, everything in the world was a great jest, a matter of jokes, castanets and laughter. It was not fitting to laugh there, but they certainly had the acute desire to do so. Marta, the godmother, looked on with the face of a Jew. She thought of her "superiority," of her personal ideas, which contrasted so greatly with the vulgar way of understanding the ceremony with which those frivolous peasants approached everything.

Suddenly the words which the clergyman spoke, the soft, pleasing tone of ecclesiastical chant, took on a true musical quality, like a recitative, and then, there inside the church, everyone heard the resonant pipes of the organ, which filled the solitary structure with a stream of fresh and playful notes. Led by the priest, the new Christian was carried across the chancel and into the church in the arms of Sebastian, who held himself majestically. The group reached the baptistry, where the friends surrounded the godparents. Old women, beggars and little children formed a sort of chorus, curious, straining, awaiting the small coins distributed on account of the baptism. For Bonis, who followed his son to the banks of the marble Jordan, everything took on the meaning of new life—a more intense, harmonious and poetic meaning. The music helped him to understand everything even more clearly, to penetrate the deep significance of things. The organ, the organ told him what he had not been able to explain himself. Why, it's clear, he said in his thoughts, the church is like a watchful lynx, so farsighted. She does know how to be a mother!

The notes of the organ seemed to play with the newborn infant, who came from a mysterious world. The chords tickled the flesh that Doña Celestina's discreet, expert fingers had uncovered, bearing the little creature's back. The quick, mischievous notes were angels who romped with their human companion, not so happy as they, but no less pure, no less innocent.

Bonis felt that the faces of even the most indifferent, even of those rascals who were waiting for the holy water, assumed then an expression of interest, of a certain tenderness. The lights seemed to sing, too, as they flickered in rhythm, burning an even brighter red. The gilt ornaments on the curate's chasuble and the baptistry grew more intense, more noble. The choirboys, tense, solemn, lent an air of circumstance to the whole ritual. The organ continued, now laughing and playing, but legitimately, since it symbolized celestial joy, the grace of innocence. But, suddenly, in the depth of that sacred and poetic laughter of the organ, Bonis could not help but fancy that he heard a sort of mocking, somewhat ironic challenge: "Let's see," said the organ. "What does the future hold? What will become of your son? Does living even matter? Is it all a game? Is it all a dream without logic or sense? Is there anything besides appearances?" And suddenly then the music took off in yet another direction. It began to say one thing and end by indicating another, until, finally, Reyes came to realize that the organist was playing variations on *La Traviata*, an opera then very popular. Bonifacio remembered *La Dame aux Camelias*, which he had read, and Armand who had loved to the point of forgetting *suo vecchio geni-*

tor,* as the opera phrases it. In fact, the organ was recalling it all: "Tu non sai quanto sofrii!"†

Poor me, thought Bonis. My son might become a total ingrate. He will surely love some woman more than me. I was surely born so that I would not be loved as I would like to be. But it doesn't matter, it doesn't matter. This is the law: we love them, they love theirs—the vanities of the world. Strange thing! Why doesn't *La Traviata* sound ugly in the church? That must be some sort of profanation—but it doesn't seem so. In *La Traviata*, for good or bad, there is love and suffering, love and death—all religion and life itself! Oh, how this organ shows us the mysteries of destiny! It returned to the mocking, ironic questions: "What will become of him? What will become of you? What will become of us all?"

"Who is playing the organ?" Marta asked Sebastian in a low voice.

"Minghetti." The godfather and godmother smiled, looking at each other.

"Whimsical fellow!" said the German, dedicating to the baritone a moment's recollection.

Bonis had heard the question and the reply. Minghetti was playing; yes, one could easily tell that there was an artist up there! What a graceful and delicate courtesy. Artists, finally, were poets. It was a shame, of course, that they tended to be rogues as well. If an occasion of incompatibility ever should arise between morality and art, in the future he, Bonifacio, would stand for morality—for the sake of his son.

Antonio Diego Sebastian was now a Christian. Doña Celestina had taken him from the arms of his uncle, the godfather, and seated on a pew beside the chapel, surrounded by friends and the curious alike, she dexterously manipulated ribbons and lace to bury once again the weak, thin body of the little creature under all those swatches of linen.

Bonifacio separated himself from the group and headed through

* his old father
† "You don't know how much I suffered."

252

the church in the direction of the sacristy, following the priest and his acolytes. That, too, was solemn. He was going to dictate the inscription in the baptismal record to establish the foundations of his son's civil status. While Minghetti amused himself by performing wonders with the organ, Bonis was thinking as he made his way through the temple: Who knows! Perhaps some day the wise, the erudite, the curious, will make pilgrimages to look with affection and respect upon the page of this parish book on which I am now going to write the name of my son, of his parents and grandparents, his place of birth, everything! My poor Antonio has no living grand-fathers, no living uncles; he won't have that love, but mine will make up for all of them.

As he entered the sacristy, he saw a woman in a side chapel sub-merged in the shadows, seated in a pew, her head resting on the altar which was embossed with churrigueresque relief work.

"Serafina!"

"Bonifacio!"

"What are you doing here?"

"What would I be doing? Praying! And you, why have you come?"

"I've come to register my son in the baptismal record. He was just baptized."

Serafina stood up. She smiled in a way that surprised Bonis be-cause he had never seen his friend wear such an expression of un-kindness, of actual malice, which accompanied that smile.

"Oh, I see, your son . . . bah!"

"What's wrong with you, Serafina? Why are you here?"

"I am here . . . to be out of my room, to get away from the inn-keeper. I am here because . . . I am becoming devout. It's not a joke. It's either prayer . . . or selling matches. Mochi is not coming back, did you know? Can you understand? I have lost my voice! Yes, lost it completely. The day that I wrote you . . . and that you didn't answer me, you know? When I begged you for those *reales* to pay for my lodging? Fine, well, that day, actually that night, since I had offered to pay, and I didn't pay . . . because you didn't answer . . . I had a battle royal with Don Carlos, that infamous man!"

La Gorgheggi was silent for a moment. She was choked with her emotions—fury, pain, shame. Two tears, which must have tasted of gall, trickled down her face.

"The infamous man had the nerve to insult me like a lost woman. He threatened me with the law; he threatened to put me out in the street. . . . I began to run. I went out into the street as I was, without a hat; then I went back because I had left everything there—my baggage, the only things I have in this world. I don't know what I caught that night running in the dew through the damp streets. Oh, with that my voice, which had been in very bad condition, left me. And from that night, I have sung . . . like your wife. I don't dare leave the lodging house because I can't pay. Don Carlos insults me sometimes; other times he makes advances. I don't want lovers of any description. All of that sickens me. . . . Mochi is never coming back. He has not answered my last letters. Just like you. You are superb gentlemen, aren't you? I beg you for four *cuartos* to avoid the insults of a wretch, and you don't answer! I don't know where to go. In the house, my creditor—who wants to be my lover—spies on me. In the street, fools follow me. The stupid curiosity of people bores me. I don't even have enough money to escape. But to escape where? So I hide here in the church. This is mine, as everyone's. You caused me to feel like this, to want peace, to dream, to hope for impossibilities. At least I am at home here, and I even pray, in my way. I do not believe, strictly speaking. . . . I want to. The saints, all of them, that Saint Roche; this Saint Sebastian with the arrows stuck into his body; that bishop, Saint Isidore . . . all of them understand me. I am not really religious, but now, for the time, lovers sicken me. I don't want lovers. I'll wait to see if my voice returns— or you. Mochi is an evil man, a traitor and a wretch; I already knew it, I always knew it. But you! I did not believe that you were one, too. Oh, Bonis, don't abandon me! I . . . I still love you . . . more than before, much more; really I do. I must be sick. The world frightens me, the theater terrifies me, lovers shock me. I want peace,

I want rest, I want respectability, but I do *not* want to live as an actress, or to eat the bread I would gain by renting my body to a stranger—to I don't know who. You, yes! Others, no. Do you want me?"

Although he was no great subscriber to matters religious and in spite of the words, the tone and the tears of Serafina which had moved him deeply, Bonis thought above all that they were in church and that the place was hardly appropriate for that type of conduct and contract. Before answering her, he looked behind him towards the baptistry to see if anyone had noticed this encounter with the singer. The baptismal retinue had disappeared. No one had given so much as a thought to Reyes' absence. He was so insignificant to all of them. Minghetti, nonetheless, continued his musical capers with the organ. That was one of his whims: to make himself irritating as a joke whenever he sat down to play.

Repulsed at the idea of discussing such matters there in church, he was still very greatly affected. On the other hand, terribly anxious not to tarnish his new dignity as a spotless father, without need of subterfuge or slackening of resolve, Bonis said in a voice that he tried to make as tender as it was firm, but which came out trembling, stammering and weak,

"Serafina, I owe it to you to tell you the whole truth. From here on, I want to live for my son. Our love was . . . was illicit. I owe a great good, a grace of God . . . having a son. I offered the sacrifice of my passion for Antonio's happiness. Moreover, I am ruined as far as my other interests go. I'll do for you what I can—you'll see! I'll make things clear to that Jew, Don Carlos. But I am ruined! The voice, Serafina, your voice, will return . . ."

Then remembering the *voice* he had once loved, Bonis was on the point of weeping, too. But Serafina's face frightened him again. That lovely woman, who for Bonis represented beauty with the addition of goodness and kindness, turned a sharp, steely gaze upon him. He saw the wrinkled lines curve about her mouth in a way that symbolized something serpentlike, almost demoniacal. He saw her pass the delicate tip of her soft, sharp tongue along her red lips, and as if expecting a poisoned wound, he waited for the slow, deliberate words of the woman who had once made him incredibly happy. La Gorgheggi said: "Bonifacio, you were always an imbecile. Your son is . . . not your son!"

"Serafina!"

But poor Bonis could say no more. He, too, had now lost his voice. What he did was lean on the altar of that dark chapel to keep himself from falling. Since he did not speak, Serafina had the audacity to add: "But, my dearest fellow, all the world knows it. Don't you know to whom your son belongs?"

"My son!" he shouted. "Who does my son belong to?"

La Gorgheggi extended an arm and pointed up to the direction of the choir loft.

"The organist."

"Oh!" exclaimed Bonifacio, as if he had felt his lover leave a deadly poison on his lips as she gave him a kiss.

He drew away from the altar. He stood firmly on his feet. Then, he smiled like Saint Sebastian was smiling, near there, pierced through with arrows.

"Serafina, I forgive you. I must forgive you everything. My son *is* my son. What you don't have and must always search for, I now possess; I have faith. I have faith in my son! Without that faith, I could not live. I am certain of it, Serafina. My son is my son. Oh, yes! *Dios mío.* He is my son! This is a terrible blow. If someone else had told me, I would not believe it, I would not feel it. You have told me, yes, but I still don't believe it. I have not had time to explain to you just what has happened to me, what it is to be a father. I forgive you, but you have hurt me deeply. Tomorrow, when you repent of your words, remember this that I tell you: Bonifacio Reyes believes firmly that Antonio Reyes y Valcárcel is his son. He is his only son. Do you understand that? His only son!"